MW00978370

Smile

Pretty

and Say

Jesus

THE UNIVERSITY OF GEORGIA PRESS

Athens & London

HUNTER JAMES

Smile Pretty
and Say
JESUS
The Last
Great Days of
PTL

© 1993 by the University of Georgia Press

Athens, Georgia 30602 / All rights reserved

Designed by Louise OFarrell

Set in 10½/14 Berkeley Old Style Medium

by Tseng Information Systems, Inc.

Printed and bound by Braun-Brumfield, Inc.

The paper in this book meets the guidelines for

permanence and durability of the Committee on

Production Guidelines for Book Longevity

of the Council on Library Resources.

Printed in the United States of America

97 96 95 94 93   C   5 4 3 2 1

Library of Congress Cataloging in Publication Data

James, Hunter.

Smile pretty and say Jesus : the last great days of

PTL / Hunter James.

p. cm.

ISBN 0-8203-1529-X (alk. paper)

1. Bakker, Jim, 1940– . 2. Bakker, Tammy

Faye, 1942– . 3. Evangelists—United States—

Biography. 4. PTL (Organization)—Corrupt

practices. 5. James, Hunter. I. Title.

BV3785.B3J35 1993

269'.2'0922—dc20

[B]   92-39494

British Library Cataloging in Publication

Data available

For my grandson,

Christopher Hunter James

CONTENTS

FOREWORD

The end of the PTL empire, as Hunter James shows, was one of the most colorful episodes in American religious history. The compelling cast of characters would suggest nothing less: cheerfully-prosperous and superficially-saintly Jim and Tammy Faye Bakker, the seductress Jessica Hahn, somber Jerry Falwell, the faith healer Oral Roberts, hard-nosed Bill Kovach (the then-controversial editor of the *Atlanta Journal-Constitution*), the theatrical attorney Melvin Belli, and the pope.

A central character is the author himself, as this is "new journalism" and the journalist's role in ferreting out the story is part of the story. This book is an intriguing memoir of a journalist covering breaking news: the reader sees the middle-of-the-night phone calls from the editor, the early morning flights, the endless waiting, the aggressive efforts to obtain the key interview. Much of the humor comes from James's world-weariness and from his encounters with the strange characters he meets along the way—the PTL true believer who thinks the overthrow of Bakker is a grand conspiracy of the "Illuminati"; the revivalists he has known in the past; the journalists he works with.

Smile Pretty and Say Jesus is most significant, though, for what it highlights about American religion. Popular evangelical Protestantism often makes celebrities of its preachers, with resultant temptations in their paths. They often do not succeed in resisting those temptations. Jim Bakker's fall from grace through the agency of Jessica Hahn, then the revelations of financial and moral corruption, and the exploitation of the faithful are surely highlights of ministerial scandal. But scandal has touched the celebrity pulpit before. Henry Ward Beecher—a former abolitionist and progressive theological liberal known as "the greatest preacher since Saint Paul"—was perhaps the most famous preacher of the late nineteenth century. He enjoyed a gospel of wealth that made him proud to be one of the highest-paid ministers of his time, even carrying uncut gems to display his prosperity. In 1874 a friend accused Beecher of seducing his wife, and the resulting trial was so notorious that the court sold admission tickets.

In the twentieth century, Pentecostal minister Aimee Semple McPherson converted her flamboyance into the $1.5 million Angelus Temple, home of the Foursquare Gospel Church in Los Angeles. In the spring of 1926, McPherson went swimming in the Pacific and subsequently disappeared for thirty-six days, emerging in a Mexican border town after, she said, escaping from kidnappers. Police found evidence that she had actually spent the time on a love holiday with a former employee in Carmel, California. Donations to the church thereafter declined.

Closer to our own times, fundamentalist preacher and raging anticommunist Billy James Hargis became the first televangelist to be implicated in wrongdoing. He appeared on 140 television stations at the height of his influence in the 1950s, but in 1976 male and female students at his American Christian College in Tulsa accused Hargis of having sex with them as part of his premarital counseling. Hargis denied the charges, but his influence waned after the incident.

Dismissing "celebrity" religion that stresses prosperity and conservative orthodoxy is easy when it leads to such outrages. But the issues involved in the dramatic decline of Jim Bakker and the stewardship of PTL by Jerry Falwell revealed internal tensions within the conservative Protestantism that has long been a prominent feature of the American religious landscape. Those issues deserve to be understood because they drive the conservative Protestantism that attracts millions of faithful, in spite of the shenanigans of the Jim and Tammy Faye Bakkers and the Jimmy Swaggarts.

Both Jim Bakker and Jerry Falwell regard themselves as part of a broad evangelical Protestantism, but that term covers many groups and outlooks. As a social movement, evangelicalism emerged in Great Britain and North America in the late eighteenth century, stressing classical

Protestant belief in sin and the need for salvation, the importance of the church, and the authority of the Bible. In the United States especially, evangelicalism became identified by its call for a personal religious experience of God's presence through his grace—being "born again." Evangelical denominations in the United States and Canada now enroll close to 50 million members.

Evangelicalism seemed triumphant and invincible after the Civil War, expressing its cultural influence in conservative, hellfire-and-brimstone denominations and in a liberal social gospel rooted in the convert's need to improve the world—to build a kingdom of God on earth. Evangelicalism, nonetheless, lost its predominance in American culture in the years before World War I, a casualty of the dramatic socioeconomic changes of the era and growing secular skepticism. Mainstream evangelical groups adjusted to the new cultural authority of scientific ideas, to "higher criticism" of the Scriptures using modern historical techniques, and to the increasing pluralism of American religion through the influence of immigrant-based Catholic and Jewish faiths.

Not all evangelicals, though, could easily embrace the modern world. Jerry Falwell is the spiritual descendant of those religious leaders who, in the early twentieth century, organized a social movement that advocated traditional evangelical beliefs they knew were under attack from theological liberalism and modern secular culture. Fundamentalists concluded that these challenges, if unanswered, would irrevocably destroy the basis of their faith. The first three decades of this century saw bitter fundamentalist-modernist warfare, as fundamentalists fought social changes and defended the literal truth of the Scriptures and the supernatural realities of the Savior Christ. Between 1910 and 1915, fundamentalists published *The Fundamentals*, twelve small books outlining their essential beliefs. The traumas of World War I triggered a mass, militant fundamentalist social movement aimed at removing liberal ideas from schools and denominations.

In the 1920s the fundamentalists were unsuccessful in combatting the changes they feared. The Scopes Trial, in the summer of 1925, was the culminating event in fundamentalist efforts to keep evolutionary ideas out of school textbooks through legislation, and it symbolized their failure. They were objects of scorn and ridicule from the national culture, progressive forces in the South disavowed them, and they became increasingly marginalized. Fundamentalists did not disappear, of course, but their efforts to counter modernism became fragmented as they pursued a variety of approaches.

Fundamentalists were drawn into closer cooperation with other evangelicals in the 1940s. The National Association of Evangelicals, the Youth for Christ, and the revivalism of Billy Graham all spearheaded efforts to achieve a Christian America—the same goal fundamentalists had in the 1920s—this time through evangelical conversions rather than direct political activities. These efforts achieved considerable respectability for mainstream evangelicals such as Graham, but militant separatist fundamentalists condemned the evangelical ecumenicism of the 1940s. Fundamentalism had always been based on the rigorous spirit of Calvinism, asserting the necessity for a clear creed of essential beliefs, and had appealed to Presbyterians, Congregationalists, and Baptists—all denominations with a pronounced residue of Calvinism. Billy Graham and other post–World War II evangelicals insisted, though, that the issue was religious conversion, and many fundamentalists left this broader movement by the 1950s.

Separatist fundamentalists, who would later include Jerry Falwell, maintained their own institutions, including Bible conferences, periodicals, missionary agencies, training schools, radio broadcasting, and, later, television broadcasting. The Baptist Bible Fellowship, the central organization for locally organized, independent fundamentalist churches, had more than 3 million members by the early 1980s, and the Dallas Theological Seminary became the key educational center for orthodoxy. During the 1970s Jerry Falwell's Thomas Road Baptist Church in Lynchburg, Virginia, became one of several "super congregations" with more than 10,000 members. Falwell extended his power in the early 1980s, emerging as a key figure in Religious Right politics through his Moral Majority, which sought a religiously-inspired political agenda and enthusiastically supported Ronald Reagan.

When Falwell entered the world of Jim Bakker and PTL, he entered a different world indeed. PTL was a modern expression of Pentecostalism, a religious tradition that dates its origins to roughly the same time as fundamentalism—the early twentieth century. If fundamentalism is given to creeds, statements of essential doctrines, and moralism, Pentecostalism is about the workings of the spirit. Its distinguishing feature is an experience of spirit baptism—the Holy Spirit—after an initial conversion to Christianity. This spirit baptism reveals itself through speaking in tongues, or glossolalia.

The movement began with an itinerant faith healer, Charles F. Parham, who preached the "second blessing" of spirit baptism. On New Year's Day, 1901, a student of Parham's in a small Bible school in Topeka, Kansas, spoke in tongues, and the movement soon developed strongholds on the West Coast and in the Southeast. Most Pentecostals in this era were blue-collar workers, not the poverty-stricken and wild illiterates of the Holy Roller stereotype, but the movement has always offered hope for transcendence to the socially marginalized. Pentecostals number between 10 and 30 million members in the United States and 50 to 250 million worldwide. The Assembly of God alone—the church of Jim Bakker and Jimmy Swaggart—reported 2 million members in the United States in 1986 and another 14 million internationally.

The spirit of Pentecostalism has even spread into the mainline denominations, touching off a charismatic movement that has revitalized many churches. In the 1940s, Pentecostals overcame their earlier ecclesiastical isolation, working with other evangelicals in the National Association of Evangelicals. The Full Gospel Business Men's Fellowship, founded in 1951, united Pentecostal spokesmen with mainline clergy and successful businessmen, giving Pentecostals a forum in which to deliver a considerably subdued, middle-class version of the faith, countering the Holy Roller stereotype. By the early 1960s, charismatics—as these modern, neo-Pentecostalists are called—had spread their influence into most all mainstream Protestant churches, although the Southern Baptist Convention and the Lutheran Church–Missouri Synod resisted that influence. Charismatics have even influenced the Catholic church. In 1977, when almost 50,000 charismatics assembled in Kansas City to celebrate their faith, Pentecostals were least in number and Catholics, including priests and nuns, were most prominent of all.

The televangelism of Jim Bakker and Jerry Falwell grew naturally out of the concerns, then, of evangelicals, fundamentalists, and Pentecostals. A television ministry became a way to fulfill Christ's Great Commission—to go into the world and spread the good news of his atonement and the need for individuals to "get right with God." The first religious telecast occurred in 1940, and Billy Graham mastered the broadcast of mass revivals in the next few decades. The 1970s and 1980s witnessed an explosion of evangelical influence on television through advances in technology—the use of videotapes, for example, and, especially, satellite broadcasting. By the early 1980s, a television viewer could choose from almost one hundred syndicated religious programs; the revenues generated by their solicitations were close to $1 billion.

Hunter James captures for us the internal world of the best-known of the electronic churches. The kingdom of PTL dissolved in the corruption of its founder, but that kingdom had represented the hopes of many true believers who turned to PTL because American society was not offering what they needed. Bakker's message was too easy: he preserved the traditional Pentecostal call for a religion of the spirit, but he claimed that the material wealth and comfort craved by consumer-oriented modern America could also be had through prayer. The temptations of acquiescence and the pursuit of sheer pleasure to which Bakker fell prey were only exaggerated versions of the temptations he taught his followers to reach for. The disturbing meaning of Hunter James's story is what it says about modern Americans, even those dedicated to preserving the religious spirit.

Charles Reagan Wilson

Part One

THE SUMMONS

1

SOOTHSAYER
Beware the ides of March.

CAESAR
What man is that?

BRUTUS
A soothsayer bids you beware the ides of March.

. . . .

CALPURNIA
What mean you, Caesar? Think you to walk forth?
You shall not stir out of your house today.

CAESAR
Caesar shall forth. . . . These predictions are
to the world in general as to Caesar.

(*Julius Caesar*, 1.2, 2.2)

Like Caesar, PTL* television evangelist Jim Bakker had to wait for a fateful day in March to find out that he should have listened to his soothsayers. On Friday the thirteenth he learned that an old and all-but-forgotten dalliance with a New York church secretary was in danger of bringing down his $172 million evangelical television network and its Heritage USA theme park. By the fifteenth—the fateful ides—he knew the worst. And now a lot of innocent people would have to pay.

*Acronym standing for "Praise the Lord" or "People That Love" and numerous invidious parodies, such as "Pass the Loot" and "Pay the Lady."

For me it began with a frantic midnight phone call from my editor in Atlanta.

"We've got another big one."

"Tornado?"

"Bigger. They found Jim Bakker with a woman. He's out of PTL and Jerry Falwell has taken over."

I stood there trying not to think about it, wondering if it was all some kind of joke. But if that is all it was, why had he waited so late to call?

The voice on the other end took on a more menacing tone. "How soon can you get on the road?"

"Where?"

"Lynchburg."

Lynchburg, Virginia. Jerry Falwell's town. Funny. It had once been my town as well. I knew it a long time before anyone had ever heard of Jerry Falwell. We had started there the same year, me as a general assignment reporter for the morning newspaper, him a scrawny twenty-three-year-old just out of Bible college. In those days I figured I'd be off to London or Paris soon. Or I could stay in Lynchburg and be a nobody. A way station on the road to nowhere. That was the way I looked at it. Falwell, meantime, would stay right there in his hometown and still manage to become the most famous preacher in America. Who would have guessed it? At the time, he was still knocking on doors along all the back streets of the town—a hundred a day, he later said—and trying to get a congregation together. A long time ago; a long time since I had been back.

By now the menace in my editor's voice had turned into something almost like panic. "How soon can you get started? We need reaction from Falwell!"

"By first light."

A lie, of course, but how was he to know?

Anyway, I had been working as a regional correspondent for the Atlanta newspapers long enough to realize that that wasn't what he wanted to hear. After four years of being wakened in the middle of the night with news of tornadoes, riots, murders, and other unspeakable disasters, I knew that he would much have preferred for me to strike out at once, racing off maniacally through the blind dark of the March morning without even taking time to pack.

From my farm home near Winston-Salem, North Carolina, it was a good three-hour drive to Lynchburg. I would get there at 3:00 or 4:00 A.M. and then spend the rest of the night walking about the cold streets or maybe trying to bribe the guards at Falwell's gatehouse. It wouldn't do any good. I tried to explain all that—the big house, the iron gates, the surly guards.

"We gotta have reaction in time for the Metro," he says, panic giving way to a kind of gloomy resignation. Or maybe it was only disgust at my failure to show a proper zeal for my work. He was right. I had been a lot better off as an editorial writer poking fun at the vagaries of human existence and at Ronald Reagan's slapdash 1980 political campaign and even—sometimes—at Jerry Falwell's Moral Majority Incorporated, which had made the preacher a political as well as a theological power.

"We gotta have something by 5:00 A.M. at the latest," he says. "Five o'clock and we can get it in the *Journal* Metro. Maybe you can reach him by phone."

Ah!

"What do you think?" he says. "Falwell's probably getting pretty anxious to talk along about now. Get some reaction and call me back."

So it was true, then: Falwell would be sitting hanging over the phone, his eyelids held open with adhesive tape, waiting impatiently for me to ring him up on what would doubtless turn out to be the most turbulent night of his thirty-one years in the ministry.

I went through the whole routine, exactly as if I thought it might work: the call to Falwell's "Old Time Gospel Hour," the dead switchboard, the desperate and futile attempt to get his phone number from the city desk at the *Lynchburg News*. No one there remembered that I had once been a celebrated reporter in the town. An ignominious development. "Maybe it would be nice to see it again," my wife says. We had met in Lynchburg; she had been a schoolteacher and part-time copy editor during the time I had worked there as a reporter. Yes. Nice to see it again. It had been a long time for us both.

But I wasn't thinking about Lynchburg, not yet. I raced off madly through the dark of the house, gulping the two tranquilizers Mary Ellen had thrust into my hand, cursing the idiocy and injustice of it all, shouting, slamming doors, kicking furniture. It was always the best way to get into a big story.

. . . *goddamn bastards calling up here in the middle of the night just because they've got some goddamn corrupt preacher on their hands like it couldn't even wait till morning by God I'll kill those bastards I'll kill . . .*

. . .

I had been to PTL only once, on assignment. I got there early one November morning just as the Christmas lights were going up: one and a half million gaudy bulbs that would transform the 2,300-acre theme park into Christmas City USA. The strands of lights hung from every shrub and tree, from tall metal standards that lined both sides of the road, from every arch and gable and portico. By nightfall the traffic would be backed up all the way to Interstate 77 more than two miles away—cars packed with gawkers willing to endure long hours of waiting in order to enjoy one of the high moments of the season. What would one call it? A feeling, perhaps, of being cleansed and renewed as they gazed upon a spectacle that from then until the New Year would blare out its tawdry and unremitting message of "redemption" all across the black night of the South Carolina countryside.

Now, thinking back on all that, I realize I shouldn't have been all that surprised at getting a panicky phone call from my editor in the middle of the night. We had been hearing for years that Heritage USA was in trouble. There had been an investigation by the Federal Communications Commission, a drumfire of anti-PTL editorials in the *Charlotte Observer,* a series of heavy-handed land-buying ventures by Bakker and his cronies, hints of near-bankruptcy, questions as to whether donor funds had been diverted to improper uses. And quite aside from everything else was the sheer, wild triviality of the place.

In a remote corner of Bakker's licentious Valhalla stood an outsized satellite dish that beamed his schmaltzy PTL Club talk show into thirteen million homes a day. On higher ground overlooking the pine barrens and red clay hills of the upper South Carolina Piedmont stood "downtown" Heritage USA, complete with amusement park, a man-made lake, white sand beaches, and a water slide almost two hundred feet tall. Just to the south, across a wide ornamental boulevard, stood the centerpiece of it all: the Heritage Grand Hotel, four stories of brick and glass and stone unable to make up its mind between Renaissance and Georgian colonial. Jim Bakker's meretricious monument to American bad taste.

You could enter the hotel past platoons of majordomos uniformed in white silk and tassels. Or you could go around the other way, through the Heritage Village retail mall, a cobbled arcade lined with "shoppes" and stores all done up in Walt Disney Victorian, pastel tints and fake façades, like a giant confection waiting to be gobbled.

I have tried to forget all that. But even now, with the fevers and passions of the PTL scandal long behind me, as I sit looking off toward a bucolic creek bottom where, at midsummer, quarter horses graze, the memories come back with a rush. I think of all the times I stood in the lobby of the Heritage Grand, my gaze drawn steadily upward through the dazzling emptiness of its vaulted atrium. For a moment I am again a part of it all, feeling a little dirty somehow, looking around at the see-through elevators, at the girls in short dresses being whisked forever out of our lives. I am caught up once more in a world of sensuous Christian pleasure, a seductive fun house adorned with elaborate mahogany paneling and crystal chandeliers and gold sconces and phony gilt-laden Queen Anne furnishings. I stand looking up at the high dais where a tuxedoed pianist bangs out pop renditions of "Tales of the Vienna Woods" or "Three O'clock in the Morning" or "Indian Love Call"; the lobby crowded as always with shirt-sleeved Christians chewing toothpicks and talking about how marvelously their lives have been blessed since the day they first opened their pocketbooks to PTL.

Alas. Neither the vision nor the reality could last for long. Bakker had found his Delilah, ignored his soothsayers, and now it had all come crashing in on him. By early March 1987, the *Charlotte Observer* had the whole story and had been phoning the preacher for days.

"We've got it all, Jim. The girl. Everything. How about a statement?"

Bakker stalled, fretted, fasted, and prayed. It was no good. Friday the thirteenth came, a bright, cold day, and the phone rang again.

It was the *Charlotte Observer.* "We're going with the story, Jim. Statement or no statement."

Bakker promised he would have a response by the nineteenth, a Thursday. In the meantime he surrounded himself with evil counselors and old friends, plotting a way out. It was still no good. The conclusion was always the same: "Nobody but God or Jerry Falwell can help you now." On the evening of March 17 he met with Falwell in a hotel at Palm Springs, California, and explained how he had been vilely tricked into the arms of Plain Jane Siren Jessica Hahn.

"Wickedly manipulated by treacherous former friends" is the way he would put it to the *Observer*. Even after being lured into her motel room he would have kept himself unsullied except—of all things—he had been stripped naked and ravished by the no-good slut, and what could he do now but place his sin—if sin it was—beneath the blood of Jesus and hope for the best?

For a while Falwell believed him. He put his hand on the shoulder of the sobbing minister and said, "You're a good soldier, Jim. God will find a way."

Later he told me that Bakker got on his knees and handed him what must have been the biggest gift offering since the dying kings of medieval times had handed over all their lands and castles to the Catholic church.

"He wanted me to take the network entirely out of his hands. 'Jerry,' he said, 'you're the only man I can trust right now.' "

That was the only part Bakker had never denied. Yes, he had asked Falwell to take the network until the cleansing power of Jesus' blood had made him whole again and lifted him with new humility out of the evil trap into which he had been summarily flung by treacherous friends and trusted former associates.

Then he would want it all back—too late. By that time Falwell and the rest of the world would have heard enough to know that, for Jim Bakker, there could be no going back.

. . .

As you took the turn off I-77 you passed at once under a huge billboard from which the cartoonlike faces of Jim and Tammy Bakker stared down at you, smiles aglow against a background of pink and bluish tints. Just around the next curve you came to the main entrance of the Heritage USA theme park. A gate giving onto a sloping drive led you past an information booth manned by waving teenagers and on down a long, wooded hill where clusters of condos and swank vacation chalets marked the way to the PTL television studio. You could tell instantly that it was no place for a fellow who wanted to be alone in a crowd.

Even as you elbowed your way furtively through the Hall of Faith and squeezed in among a packed audience awaiting an 11:00 A.M. airing of the "PTL Club" you found yourself unavoidably caught up in the camaraderie of the place.

"Smile pretty and say Jesus!" admonished an advance man as he came out from behind a purple curtain. "Now is the time for everyone to turn and take their neighbor's hand! Reach out for Jesus! Take the hand of your neighbor! Jesus don't want no strangers here!"

The crowd cheerfully complied while I busied myself with my notepad.

Later, as I climbed aboard a tram that sped visitors about the grounds, it happened again. A bright-eyed teenager wearing a flowery dress that said Jesus Saves reminded everybody to "loosen up and find a new friend today."

"Smile pretty and say Jesus! Our Jesus don't want no strangers here!"

One such stranger turned out to be a machine shop operator from a small place in western Pennsylvania. "Name's Herb," he said as he shot a wary glance at his wife. "Herb Overby. A real nice place they've got here." Again a wary glance as he jabbed my ribs and lowered his voice. "Yup. But they say a fellow can get mighty thirsty around here if he don't have the gumption to bring his own bottle."

No booze, no cigarettes, no carousing. Except for the people who ran the place. Of that, however, we had as yet heard only the barest of rumors. And I wouldn't have a chance to see Bakker today. Richard Dortch, his second in command, would explain during a prolonged lunch that the PTL chairman had secluded himself from an admiring public so that he would have time to fast and pray and mull over next year's budget.

Dortch had sat in for the Bakkers on the set of the "PTL Club" that morning. "Jim and Tammy regret so much that they can't be with you today. They send their love. But you knew that already, didn't you? Isn't that wonderful? Let's give them a nice big hand."

A thin girl in bracelets and bright lipstick came to the microphone to sing about Jesus and glory. "How wonderful," Dortch said as she returned to her seat. "Isn't that simply marvelous?" He called for more applause. "Let's let the whole world know how we feel about Jesus!"

Next up was a bespangled fat man who put me much in mind of a pedophile, what with all the diamond rings hanging off his fingers and the piece of gold filigree about his neck. He belted out another song about Jesus. Then Dortch again: "Simply wonderful! Isn't that simply too marvelous for words!"

There was only one message on the show that morning, the same as every morning: forgiveness, mingled with blatant appeals for money. The guests were mostly reformed drunks and knockabouts who wanted to talk about their troubled trek through life, and all about how their burdens had suddenly fallen away when they found in themselves the power to forgive.

Over lunch Dortch would explain that he had once gone so far as to forgive the *Charlotte Observer* for its hostile editorial campaigns. After Bakker's fall, Dortch would take over as president of PTL and as host of its television show. He would last only a month. Even before his brief fling with stardom we'd heard talk—soon proved true—that he had acted as bagman for the $265,000 in hush money that found its way to Jessica Hahn.

Though he was serving only as Bakker's understudy at the time I knew him, he was already quite a celebrity with PTL regulars. I found that out as we were on our way to lunch. We had met under an awning on Main Street USA, a cobbled walkway that traversed the Heritage Village shopping mall. As we moved past the Heavenly Fudge Shoppe—"The next thing to sin," the advance man had said—and Der Bakker's Bakkery he was constantly stopping to pose for snapshots.

He was awfully good at it. One moment he would be walking along talking about the great pain Bakker had suffered from the clamors of a vindictive press. Next thing you knew he would have spotted a camera off in the crowd somewhere and would have come to a jolting halt, his whole body thrust suddenly forward in a fevered and accommodating pose: a glint of teeth, one hand shot forward in a rigid greeting, his right leg raised a little behind. Like a shot putter polishing his style for the Olympics.

Then the world would start up again. He would fall into the old gait, his voice solemn as he took up the familiar theme of Jim Bakker versus "the media." I nodded obligingly, as though I was by no means to be counted among their number. We had a pleasant lunch even without the martinis, and I had begun to feel that Dortch wasn't such a bad sort. The talk kept going back to the *Charlotte Observer* and its unprincipled editorial policy. The whole business had got so out of hand that PTL had decided to withdraw all of its advertising from the paper—about

$100,000 a year—and put it in billboards. Dortch had briefly lost his Christianity and written a nasty letter condemning the editors for their "prosecutorial tone." A momentary silence as he looked up at me and explained how he had no more than stuck the letter into the mail when he found it in his heart to forgive.

"You see, the Lord had admonished me, and I understood that I was not being a Christian from my perspective. The perspective of the *Charlotte Observer*—despicable as it was—was not the point."

Dortch made Bakker's extravagance seem almost defensible. In recent weeks there had been a great outcry about the chairman's purchase of a $449,000 condominium in Palm Springs, California. But that was nothing, Dortch explained. A mere trifle, seen in perspective. Any executive of a secular corporation the size of PTL would have been willing to pay far more and would have lived far more enviably.

At the time neither I nor anyone else covering PTL knew about the more than $2 million Bakker had drawn in salary and bonuses during his last year as chairman of the ministry. Maybe Dortch could have made that seem respectable too. After all, the pressures of the gospel business were mighty intense these days. How was a big name like Bakker supposed to find time for himself? He wasn't like other men. He couldn't just go off and lackadaisically check into a vacation hotel like anyone else or take a weekend off to relax at the coast. His adulators would be on him in an instant.

"God bless you, Jim. God bless you. How do we make out our checks?"

So he needed all that: the $449,000 Palm Springs condo; the Gatlinburg mountain retreat; the $1.3 million lakefront parsonage in Tega Cay, a resort community just below the North and South Carolina line; and the Florida beach house with floor-to-ceiling windows that provided a view of the ocean from every room—places where he could escape his adoring public and spend long hours studying the Scriptures and communing with his Maker.

"Well," I said. "He could always try donning a beard or a fake mustache."

Dortch bristled, raising his fork in a gesture of defiance.

"Jim Bakker live like that? Monstrous! Unforgivable!"

It was only a joke. How could I have known that Bakker had been very good at "living like that"? I hadn't yet heard about his wigs and panty hose and fake boobs and all the rumors of his secret nocturnal visits to Charlotte's whorehouses and massage parlors.

But maybe Dortch had. He turned back to his food and again talked somberly about Bakker's need to find privacy in an atmosphere congenial to fasting and prayer.

"There's simply no way he can do that in a public place. I don't think we should expect that of him. My word, that would be extremely unfair."

.   .   .

Even with all the evidence laid out before them, many of PTL's "faith partners" would never for a moment believe all those stories about the massage parlors and the whorehouses and the steam rooms where Bakker supposedly cantered naked with his pederastic hangers-on.

To those who truly believed in Bakker such talk was all part of a conspiracy dreamt up by Jerry Falwell and Jessica Hahn during their days as founding members of a witchcraft cult. And even those who did believe it would never feel right about blaming him for his indiscretions. He had suffered too many hardships as a poor boy in a Michigan slum. He had grown up in an orange cinder-block house with purple shades (in some such fashion he would always recount the story) and had been ashamed of his childhood. How, then, could one blame him for being staggered by all the great wealth that had suddenly come his way, thanks to the redeeming power of the Lord Jesus?

There had been other successful prosperity preachers. The most famous were Oral Roberts, whose money-making stunts were also creating a scandal during this year of PTL, and Bakker's old boss Pat Robertson, who had built the giant Christian Broadcasting Network at Virginia Beach and was now thinking of running for president. But Bakker had been far and away the most unsavory.

"God wants his people to go first class," the grinning necromancer would say as he stood before the PTL television cameras and lovingly fondled his vintage $63,000 Rolls.

"The more you give to Jesus, the more Jesus will give to you!"

Serious men of the gospel would gasp. "A damnable heresy, this prosperity gospel," Falwell would later remark.

But Bakker would keep right on raising the ante, and each time the faith partners would dig a little more deeply for the donation that would return itself a thousandfold.

"Cast your bread upon the waters and it will return to you after many days!"

When he started making more money than seemed respectable even for a prosperity preacher he created a secret bank account that would keep the worrywarts at bay and himself awash in sybaritic ease.

Sometimes the donations coming in from faith partners never even made it into the secret bank account. Bakker associates would later testify that much of the money received in cash would simply be stuffed into one of Bakker's "money suitcases" and set aside for the next plane ride out.

"I am come that ye might have life and have it more abundantly!"

Half the world had heard about it by now: the Bakkers and their fast life under the South Carolina sun. The big cars and fancy houses, the shopping sprees, the mink stoles, the $2,000 Gucci handbags and the air-conditioned doghouses and the big parties. (He had once flown in $9,000 worth of truffles from Belgium for a bash at Café Eugene in Charlotte.)

And the tearful blandishments of wife Tammy, and her fake hallelujahs, as she stood there in her leopard-spotted jumpsuits and her spiked heels and her diamonds and her beehive wigs and all the rest, pleading shamelessly before the cameras: *We've spent it all every dime we've put every cent into PTL everything our money our lives our sacred honor*

Again the partners would unleash their "dollar power," and again the tears would come squirting out—tears of joy this time as she cranked out another song about Jesus, her pancake makeup all melting and her iridescent eyelids glowing hotly beneath the klieg lights. So that next time there would be more cars and even fancier houses. Three black Cadillac limousines, a Corvette, another Rolls, a houseboat, more gowns and stoles and satin petticoats, and finally the $449,000 California condo from which Bakker had phoned to confess his sin—if sin there was—to the mighty Falwell.

Through it all Tammy Faye stood looking out at us, woefully prisonpent from behind her bars of melted mascara, her whole face a smear of tearful penitence and her flywhisker eyelids coming apart as she pled for the tithes and offerings that would redound ten thousand times on their donors.

"I'm gonna sing a new song about Jesus and its gonna be bigger than all the others and you can say you heard it first on PTL and it is part of our new album that comes free with your next donation. So please send money please . . ."

Then off they would go for another $350-a-night vacation in Hawaii, never forgetting to send back happiest returns through their emissary Richard Dortch, who would appear onstage one morning holding the telegram. "Jim and Tammy say they are having a wonderful time. They wish all of you could be there with them. Isn't that wonderful? My goodness. Can you imagine that? Isn't that simply wonderful?"

Back from Hawaii or the Caribbean or the Tennessee mountains, they would suddenly be broke again. The money had all gone for foreign missions, they would explain. Soon Tammy would be back in front of the cameras, wearing a hot-pink sweater dress or maybe a white silk gown trimmed in scarlet chintz, crying and saying, "We've given everything. Please help us please . . ."

And again the faith partners would make their pocketbooks sing.

I am come that ye might have life and have it more abundantly!

.   .   .

Like I say, I probably shouldn't have been surprised at getting so many late-night phone calls or at any of what was to happen in the coming weeks. After my lunch with Dortch I had another chance to look around the place. I had already begun to feel a little unclean. No cigarettes; no whisky. Only the fetid, cloying stench of PTL wholesomeness and good fellowship. I kept thinking of what an old eastern North Carolina newspaper editor named Hoover Adams had told me once: "Why, son, anybody who wouldn't be impressed with Heritage USA wouldn't be impressed with anything, not even with the gates of Paradise itself!"

In one shoppe you could buy an exclusive line of Tammy Faye cosmetics and panty hose; in another, Saks Fifth Avenue originals at discounts. At Perry's Jewelry Emporium you could pay New York prices—and be damned glad of it too—for diamond earrings and emerald-studded stickpins. Among the knickknacks at a PTL souvenir shop was a purple metal-flake license tag that read Ask Me About Jesus. In the bookstore the PTL albums and cassette tapes and the inspirational paperbacks fetched a tidy sum even if you were lucky enough to own a PTL discount card. Among Bakker's best-selling cassette titles was a work I first took to be autobiographical: *The Church's Greatest Thieves*. Ten dollars, not including your discount. Down the street, at a toy store, $750 would get you a life-sized stuffed giraffe, and for only $550 you could get a Lassie lookalike.

You could be a partner in this Byzantine enterprise for only $15 a month. But to feel really a part of it you had to give a great deal more. A $1,000 donation would make you a Silver Partner and guarantee you three free nights a year at the Heritage Grand for the rest of your life. Plus discounts. Pay $3,000 and you could become a Golden Partner. Six free nights a year at the Grand or at the twenty-story yet-to-be-built Heritage Towers, a cleverly mismanaged project that would stand uncompleted for years after Bakker had fled.

A lot of faith and a lot of money. "They don't allow any poor Christians here," a young man named Will Close told me over coffee on the afternoon of my visit. "But they're attracting a lot of them to the area, and the burden of looking after them falls back on our relief agencies."

Will was the heir of an old textile family that had built the nearby town of Fort Mill. As we sat talking in one of his family-owned restaurants he anticipated a lot of Falwell's later condemnation of Bakker's prosperity gospel as scandalous, heretical, and, more often than not, financially disastrous for believers living on fixed incomes.

"People listen to Bakker on TV and they believe what they hear," Close said. "Some of them sell everything they've got and load their families in a battered old station wagon and come down here. But here's the catch: when they get here they find out they're not allowed to stay at PTL. Bakker ships all these poor people away from the main part of town. I guess he doesn't want them cluttering up the nice clean streets of PTL. And so they wind up on our churches and welfare organizations. That's the part of it you don't see."

. . .

The woman standing at the JB Wiener Wagon seemed at first to have wandered onto the grounds of Heritage USA by mistake. Her diamonds and furs were quite in keeping with the garish atmosphere of the place. But her elegant coiffure, her statuesque bearing, and her lofty manner of speaking hinted at a more subtle provenance. She had been all over. She had visited all of the great cities of Europe and had worshipped in the fine old cathedrals at Nuremberg and Strasburg and Cologne. She had cruised the Adriatic, supped at Venice, and explored the ruins of Yucatan. She had dined in palatial splendor on the Côte d'Azur and sipped good *Deutsche* schnapps under dripping awnings along the Kurfurstendamm. She had seen most of the world's great tapestries, much of its elegant statuary, and all of Titian.

But she was home now, back at Heritage USA, the only place ever to make her feel as if she belonged. "I can hardly tell you," she said, "how empty life would be for me without the pleasure and, really, the sense of fulfillment I get from coming here."

Me, I got out of there just in time. The cars were already beginning to back up for the first night of Christmas City USA. I had begun to feel really dirty now, as though I had strayed by chance onto the back streets of Quasimodo's Paris. In what other part of the world could Bakker and his pals have possibly foisted off their sucker game with such astounding success? A great country, the good old U. S. of A.: you get all kinds.

As I went back up the long, sloping drive past the incoming traffic and the gatehouse full of waving teenagers I could see the first ominous glimmer of the farewell sign I was already anxious to forget:

GOD LOVES YOU

HE REALLY DOES

HURRY BACK

LOVE

JIM AND TAMMY

It was good to get out of the place and even better to know that I would never have to see it again.

Or so I kept telling myself at the time.

2

Day two of the PTL scandal found me walking the streets of the town where I had broken into the newspaper business more than twenty-five years earlier, the town most of America would never have heard of if it hadn't heard of Jerry Falwell first. Maybe on another day it would have been a pleasant diversion to go back and rummage through a dimly re-membered past. Not so on this cold March afternoon. At the moment Lynchburg, Virginia, was the place to be only if you were a twenty-eight-year-old hungering after a front-page byline. I was past fifty and no longer aspired after that commodity—but I was to have it, by God, whether I much cared for it or not!

My editor had rung before dawn, alarmed to find me still at home. "Just going out the door," I explained. He hung up and I took an extra dose of tranquilizers and lay back down and fell into a welcome if troubled sleep. By the time I got to Falwell's town, somewhere along toward noon, most of the other newspeople were already there. Camera crews and sound trucks had come in from Richmond and Washington and Charlotte. Some of the biggest names in American journalism would be there later that day, by video hookup if not in person; and I was to be a part of it all, contrary to every decent instinct. Nor was that the end of it. As my editor had informed me, I was somehow to steal a march on the whole crowd.

"Get to Falwell any way you can! We've got to have something from him direct!"

At Falwell's "Old Time Gospel Hour," a labyrinthine brick complex on west Langhorne Road, I attempted to fulfill my mandate in the best tradition of American journalism. I growled at the receptionist and flung myself rudely across the lobby through a pair of heavy doors that opened onto an inner hall—only to be met by two defiant security guards.

Sorry, buster.

I'd known from the start what kind of reception I would get. Still, it was to be taken for granted that I would unhesitatingly browbeat the truth out of Falwell's associates if not out of the great man himself.

"Can't go nowheres in here without a badge," one of the guards said.

He showed me back to the lobby. The girl at the switchboard was courteous and condescending. Seeing Falwell would be impossible, of course. But have a seat and she would ring Mark DeMoss, Falwell's administrative assistant, and find out if he might have a moment to spare.

"Sorry. Mr. DeMoss is quite busy right now."

I took the badge, strung it from my lapel, and retreated to the waiting area, drumming my fingers impatiently on the arm of my chair. I sat there for thirty minutes or more, leaping up at intervals to demand satisfaction and being told each time that DeMoss was "still tied up."

I had been there for almost an hour when she called me over and said DeMoss was finally on the line. I could tell by his voice that he was young, probably twenty-five or twenty-six at most. He was snappish and perhaps even a bit disdainful of my high standing in the world of journalism: I was just one more in a mob of reporters that had been swarming in by jet or limousine all morning and wantonly disrupting his day. I reminded him that Falwell had appeared on CNN's "Daybreak." Was I to be denied equal access?

Equal access denied. But come back in an hour or so and maybe he could scramble around and find a minute or two to deal with my importunities.

Mary Ellen, looking more than ever like the girl I had met in that town more than a quarter of a century earlier, had gone out with me for a late lunch. Though brought up by Virginians in the Alabama Black Belt, and thus a stickler for proper behavior, she had been decent and understanding about my display of bad manners. The streets of Lynchburg were no longer so familiar, and we could find none of the restaurants we remembered from our first days there—and indeed the town had changed in many ways. Anyhow, there was little time for dawdling; there would be little time for anything in the weeks to come. We were back at the

"Old Time Gospel Hour" promptly at three-thirty. I dashed through the security doors and was again manhandled by a guard.

Not this time, Mac.

Git that white trash outa here. I guess that's what they were thinking. No manners. Childishly inane and trivial. *Just git him on out!* But what was I to do? Being childish and trivial and unmannerly is the first responsibility of any newspaper that expects to get itself taken seriously.

Certainly that was never more true of any newspaper than of the *Atlanta Constitution.* My editors would be sure to demand a full accounting. Under an editorial regime that had come in from the *New York Times* a scant three months earlier, reporters were to be judged by a single unremitting standard: the amount of gall and pure orneriness they were able to display in pursuit of a news story. Soon the new editors would draw up a white paper and call me in for a review. We feel that you need to be a little more aggressive in this area, they would say. Or in this. And sign the paper, please, so that we will all know where we stand.

The security guard again conducted me back to the lobby. My wife pretended to be reading a copy of *Parental Guidance.* Others sat whispering behind their hands. *I tell you Ethel there's nothing worse than a sorry white man.* I fingered my badge and waited, still popping up every ten minutes or so to demand satisfaction. Four o'clock grudgingly turned to four-thirty and then to five o'clock. No word from DeMoss. But at least none of the big-name journalists had come in. Maybe they had already been there and gone, or reached him by satellite, or decided he wasn't worth the wait. It would take one more fine excuse to satisfy my editors that I had exhausted every trick in the *New York Times* repertoire of snoop reporting and still hadn't got inside. Anyway, there was nothing to do now but sit it out. It was almost six before I finally got into his office.

Not a bad sort, DeMoss. Perhaps we had misunderstood each other. We each apologized, almost to the point of being fulsome. I hated thinking about it. I hated thinking about how to explain a wasted afternoon to my editors. I later learned that DeMoss had been born rich—the son of one of Falwell's old patrons—and that this was his first crisis. He would mature greatly in coming months as the PTL effusion blossomed forth in all of its noisome glory.

For the moment, though, he sat eyeing me suspiciously from behind his desk. Why did I need an exclusive? There was to be a 9:00 P.M. press conference at which Falwell would fully discuss his role in the rapidly developing scandal. Wouldn't that do for me as well?

A deadline problem, I lied. I would need only fifteen minutes.

"I'm just not sure. Come around to the church tonight—say about eight o'clock—and we'll see."

.   .   .

The church was Thomas Road Baptist, an institution hardly less renowned than Jim Bakker's South Carolina theme park, and in Lynchburg, at least among the people who counted, hardly more respectable. It was one of America's true monster churches—more than twenty thousand members and five sermons every Sunday, all but one by Falwell himself. But the better sort in Lynchburg had never much cared for fundamentalist preachers, not even the kind who could elect presidents and tell the People for the American Way where to head in.

Lynchburg was an old place on the edge of the Virginia hunt country, built on terraces high above the south bank of the James River and crouched amid a cluster of hills at the foot of the Blue Ridge Mountains, a town sort of lost and forgotten by most of America until Falwell had come along and brought it his peculiar measure of fame.

Once a promising inland port city, it had lapsed into obscurity after the Civil War. Yet it still enjoyed prosperity of a sort. During the early 1900s it was known mostly for its tobacco markets, later for its ironworks and shoe factories, and finally for the ministries of Jerry Falwell. During the year and a half that I was there, back in the late fifties, Falwell was still an obscure proselytizer knocking on doors in the back parts of town like a seedy bill collector or vacuum cleaner salesman, getting knives and guns stuck in his face and big dogs sicced on him and still managing to preach every Sunday to lank, slack-jawed factory workers and their wives in the corner of a drab cinder-block building that had once been home to a soft drink bottling company.

He was a pretty rough character in those early days. So we'd always heard. Half-boots, swept-back hairdo, polyester suits. So I guess there were a lot of bloody fights in some of those back alleys. His father had been hugely successful as a con man, with plenty of money in the bank, and the young Falwell had grown up as a big, rough-talking, hard-drinking gang leader down Rustburg way. So I always figured he must have kicked plenty of guys in the teeth getting them to come up to God.

I moved around a lot during my first year in Lynchburg, eventually finding myself in one of those rough sections where, at any moment, you might expect Falwell himself or maybe only one of his surrogates to come knocking at the door. "Are you saved, young man? No? Well, if you would be so good as to come with me, please."

I didn't start out that way. Truth is, I started out in the fancy Rivermont Avenue section, the one place where Falwell and his crowd were never welcome. Rivermont Avenue ran all the way from downtown Lynchburg past the dismal slums of Red Line and along the steep banks of the James River almost to the foot of the mountains. It was truly Old Family Virginia. All the best homes were along that street, all the old names, with pure bloodlines going all the way back to the founding of colonial America.

Even with all their money the Falwells never made it big with the Rivermonters. Falwell thought he knew part of the reason:

"To my dad the rich Republicans who lived across Lynchburg in the Rivermont Avenue section . . . were carpetbaggers who threatened the future of the nation. . . . He scrambled to build a little business empire of his own, and he often said that the wealthy men of Rivermont were surprised at his success. He was a self-made man without a 'proper education.' "

I barely qualified as an acceptable addition to the Rivermont milieu— barely, I say, because I'd been taken in as a reporter on the staff of the *Lynchburg News,* a paper founded by one of the really big names in those parts: the late Senator Carter Glass, who'd started out his political life as a populist loud in his cry against railroad monopolies and the Wall Street money power before ending it in the finest Old Family style, defender of all the proper Virginia traditions and, by now, a committed Democrat who helped create the conservative political organization that would run the state almost as an oligarchy for the next half century. The Harry Byrd machine, as it came to be known after Glass had passed from the scene.

During my brief three years as a Virginian, first in Lynchburg and later in Richmond, Glass was little more than a hazy memory everywhere except in his hometown. There, to be sure, he was far from being forgotten.

The town had belonged to him and his family a long time before it ever belonged to Jerry Falwell. He had left an estate worth millions, including the town's two dailies. Given my youth, my North Carolina origins, and my inferior intellectual acquirements, I knew from the start that my status among the Rivermonters was far from secure. I kept thinking of what William Faulkner had said on his first day as a writer-in-residence at the University of Virginia: "Virginians are all snobs. I like snobs. They spend so much time being snobs they don't have any left over to meddle with you."

Yet, in spite of everything, I managed to hit it off pretty well during my first days there. With the help of my managing editor, a personable fellow named Peyton Winfree, I finessed a room in the home of a genteel lady related to Senator Glass himself. I guess the lady—I believe she was a niece—was close enough to claim kin but not quite close enough to have had any part in the will. Otherwise, why would she be taking in boarders?

Actually, the way it was explained to me, she was doing it as a favor and had helped other young men in the same way. But I could see that she probably also needed the money. It was a real gloomy place, that old house, even if it did sit right at the end of one of the best streets in town, only a block off Rivermont Avenue and just across from the campus of Randolph-Macon Woman's College. I could see in an instant that she had gone a long way toward falling into that not-unfashionable social state known as genteel poverty. Falwell would have been about as welcome there as some sleazy character peddling used condoms.

I have to admit that Rivermont was a swell place in a lot of ways. But I don't know. I spent almost six months there and always felt a little stifled somehow. Was this any place for a guy trying to make himself known as a New Voice from the South? I guess the truth is that from my first day there I was already looking for a way out. Maybe I figured I would learn a whole lot more about life on Falwell's side of town. Anyway, I eventually made my excuses and left one bright Sunday morning, without any clear idea of where I was going.

Well, I went back to the good part of Rivermont many times after that, but only as Jerry Falwell might have gone, as a second-class citizen, or, I guess I should say, as a reporter on assignment, which was much the same thing. I went into a lot of the big houses and would always stand there a little awkwardly while one of the aristocrats went off to announce that "the photographer is here." Goddamn them! Just because I happened to be lugging one of those old-fashioned Speed Graphic cameras that immediately got you classed as some kind of dirty little news hack who might have just stepped out of a 1935 B-grade gangster movie.

New Voice of the South to you, my good man!

Except I couldn't tell them that or explain that a real photographer hadn't been available to come along and take the pictures. Or, what was closer to the truth, that the city editor just hadn't figured the story was important enough for him to send a real photographer. Anyway, I always got the feeling that everybody would have felt a lot better about it if I had knocked at the back door, along with all the hired help, rather than at the front. The same as Falwell or as William Faulkner himself if Faulkner's name had been Bill Jones.

· · ·

So now I was back, after twenty-five years, slouching gloomily about the aisles of the Thomas Road Baptist Church. Jerry Falwell's side of town. I waited for DeMoss in the big sanctuary until I realized he wasn't coming and then went off on my own to find Falwell.

He had just come in from a 7:30 appearance on CNN's "Crossfire" and was awaiting a 9:00 P.M. press conference when I presumptuously barged into the tiny alcove where he and an aide had taken refuge. He smiled and greeted me warmly, his face still masked by the thick coat of pancake makeup he'd worn on "Crossfire." He remembered me at once; not from the old days—we had not known each other then—but from my coverage of his big 1984 libel trial against *Hustler* magazine in neighboring Roanoke.

Falwell, known less as a preacher in those years than as a rousing trumpeter for Moral Majority, Incorporated, of which he was founder and chairman, had sued *Hustler* and its publisher, Larry Flynt, after the magazine smeared him with a fake testimonial based on a popular Campari aperitif advertising campaign of the day. The Campari people had made brilliant use of sexual double entendre. Celebrities talked about their first encounter with Campari as though they were recounting their first adventure with a member of the opposite sex. And now *Hustler* had decided it was Jerry Falwell's turn. *"Jerry Falwell Talks About His First Time."* The ad depicted him as a drunken lout copulating with his mother in a Lynchburg outhouse. People didn't like to talk about it at church or even on the streets and perhaps not even in the parlors of Rivermont Avenue. "Not in the best of taste, my deahs, but then he *is* a Falwell, you know."

"Well, I guess I have to ask you," I said. "Jim Bakker and his women. I guess there must have been too many of them to count."

"My word, I don't think so. I can tell you that he spoke to me of only one."

"Jessica Hahn?"

"Yes."

"Was she a regular?"

"His statement to me was that he had only one encounter with Jessica Hahn. One unfortunate incident for which he seemed truly contrite and penitent. He asked me who he could trust in this time of crisis. I told him that was between him and the Lord. And he said, 'There's no one else, Jerry. You'll have to take the ministry.'"

"If you were to find out there were others. Or if he had been seeing Hahn on a regular basis . . ."

"It would be a dark day for the Christian ministry and for the world of televised evangelism."

It was already a dark day—the darkest, as he was quick to confess, that he had ever faced, and maybe even darker for the "body of Christ" than for him personally.

"I'm sure you must have heard the stories about all the others," I said. "The other women, I mean." I had not heard them yet. I was only guessing. But I was sure there must have been others. It only made sense for a guy like Bakker.

"I hope those are only stories being spread by the enemies of Christ, and I truly pray that we may be spared further headlines of that nature."

He must have known the truth—that he had been lied to going and coming and that he had been forced to protect Bakker if only for the greater good of television evangelism.

The squeaky-voiced little PTL host had always assumed he could do whatever he wished and explain it away in any fashion he chose and that the world would automatically accept his version of events as indisputable, no matter how much evidence had been amassed against him. But what about Falwell? Had he truly been taken in by Bakker's trumperies? We would not be long in finding out.

He had been more than tolerant of my presence and was thoughtful enough to avoid troublesome topics. Like whether I had yet found the Lord or voted for Ronald Reagan. He had hoped to find time for reflection and prayer before meeting with reporters at nine. No chance of that now. Long before that cold March evening I had begun to like Falwell in spite of myself. I'm not sure when I began to change my mind about him; maybe as early as the 1984 trial in which he had attacked Larry Flynt with what turned out to be only limited success.

The *Hustler* people had managed to get the trial moved to Roanoke under the mistaken impression that Lynchburg was solid for Falwell and that it would be impossible to find an impartial jury there. It may have been harder in Roanoke, where the Rivermonters had no clout and no local envy prevailed. Sentiment appeared heavily on his side, and well that it was so; for, as it turned out, he had a pathetically weak case. The libel laws afforded him no refuge; he was too much in the public eye and hence, under a series of Supreme Court rulings, was fair game for vitriolic publishers. The verdict came down in his favor, though it was a verdict for which little could be said: only $200,000 out of the $45 million he had sought—$200,000 for "emotional distress," and nothing at all for libel.

"Lilliputian!" snarled Falwell's New York attorney, Norman Roy Grutman. "A mere bagatelle—and worlds away from the Blue Ridge mentality of what is proper." The irrepressible Grutman had been somber while awaiting the verdict—perhaps foreseeing the result, perhaps realizing after he had time to reflect on it that his exaggerated style was too "hot" for the Virginia hill country.

"The people in these marvelous old hills remember when a dollar was still a dollar," he said at a closing press conference. "I'm sure they thought in their hearts that they were punishing Larry Flynt. They were not, of course."

Grutman had won the bagatelle and spared Falwell an embarrassing down-home defeat by arguing under a law not directly related to libel that the preacher had suffered irreparable emotional damage as a result of the *Hustler* parody. Even a small-town Virginia jury would have had a hard time believing that line of reasoning if Falwell hadn't had a Grutman to pull it off. Few had seen his like before. For weeks after the trial the people at the courthouse would marvel at the oratorical wizardry of the Amazing Roy Grutman, master of four languages and the favorite lawyer not only of Falwell but also, strangely, of *Penthouse* publisher Bob Guccione.

Three years later, after he had signed on as chief counsel for Falwell's PTL regime, the whole nation would come to know the Grutman that a contingent of Virginia reporters and I had seen in the Roanoke courtroom. From opening statement to summation the performance of this onetime Shakespearean actor was a masterpiece of invective, bombast, lamentation, and muted despair. I remember coming up behind him on opening day. He had been the first to arrive at court; a squat man in his mid-fifties, striding slowly about the plaintiff's table with a faint show of restlessness as he waited for the judge, jurors, and *Hustler* attorneys to appear. He swung on me with an owlish glare and characteristic smirk, soberly assuring me in a thunderous baritone that I was about to witness the last great battle between good and evil.

Armageddon come to this little Blue Ridge Mountain town?

"Indeed, sir!" He glared at me with quivering jowls. "At least for this type of man and this type of publication!"

None of us could have known that the last great battle would have to await the coming of the PTL scandal, whereupon it would be shifted to the grounds of Heritage USA. But the Roanoke trial was enough of a battle for the moment. Before it was over people would almost have forgotten about Larry Flynt and *Hustler* and Jerry Falwell. Grutman was very nearly the whole show, bedazzling jurors and spectators alike with the splendor and outrageousness of his rhetoric. "Whither America!" he would say as he roared out his indictment of the magazine publisher who liked to think of himself as Mr. Sleaze. "Are we even now in the bosom of deepest chaos buried? Are we even at this moment being transformed into a planet of the apes!"

Then he would turn to his favorite playwright for supporting evidence:

> Who steals my purse steals trash; 'tis something, nothing;
> 'Twas mine, 'tis his, and has been slave to thousands;
> But he that filches from me my good name

Robs me of that which not enriches him
And makes me poor indeed.

Grutman was something of a hustler himself, neglecting to remind the jury that Shakespeare had put those words into the mouth of the most venomous scoundrel ever to engage the passions of theatergoers.

Was Falwell now to be branded an Iago?

I had often derided him as such in editorials: a malevolent tyrant anxious to napalm the pornographers, pistolwhip the abortionists and evolutionists, castrate the homosexuals, and throw at least half the Supreme Court in jail. The press had uniformly hated Falwell for his work in behalf of the Moral Majority and Ronald Reagan. Now I found him gracious and accommodating. After our first conversation he would throw up his hand each morning in a cheery greeting as I sat there uneasily amid a nest of liberal newsmen. I would always sit at the back and make myself as unobtrusive as possible. It was quite embarrassing. Once, in front of almost everybody in the courtroom, he had described me as a "great American journalist." The other reporters assumed we were old friends and fellow Christians and began to take seats on the other side of the room. Naturally they were all pulling for Mr. Sleaze; somehow I could not bring myself to do so, despite the seeming likelihood of Flynt's victory. In this type of case the First Amendment guarantees were always on the side of the press.

Maybe I had begun to undergo some sort of conversion experience. Not the orthodox kind, to be sure, and mighty slow going at that. Maybe I realized even then that I would no longer be able to write editorials ridiculing Falwell for his conservative politics. I would go on trying to hate him for a while, but somehow all the old relish was gone.

The Rivermonters were less forgiving. In Lynchburg the better sort would never have accepted him as an equal even if he hadn't been a persistent embarrassment to them with his widely popular fundamentalist television show. The Falwells had been among the earliest settlers in Virginia, but it was only in recent decades that they had acquired land and money, and, as I say, none had ever run in the best circles. They were a country family—the home place still sits on a hill one mile south of the town limits—that had built a reputation for low morals and fast dealing.

Falwell's father, Carey, had hit it big during the twenties. He laid the basis for the family wealth by organizing a sixteen-county oil distributorship. He owned gas stations, restaurants, guest cottages, grocery stores, a transportation line that would eventually become part of the Greyhound-Trailways system, and a mountaintop dance hall that could serve a thousand at a sitting. He acted as host to traveling carnivals, kept a pet bear, sponsored cockfights, and, during Prohibition, hauled bootleg liquor in false bumpers built onto his buses and oil trucks. He was loud, profane, often drunk, and an infidel until the day of his deathbed conversion. He also shot and killed his younger brother on the night before the 1929 stock market crash.

In Lynchburg, the shooting rivaled Wall Street for front-page news. The younger man, a drunkard and Veronal addict, had developed feelings of persecution after being in and out of trouble with the law. A quarrel with his brother in one of the family's restaurants led to an exchange of gunfire and to his death.

"Self-defense," the judge proclaimed, and no one doubted the justice of the ruling. But Carey Falwell brooded on the deed and turned more heavily to drink.

"For him the sorrow had just begun," his son was later to write. "Eventually it would kill him."

The young Falwell grew up pampered and gregarious in a house full of servants. Mostly he spent his time idling about the estate, terrorizing his teachers, and throwing himself into other aimless pursuits that during the late forties and early fifties passed for sin: beer busts, fast cars, and all-night poker games. Afternoons and evenings, he and a gang of fellow rowdies would hang out at one of south Lynchburg's hot spots, the old Pickeral diner, with little to do except feed the jukebox, watch the stoplight change, intimidate motorists, and flip their gold dollars* high in the air while hurling ribald invitations to the neighborhood girls.

Those who knew Falwell during his PTL days and came to respect his deftness of mind, his adder-tongued wit, and his ability to dominate all encounters with the press will not be surprised to learn that amid all the tomfoolery of his high school years he found a way to finish at the top of his class. He had also quit church and thrown himself even more

---

* A popular condom of the day, encased in gold foil wrapping.

fully into the perverse life of the streets. He lost his chance to deliver his class's valedictory address when school authorities learned that he had been stealing lunchroom tickets all year from a safe to which he and his gang had shrewdly gained the combination.

On the day he was found out he sat in the school's administrative office, swollen and bloody from a near-fatal automobile accident, listening with feigned amusement as the principal handed him the bad news. "Tell me, Jerry, how do you think it would look if we allowed a petty thief to deliver our honors address? Sorry, Jerry."

An enduring lesson for the young Falwell and, to judge by his performance in later years, possibly the most famous valedictory that never got delivered at Brookville High.

Out of school, he showed no inclination to change. He drifted with ease through two years at Lynchburg College and thought vaguely of going off to Notre Dame and becoming an engineer. But mostly he lived a life of the streets, coming in late on Saturday night and lying slothfully abed all Sunday morning. His born-again mother, who had fought tirelessly to prevent her family from tottering headlong into the abyss of wholesale unrespectability, learned to tolerate his errant ways and perhaps even to forgive him and his twin brother, Gene, for the "sorry blood" they had apparently inherited from the other side of the family.

Unable to get them to church, she fed them a healthy dose of Charles E. Fuller's radio sermons in their sleep. Falwell would later say that he owed everything to Fuller, an inspirational preacher whose "Old Fashioned Revival Hour" was standard listening fare in most fundamentalist homes during the early fifties. Falwell's mother would turn up the volume as she left for church, and he would lie there half asleep listening to Fuller's message of sin, conviction, penitence, and redemption through the blood of the risen Christ. America's first documented experiment in subliminal conversion. It did not happen all at once. For a long time, as he would later remember it—and he would never tire of the story—he had lain there wishing that just once he could wake up "without a Charles Fuller sermon echoing up and down the stairway."

Then one morning it hit him a little differently. It was one of the times his mother had managed to get him downstairs for breakfast. As he sat there over his eggs and ham and a platter of hoecakes laden with molasses he felt a new stirring inside him. "I felt like crying, but I wasn't sad. I felt excited, but there was nothing exciting on my schedule that day. . . . I know God is always present in our lives. Sometimes we feel Him. Other times we don't. That morning I felt Him there but didn't know what I was feeling."

He talked about all that one day shortly after the eruption of the PTL scandal, as we were driving up the mountain to Liberty University. He had founded the school fifteen years earlier as a parochial Bible college. Since then it had grown into an accredited—though still determinedly fundamentalist—university with more than eight thousand students. In years to come, he said, it would have thirty or forty or maybe even fifty thousand and would be to fundamentalist America what Notre Dame was to the Catholics or Brigham Young University was to the Mormans.

His GMC station wagon smoothly took the steep grade on that cold March morning. As we swung around the crest of a hill the campus hove into view, a cluster of low beige-brick buildings spread out far below in a wide valley, the sun coming down hard now and the great wall of the Blue Ridge Mountains rising far to the west. He fell silent for a moment, sweeping the valley with a long, thoughtful gaze. We came off the mountain in a blaze of sun with Falwell once more in a lively mood. The talk had turned again to the incomparable bounty of the Lord and how He had blessed Liberty with almost five thousand acres on which to expand and how within another year the school would enter NCAA Division I athletic competition, scheduling teams perennially found in top ten rankings. "And we'll be going after the best born-again athletes we can find."

Getting accredited hadn't been easy for an institution that openly scorned the concept of academic freedom, not even for a chancellor named Jerry Falwell. How had he managed it? Through purest guile, he explained, smiling blandly and ironically, learned at the footstool of his "good old daddy."

There were no political liberals on his faculty, no Darwinists; and no student could graduate without taking at least six hours of "creation science." What this meant was that the Falwellian view of biology had to be taught as "philosophy" to keep from running afoul of Virginia's accreditation standards. In other words, the trained Liberty University biologist who taught evolution as a rank heresy doubled as a philosophy professor in order to teach students that the biblical view of creation was essentially correct.

"Our people are all Ph.D.s," he said. "They can provide a kid with all the information he will need when he goes on for a graduate degree."

Falwell had known there would be trouble from the American Civil Liberties Union. And there soon was. The organization filed a complaint with the Virginia Council of Higher Education, arguing against the accrediting of Liberty graduates as public school teachers.

"The way we were going at it, they said that that was nothing but a circumvention of the issue." Falwell smiled again at the ruse. "We teach in our biology classes everything a kid can learn at the University of Virginia. But you don't get out of Liberty without taking those six hours of creationism."

We came on down the mountain and turned into the campus gate. Falwell swapped pleasantries with a security guard and then drove on in silence. What was he thinking now? Perhaps about all the hard years of his early ministry and about all the faith and turmoil and hard work that had gone into the building of his church and university. Or maybe about the difficult struggle that lay ahead: criminal indictments coming, PTL functionaries going to jail, the Body of Christ being mowed down like the flower of medieval chivalry before the sword of Saladin and his Islamic hordes.

"God's housekeeping," he said ruefully. "It may be two years—three years—longer—before we can recover from this blow. It's our Watergate; the effects may be even more devastating."

Even with all the gloom hanging over him no one could doubt that Falwell himself would recover. He always had. He had come a long, long way, by a lot of different routes, and he gave Charles E. Fuller all the credit. The memory of the "Old Fashioned Revival Hour" had informed his ministry at every turn and inspired him to experiment with television as a medium of conversion long before most preachers had grasped its potential.

"Four or five years of listening to Charles Fuller finally convinced me that I needed what he was talking about. I became aware of the fact that there must be millions of Jerry Falwells out there, who don't go to church, who aren't going to look for a church, who somehow had to be reached in a different way."

. . .

Nothing was ever the same after Fuller came into his life. He found no joy in the streets. Beer soured in his belly, and the songs of the Pickeral left him feeling vaguely dispirited and uneasy. Stories that had once seemed amusing now seemed pointless and insipid.

On the same day he'd first felt the powerful stirrings of the Almighty he found a church known for its devotion to Fuller's old-fashioned gospel and went up to be saved. Such was the force of his personality, even in those days, that he coaxed a fellow gang member into accompanying him on the long trip up to the altar. Within a week most of the others were there, crowding the communion table, learning about salvation and Christian sacrifice. Then it was back into the streets as Falwell and his old gang scattered about the town and began knocking on unfamiliar doors—in a sudden burning compulsion to save Lynchburg, America, and the world.

Yet the old Falwell did not vanish as suddenly as legend would later make it appear. In the early days of his ministry he was still wearing his tooled, western-style half-boots and Elvis Presley haircut. He had his father's unfailing instinct for promotional gimmickry and used it shamelessly to pack his church. One Sunday morning guest was a seven-and-a-half-foot wrestler, introduced to the congregation as the "world's tallest Christian." Black-belt karate masters also shared his pulpit, smashing hundred-pound blocks of ice in dazzling exhibitions of an Oriental art not yet the standard fare of the kung fu movies.

More magic than art it might have seemed to the Thomas Road congregation. "Blessed are they whose faith rests wholly in the Lord," Falwell would say, "for to them shall be given power to do works far more wondrous than these."

In 1984 a writer for a national magazine described the tone of Falwell's early ministry as "bullying." A fellow Lynchburg pastor, the Reverend John Killinger of the First Presbyterian Church, likely would have agreed. When he attacked the Thomas Road minister as a kind of sideshow entrepreneur, Falwell "struck back with typical venom," the writer said, "mispronouncing Killinger's name as Dillinger."

"Falwell's aggressive tone may have given some of his supporters violent ideas. Killinger and his family started getting death threats."

The writer must have heard a lot of those old stories we were hearing in those last days before I left Lynchburg. A lot of people had seen that in him before most of us had ever heard the name "Falwell." As a twenty-three-year-old graduate of Missouri Bible College, the aggressive and indefatigable preacher came straight back to Lynchburg and again started knocking on doors. Again he looked into the faces of angry drunken men cursing him and poking him in the gut with a shotgun. *Git the fuck on outa here you . . .* He even took to carrying a stick to beat off the angry dogs.

"But at least two or three times a day I would hear a stranger say, 'Please, come in. God must have sent you here. I've been praying that someone would come.'"

The world knows the rest: Falwell, Thomas Road, and Moral Majority, Incorporated. Long before he had become active in New Right causes his name was a national byword. His "Old Time Gospel Hour," a barely disguised version of Charles E. Fuller's "Old Fashioned Revival Hour," was the biggest of the television ministries, and his church membership had risen to more than fifteen thousand. Now, on a fateful morning in 1973, the issue of abortion on demand had come along to fire him with a new sense of mission. He found the news of the hated *Roe* v. *Wade* decision next to Lyndon Johnson's obituary:

SUPREME COURT LEGALIZES ABORTION

He put the paper aside and went to the window, looking out across a wide, billowy sweep of lawn, at streets on which going-to-work traffic was just beginning to appear. At forty, he had already done the work of two lifetimes—more work than a less ambitious man might have accomplished in a dozen lifetimes. But there was a deeper restlessness in him now, a persistent gnawing that his daily reading of the Psalms would not still—that was already rapidly growing into a passion even as he sat over breakfast. He thought of all he had been taught about the separation of church and state. Yet nothing seemed very clear anymore. All he knew was that he had seen too much and stood aside too long while all the big battles were being fought.

The street marchers and draft-card burners and drug cultists of the sixties had shaken mightily the stable and predictable world of his youth. Now the Supreme Court had brought it to the verge of apocalypse. A license to murder. What else could you call it? And now he, too, would soon take to the streets, organizing mass rallies, registering voters, frustrating talk-show hosts with his imperturbable certitude, confronting jeering mobs—"Babylon rose, Babylon fell; racist Falwell, go to hell!"—

and hating himself for all the times he had thundered against the idea of preachers getting mixed up in politics.

He felt as the Old Testament prophets had felt when they looked out on a world far gone in moral decay. Who would bring back the old ways? Surely there must be a moral majority out there somewhere. By the early eighties he was traveling up to 400,000 miles a year, mingling with Catholics, Jews, and anyone else who believed, with him, that the nation had dallied too often with false gods and was about to be spewed out the mouth of an angry Yahweh.

He was still far from saving the world, America, or even all of Lynchburg and seemed constantly on the verge of outgrowing the benighted fundamentalist precepts that no man had espoused more eloquently. Yet he would never entirely get rid of the Jeremiah that burned in his bones, just as he would never entirely overcome the stigma of having been born a Falwell. He would never have overcome that anyway, not in Virginia, not on Rivermont Avenue. His future mother-in-law, herself born to the old-time faith, came down with one of her "little spells" when she found out her daughter was sweet on Falwell and spent months devising stratagems to keep them apart.

On the morning that we drove up to Liberty University I tentatively broached the subject of his dubious social status. Was it true, as the magazine writer had said, that the Falwells had amassed considerable wealth without ever having achieved much standing in Lynchburg?

Yes. All true. Famous as he was, he still hadn't risen far enough to become socially acceptable to the people on Rivermont Avenue—all those self-important characters who had sneered at his family and shunned his ministry and, with precious few exceptions, had never yet made him feel welcome in their homes.

"The Rivermont Avenue crowd," he said, chuckling. And that was all, because I guess he remembered my telling him that I had lived there once, even if for only a couple of months, and that he didn't need to say anything else. Or maybe he figured it was just best for us to share our humiliation in silence.

3

"Hold for Mr. Grutman, please!"

The phone call had come unexpectedly on a Tuesday morning in late March. Before I had time to reflect on this strange turn of events or to grab a notepad, Grutman's powerful baritone came surging over the wire. He explained that he was "often wrong about people" but that in our earlier meeting at the *Hustler* trial he had taken me for a rare breed: a newsman with integrity. It was the most demeaning of insults, of course, coming as it did from someone outside the profession; but I didn't have time to think about that either.

Grutman had phoned, as he explained it, because he couldn't trust the perfidious New York press and, in short, to offer me an exclusive that in coming days would be the stuff of blazing headlines all over the world: evangelist Jimmy Swaggart's secret plot to destroy Bakker and promulgate a "hostile takeover" of PTL.

I was in no mood for an exclusive. I would rather not have had it. Bring the Xanax, dear! Why, I wondered, had he picked me out as the only "fair and responsible journalist" at the *Hustler* trial? Because none of the others had been willing to admit (though I myself had provided only the barest hint) that the time had come to bash the very daylights out of the People for the American Way?

Grutman's "exclusive" would prove to have all the resiliency of quicksand. But for the moment it rang true enough. The blatherskite Swaggart had been all over the news in recent days, saying nasty things about

Bakker's "carnival sideshow" and giving it out that the only business of television evangelists was "to preach the word of Jesus." At the time Grutman was still representing both Bakker and the new PTL regime—Falwell had called on him for double duty—and the story of Swaggart's attempted takeover, if that is what it was, would make big headlines in our afternoon editions:

JIMMY SWAGGART CONSPIRES TO BRING DOWN BAKKER

So, a big break at last. I was getting the story because I alone had stood out from all the simpering liberal newsmen who had been pulling for Flynt in Roanoke. To hell with your exclusive, Grutman! I didn't say anything. Instead, after thrashing around to find pencil and paper, I frantically and only half successfully tried to get it all down. By Grutman's account, Swaggart was out to smear Bakker as a first step toward seizing the PTL television satellite for his own Baton Rouge ministries. No doubt he had decided that it would prove a useful instrument in the conversion of mankind from unbelief and that it would also enhance his popularity in the whorehouses of New Orleans.

I did not actually know about the whorehouses yet. Later I would wonder how much Falwell had known. I would realize from something he had said during our trip to Liberty University that he apparently had heard all about Swaggart's weakness for women of the street and was only hoping it wouldn't get into the headlines. But I doubt if even he could have known the whole truth or fully grasped the vast hypocrisy of the man. After accusing another television evangelist of womanizing, Swaggart had been caught coming out of a New Orleans bordello by the same fellow.

He shook it off. When the word got out, much later, and he could no longer deny his failing, he would go before his congregation and weep pitifully for forgiveness. A simple matter to win over his own people, but that was only the half of it: he would lose the support of his mother church, the Assemblies of God, as Bakker had, and his ministry would soon be in decline, so much so that he would again be driven to seek consolation among the loose and tawdry women he had supposedly renounced in a blubbering fit of remorse. This time he wouldn't even try to make an excuse. When someone spotted him on a California street with one of his women and asked him what it was all about, he shot back, in effect: *Ain't none of your fucking business, mister.* And there would be no more weeping at the altar.

But we didn't know any of that yet. We did not know that while he was railing against Bakker's "soap opera down in South Carolina" he was himself out cruising the seedy New Orleans whorehouse district looking for action. Meantime, I was to have my exclusive and Grutman would do his part by making himself inaccessible to the clamorous scoundrels of the New York press. He would set out at once to lose himself in some obscure Vermont hamlet or New Hampshire cove. Or maybe he would take the voyage to Europe that he had been putting off for a long time. Never fear. I would have plenty of time to savor the glory of my windfall.

Grutman's story, in brief, was that Swaggart had tried to engineer his takeover by furtively accusing Bakker of the "most egregious kinds of sexual misconduct." He went on to explain that it was Swaggart, apparently, who had first spread the word of Bakker's midnight visits to a Charlotte massage parlor. And he had it all in writing.

As his voice stormed over the wire I kept thinking about the Grutman of the *Hustler* trial: his massive scowls, his anguished shows of feigned indignation and hurt pride, his air of barely concealed contempt for the defense witnesses, his subtle literary allusions, even his portentous silences as his gaze floated slowly to the ceiling: How long, O Lord! How long?

Maybe he knew the whole truth about Swaggart and maybe he didn't. Or maybe he was only being typically Grutman-like as he unloosed a withering stream of invective against the Baton Rouge preacher: Ugly and un-Christian. A despicable fraud. Egregious and unforgivable, a damnable hypocrite, a very dungheap, a cankerous and indelible blot on the escutcheon of Christian fair dealing.

All true, perhaps—yet for all the wrong reasons, because no one ever was able to show for certain that Swaggart had any real designs on Heritage USA.

I phoned in the story just in time to make the *Journal* Blue Streak. Last run of the day. Copyrighted.

But the paper had barely hit the street before my "exclusive" began to fall apart. Grutman again. Instead of beating it off to the wilds of New England or to some snowbound Alpine village as he had promised, he was on all the networks telling the same story. An egregious and damnable fraud, this Swaggart. And he had it all in writing. Damn you, Grutman. *Damn you Grutman damn you do you hear me you egregious and damnable fraud*

He had left us nothing for the morning editions. Shortest-lived exclusive since the old *Washington Times Herald* announced in a famous misprint that FDR had been confined to bed with a coed. An indelible blot on the escutcheon of my near-glory as a great American journalist.

Even so, in this business it was no small thing to be first. At least it would show that I was on top of things. No one would have to know that the phone call had come without my bidding. Bill Kovach, our overly ambitious editor in chief, recently acquired from the *New York Times* (actually one of their big-name castoffs, as we were later to learn), would probably be on the phone that same afternoon. Or maybe he would wire congratulations. Nice job. Keep it up. We've got big plans for you here. Real big.

The call did not come that afternoon, nor the telegram in the evening. By next morning I still had heard nothing. Quite a letdown. My editor had always called Kovach "the most powerful man in American journalism." At least until he got to know him a little better. So I guess it stands to reason that a guy like that couldn't allow himself to get excited over an exclusive that had already lost its impact by the time it reached the streets.

Still, even the illusion of a mighty journalistic effort should count for something. Finally, as I was preparing to leave town on another assignment, I got around to asking my immediate superior about it.

"How'd Kovach feel about the copyright?"

"Dunno."

"He didn't say anything?"

My editor grunted something that sounded like "No." Then: "He did say a little something."

I waited anxiously. "Well?"

"Wanted to know what you've got for him today."

"What the hell is he talking about?"

"Wants something new. The inside stuff on Falwell. Wants it fresh for the afternoon editions."

"There's no time."

In reply, only a massive and eloquent silence that had become the familiar postscript to almost all our conversations.

"Didn't you hear me? No time, Brice. I'm telling you, there's just no time."

"We'll need it by ten."

"It's already nine-thirty."

"Wants it quick. Wants it fresh. What the hell. Get Falwell on the phone. He's probably got plenty of new stuff ready to go by now."

Cancel all other assignments. Knock out something fresh for a 10:00 A.M. deadline and then beat it back to Virginia in all haste lest Falwell escape to some secret hideaway and deny us access to all of the other late-breaking PTL "dirt."

I didn't make deadline. But I was back walking the streets of Lynchburg that same afternoon. The day had turned windy and cold after a week of springlike weather. My last instructions from Kovach, as filtered through his second in command—a blustery fellow known as the Sonny Corleone of the newsroom—and finally through my own editor, were somewhat as follows:

"He's gonna hang on Falwell like his goddamn fuckin' shadder. You unnerstand? He lets him outa his sight just one goddamn second and we'll have his balls. Unnerstand?"

As always, security was tight at the "Old Time Gospel Hour." I haunted the place like a gaunt and angry specter, roaring through the lobby and forcing my way into the inner corridor only to be thrown out by a couple of guards who didn't give me time to explain that I was there on orders from the "most powerful man in American journalism."

Where's your pass mister you gotta have a pass to come in here

I got DeMoss on the phone and raged that it's my balls DeMoss, I've got to see Falwell. Impossible. Big meetings all afternoon. Give me a time, then. Can't say just yet. Call back later.

I knew he was there. I had seen his GMC station wagon parked just outside the door. The same wagon we'd taken up to Liberty University the week before. Maybe I could just wait for him out front. I knew it would be all right if I could see him face-to-face. He had told me as much on the night before our trip to the university. We'd set up a rendezvous for 8:00 A.M. in the parking lot behind his television studio. "But don't call Mark," he said. "He'll be trying to protect me."

So I knew it would be all right if I could just keep DeMoss out of it. Easy enough to do unless I cared less about my privates than about the cold March wind. Sure, one could argue that I might have spent the time more profitably at home reading *Capitalism in Crisis* in front of a good fire. But the fate of economic systems and even of mankind itself seemed insignificant now that a PTL fever was sweeping the land.

I waited there all afternoon, scrunched against the wind. It would be all right. He would have to come out sooner or later, and then everything would be just fine.

Actually there was reason to see Falwell that day. We had learned through confidential sources in Columbia, South Carolina, that in one recent year Bakker had taken $1.5 million out of PTL in salary and bonuses. An unconscionable amount of money for any kind of preacher. Did Falwell know? His auditors had been on the job for more than two weeks. Perhaps by now he had heard the news and would be willing to comment.

He'd better comment. Or I could expect the worst. *Gonna be his balls you can be damn sure of that.* Corleone, like Kovach, was new in Atlanta, a loudmouthed posturer who had brought tension and fear to the newsroom and who had long been proud of his reputation as the backroom brawler of American journalism. "We're taking names and kicking ass," he kept telling interviewers. "We're gonna make these newspapers world class." You could see him sallying forth from his glass office at any hour over almost any issue, spinning about the newsroom like a dervish gone mad with hashish, shouting and cursing with an inimitable flair that I guess was his understanding of how big-time editors are supposed to act.

Taking names and kicking ass. Ain't nothin' 'bout us that ain't world class

Suddenly nobody's job seemed safe. So I waited there by the GMC, hoping it would be all right. Sometimes I would stand casually leaning on it; other times, thinking I might arouse suspicion, I would slink off to some far corner of the mall-like complex, drawing my coat up and trying to stay out of the wind. The memory of all the old detective movies I had seen—Sam Spade lurking behind chimneys in murky alleys—came vividly to mind. Perhaps someone would see me there, in that same furtive pose, like some disreputable character from an old Bogart film, and figure that mischief was my game. And then the cops would come: "OK, fella, hows about a little ride down to the precinct?"

I must have waited four hours or more. It would be all right if I could just get to Falwell in time for my second deadline of the evening. Death and damnation if I could not. I'd heard not long before how DeMoss and Jerry Nims, Falwell's other chief aide, who had been put in charge of the PTL financial investigation, had visited Atlanta to complain about my constant harassment of the people at the "Old Time Gospel Hour."

"Somebody's forcing him to do it," DeMoss supposedly had said. "We want it stopped."

Kovach's new editor kicked them out. Keep a stiff pecker and stand behind your people out there on the front line. I guess that's one thing you could say for him, anyway. So I kept waiting, on into the shank of the afternoon, the wind blowing more sharply out of the mountains now and dusk settling heavily over the city. The last of the office workers had departed; nothing left now but Falwell's GMC and me watching from the corner, trying to fend off the bitter March cold and hoping nobody would get suspicious.

Then I saw him: a portly man striding briskly from the front of the building and heading straight for the GMC.

I came up on him in a hurry, a little anxious, yet knowing it would be all right.

He turned as he opened the door and looked me squarely in the eye. It wasn't Falwell.

"Sorry, I thought . . . Sorry . . ."

It was a much younger man—blond, squarish—who had come, apparently, to drive the wagon to wherever Falwell was. When I realized the truth I pressed him for a clue as to the minister's whereabouts.

"Ah," he said in good Deutsch. "*Er is lang aus gegangan.*"

The young man, I gathered, was a Liberty exchange student from Bavaria and part-time Falwell driver. Lynchburg got all kinds these days. He nodded apologetically as he climbed into the wagon. No, it would not be possible to see Dr. Falwell that evening; he had been gone for hours. "*Entschuldigen Sie, mein Herr.*" I stood there being buffeted severely by the wind, feeling a premonitory ache in my balls, watching morosely as the Bavarian drove off into the heavy and forbidding dusk, thinking about all the time I could have invested in *The Age of Revolution* or in *Medievalism and Modernity*.

So there was nothing left now. And the future of my privates hanging in the balance. I spent the evening dialing the unpublished number Falwell had given me and getting his recorded message. It just wasn't any good at all. He was probably in South Carolina by now; he had probably called a press conference and already broken the big news about Bakker's scandalous salary. It would all be going out over the wires with me standing on a cold street in Lynchburg, and Corleone anxiously hanging over the news terminal, saying, "We've got him by the nuts now. Just tell the sorry sonuvabitch to bring his own knife the next time he comes in."

Next morning I rang Falwell's secretary and learned that he was still in Lynchburg and that I might be in luck: he was to address a student assembly at ten o'clock that morning at Liberty University. I beat it out there in one big hurry. Maybe it would still be all right. At least nothing had come out about Bakker's big salary.

I talked to the Liberty ushers and got a spot near the podium. A good way to grab the chancellor on his way out. The guest speaker that morning was the California evangelist and exorcist John McArthur; a good speaker in a timely hour. It was a disappointment that he chose to say nothing about his great work at casting out devils. I was also a little surprised that Falwell had overlooked a chance to appoint him to PTL's new board of directors—the one spot where his experience would be a definite asset.

I watched for my chance with Falwell. Luckily, he recognized me as he came down from the podium. I explained that I had important new information on Bakker and needed to talk.

He thought for a moment. No, it would not be possible that afternoon. Where was I staying? The Radisson? Very well, then. He would ring me there that evening.

Before I could say more we were swept off in different directions by the crowd. So it was no good after all. I had let him get away without providing enough detail to incite his interest. Busy as he was, he would never remember to phone. Nothing to do but wait until morning and then rush back out to "Old Time" and start pounding on the doors again.

I went out for dinner and martinis. I staggered back to the room about eleven and had been there only a short while, fumbling around drunkenly for my paperback copy of *Decline of the West,* when the phone rang. It was Falwell.

He explained that he had business early next morning in downtown Lynchburg and could meet me at the Radisson for breakfast or coffee.

He was there promptly at eight, smiling and friendly—and alone. We adjourned to the restaurant and I immediately brought out the incriminating evidence against Bakker. One and one-half million dollars in a single year. (That was only part of the story; later figures would show that he had collected $4.8 million between January 1984 and March 1987.)

Falwell's startled reaction was a convincing sign that he'd heard nothing about it until now. "What? Are you sure about those figures?" He leaned over for a closer look. "If that is salary from PTL it is truly astounding. Truly."

But he could add nothing for publication. He had not talked to his auditors, and, in any case, he had obligated himself to say no more publicly until they had completed their investigation. He would disclose all details two weeks hence at a big press conference scheduled for Heritage USA. I explained tactfully that it would be all over for me if I were to phone the office with no reaction from Jerry Falwell. He laughed his familiar noncommittal laugh and motioned for the waitress to bring more coffee.

For once he seemed in no hurry. He was somber, reflective. The longer we sat there the more evident it was that the news about Bakker's salary had come as a serious jolt, one more piece of information to help confirm the many scandalous rumors he'd been hearing for the past two weeks. Maybe he would just have stayed out of the whole nasty mess— he would later confess as much—if he could have foreseen where it would end.

"You know," he said, "it burns me sometimes. These limousines and these big-shot preachers and these two-million-dollar homes."

The issue had come up during his recent appearance on ABC's "Nightline," Sam Donaldson presiding. "They started with a picture of Oral Roberts's home; $2.4 million. Then Swaggart's home. That was only $1.5 million. I was prepared for what was coming next. Macel [Falwell's wife] had told me ABC had had its cameras on top of our fence shooting all afternoon. But they didn't use the picture because they'd found out the house was bought by one of our parishioners and given to the church as a parsonage."

It was quite a nice place. I had seen it from beyond the iron gate: a 250-year-old neoclassical plantation house, with a wide veranda across the front, set on a hill amid a stand of white oaks far older than the house itself. Not far from the spot a haggard band of Rebels had fought a pitched battle with the Yankees during the last days of the Civil War.

"I could buy a big, fancy car," Falwell said. "I was raised in a wealthy home. But the issue is—and the imagery we need to present to the world is—that we're not in this thing for the money." He had pressed the point on "Nightline." "'Why didn't you show my house, Sam? You had your cameras over there today shooting. Was it because it was only a $160,000 house that had been given to the ministry by a businessman?' And he said, 'Well, you do own an airplane, don't you?' And I said, 'No, Liberty University does.'"

He still seemed in no great hurry to be on his way. He sat there letting his coffee grow cold. The waitress had come with a third refill. Except for the morning we'd gone off alone in his GMC it was the first time I'd seen him when he wasn't surrounded by protective aides or admiring parishioners.

"We've had headlines in the Seoul newspaper," he said. "Headlines all over the world. Front-page headlines in the *London Times*. We've heard from churches all over Europe. We've heard from Asia. We're not talking about a little rupture or incident. We're talking about a problem of major proportions, and it ought to be a message to each and every one of us who loves Christ: Be sure your sins will find you out."

He took a sip of the cold coffee and leaned forward. "We can't say any longer: 'I'm my own boss; it's my own business what I do.' It is somebody else's business. Reverend Bakker found out it is somebody else's business. The whole world is making it their business. And properly so. The world has a right to expect that from us. And we have a right to expect better of ourselves. We have a right to believe that we're not going to keep hearing all the garbage and rumors we've been reading in the newspapers every morning—something that contradicts everything the gospel represents."

He paused for only an instant and went on in a stronger voice, almost as though he were in the pulpit. The waitress backed off to watch. "Be not deceived! God is not mocked! We're the ones who are the butt of the world's mockery, and we're the ones who will eventually have to pay the piper."

Yes. All that, and we still didn't know the worst about Swaggart. At least I didn't.

Time to go, and I had just now got around to asking him whether demonic possession might have been a factor in the PTL scandal. Was that why he had brought in John McArthur? Was Bakker himself a victim of demonic possession?

He dismissed the thought with a shrug and another deep-throated noncommittal laugh. You had to wonder what he was holding back. I knew he was a profound believer in possession. But he wouldn't talk about it except in the vaguest sort of way.

"I think it is very real. I have never had an experience with it. Most of it occurs in Third World countries where there is just terrific spiritual darkness."

Third World? Terrific spiritual darkness? My thoughts immediately flew back to the bleak pine and broom-sedge fields of the upper South Carolina Piedmont and to Heritage USA, gaudiest of man-made landfills. Not technically a part of the Third World. But certainly a place of great spiritual darkness if even half of what we had been reading was true. Falwell knew more about that than any of us. It was just that I couldn't get him to talk about it for publication, maybe because he had already envisioned what it would look like in the headlines:

FALWELL CITES DEMONS AS CULPRITS IN PTL SCANDAL

So he must have known a lot more than he was willing to admit. Was it really only an accident that McArthur was in town? Any sensible observer who had followed the PTL controversy could not entirely dismiss the thought that demons were almost certainly mixed up in it somewhere. The fundamentalists had always said you couldn't trust the Pentecostals to keep satanic influences out of their services. With all that speaking in tongues and laying on of the hands and divine healing—well, you just never knew when you might be inviting the wrong crowd in for worship. And then try to get rid of one of those fellows once he'd got his feet under the altar or latched onto your innermost being.

For the first time Falwell seemed anxious to be on his way, explaining frankly that he would be at a loss to exorcise a demon even if by chance he were to meet some poor tormented PTL faith partner unlucky enough to have fallen into the hands of such a being.

"I would definitely defer to someone else. The Catholics have had a great deal more experience with that than we have. My word, for me to interfere in something of that sort—well, I think that would be decidedly unwise. That certainly is not one of the things I pretend to know much about."

Well, anyway, he couldn't risk talking about it openly when most of the people at Heritage USA were committed Bakkerites who had been looking for almost any excuse to bring him down. Let him drop even the slightest hint that Bakker's theme park was the most notorious demonic outpost of the Western world and he'd never be able to explain himself satisfactorily to all those Pentecostals he was still hoping to bring over to his side.

I watched him as he got up to leave, fidgety and quite definitely in a hurry now, though obviously much too polite to break into a dead run. The manager of the restaurant came up with a bow of great courtesy and announced that our coffee was on the house. What small-town motel restaurant wouldn't be honored to have an authentic American hero on its premises? What reporter would not compliment himself on being mistaken for an "insider" who had by some means gained a private audience with the great Falwell? But what good was it after all? I'd got almost nothing out of him. He had smoothly put me off at every turn, assuring me repeatedly that every secret piece of information would be made public at his late-April press conference.

I would be there for this momentous event, but only as one of a multitude of reporters and big-city TV cameramen. Even if he were to announce that an exorcist had been hired to sweep the place clean of demonic influences, my story would inevitably be little more than a rewrite of what would already have become old news on the television networks. No copyright. No Pulitzer. No pat on the back from the editors. Only the dark and bloody knife, the secret castration downstairs behind the great rolls of newsprint with the presses running so that nobody would hear the screams.

"And just make sure you don't go outa here walking funny and getting blood all over the floor. You hear me?"

5

Maybe it didn't even matter what I phoned in to my editors. Lacking confirmation from Falwell, the *Journal-Constitution* cravenly refused to expose PTL as a place of "great spiritual darkness" and as an outpost of demons—or even to print the story of Bakker's financial excesses. The *Charlotte Observer* was slightly more courageous. No mention of demons. But within the week it would have the news of Bakker's secret monetary account on its front page, quoting "sources."

By then there was even more improbable news. On April 24, a Friday, respected television minister John Ankerberg appeared on "Larry King Live" to divulge a story from the deepest stews of debauchery and demonic excess—which is to say, from backstage PTL: a tale of fevered homosexuality, adultery, whoremongering, mate swapping, and other diversions seemingly patterned on ancient rituals of satanic sacrifice.

The day before, in Nashville, Tennessee, Ankerberg and Falwell, together with four presbyters from Bakker's headquarters church, the Assemblies of God, had spent hours listening with stupefaction as former intimates of the PTL evangelist trooped forward with stories of his financial and sexual intrigues. Could such things be? Every witness, it seems, had sworn to the truth of his statement and was willing to stand by it in court. Falwell, who had led a privileged though by no means reclusive life, recoiled with physical revulsion when he learned the worst, realizing, perhaps for the first time, how roundly he had been taken in by Bakker's self-serving version of the Hahn affair.

Ankerberg had been scheduled for a thirty-minute segment on the hour-long show. When the other guest, ABC's acerbic, news-wise Sam Donaldson, realized what he was hearing, he immediately got on the phone to King's associates. His message: Let Ankerberg have the whole hour.

Even people who had habitually sneered at Bakker initially turned away in disbelief. Others would never believe it at all. All a put-up job, they would say. What could you expect from a Falwell? The most dedicated of Bakker's followers had believed from the start that Falwell and Jessica Hahn were in it together, trying with all their might to steal PTL—part of a plot they had cooked up way back when they had been coworshippers at the shrine of a latter-day druidical cult known as the "Illuminati," originally an eighteenth-century Bavarian quasi-religious sect associated with freemasonry and renegade Jesuits.

Although outlawed in the land of its birth, the Order of the Illuminati, as Bakker devotee Paul Wood explained it, had experienced an insidious rebirth as an appendage of the International Society of Druids and other powerful British conspiratorial forces. Now it was bigger than anything, bigger even than the group that had spawned it, bigger than the "Old Time Gospel Hour," bigger than Ted Turner, maybe even bigger than the Trilateral Commission, which had always been a favorite target of theorists who liked to believe that the whole world was being dragged down by a multinational conglomerate of big-moneyed interests taking orders from Wall Street and political big shots like George Bush.

Skepticism about Ankerberg fed on itself. Bakker loyalists came to believe, and may still believe, that Falwell's plot to steal PTL was the inevitable prelude to the last great battle between good and evil. You could find it all in Revelation. The years of the Tribulation had come, and now we could confidently anticipate the years of the Great Tribulation, sponsored by the Illuminati and featuring the savage oppressions of the Antichrist, hard days during which men would swap their faith in Christ for the merest scrap of bread or meat. And it was all taking place right in front of our eyes, at the very gates of Heritage USA—the road to Armageddon leading straight through the blazing sun of the South Carolina Piedmont, past broom-sedge fields and pine thickets and cheap motels and a tawdry billboard stamped with huge, pinkish, cartoonlike images of Jim and Tammy Bakker.

Ankerberg's tale of deceit, lust, and carnival-like charlatanism was like an intricately woven mosaic from which no one could turn his eyes, believer or nonbeliever. Skeptics laughed while Bakkerites gasped with anger and vowed revenge. In one way or another almost everyone felt the impact; and now that the torrent had burst, nothing would be quite the same again, not when it came to television preachers. It was as though we had been overtaken by a whole new kind of midsummer madness, a dizzying moment in which the world would turn its attention from war, revolution, the Bomb, Middle East terrorism, Washington scandals, natural disasters, and the gender gap to focus on two more abiding obsessions: wholesale fornication and a craving after God.

Not since the novels of Erskine Caldwell had we seen the two so intimately bound up together. Walk across the grounds of Heritage USA and you would almost always find somebody willing to share the dark secrets of Bakker's last days at the ministry. From former PTL administrators, performers, and stagehands we began to discover a Bakker consumed by passions and manias that went way beyond our most lurid imaginings, a man far gone in greed and lust, tormented by jealousy, impious to the point of blasphemy, given to nasty swings of mood and even paranoic behavior, a dipsomaniac unable to face his audiences without a bolstering slug of good vodka or brandy.

The funny thing about Bakker is that as good as he was at inspiring a fanatical loyalty among the faith partners, he never felt comfortable in crowds. Don't press me too close, brother; give me a little wine for my stomach's sake. The conviction that his own people were bent on his destruction, either through deft infusions of poison or by shooting him in the back, grew on him in 1981 after a cabal of fanatical Moslem commandos gunned down Egyptian president Anwar Sadat. Why, he kept asking, had Sadat's presumably loyal security forces failed to protect him adequately? Why had they been so tardy in their pursuit of the murderers? Don Hardister, PTL's onetime chief of security, was about the only man in whom Bakker placed implicit faith. The people Hardister hired as assistants or brought in as temporary replacements Bakker regarded with distrust, and even with fear. How was he to know, as he once told Hardister, that "they aren't ax murderers or haven't killed a lot of people?"

Maybe it was not always like that. Maybe there were moments of reprieve. There may even have been times when he lapsed into remorse or felt more guilt than he would ever be able to admit. We knew nothing of that. All we saw during those spring weeks when he was keeping to himself, locked up fetuslike behind the oleander-splayed walls of his Palm Springs condo, was the Bakker of caricature: vindictive, childishly self-indulgent, big-cocked ("Wisht I had me one like that," a confidant said), and thoroughly weary from long hours of whipping himself off.

His spending habits had become a private scandal long before the world had heard even the first murmurings of his disgrace. "Control Jim Bakker and the way he and his people spend money?" said Gary Smith, a former PTL financial manager. "Impossible!"

Apparently it was only in his last years as host of the "PTL Club" that he turned to drink as a way of keeping up appearances with the faithful. The fears and phobias that had been building up deep inside him during all the years of struggle seemed to take hold of him all at once. He had reveled in the agony of a deprived childhood. A lot of it was lies, but in dwelling on it for so long he had transformed it into something that transcended mere fantasy. Bakker was a born maker of myths. His greatest achievement was the myth of his own life. Toward the end he needed the myth, as well as the liquor, to keep him going: self-doubt and self-pity seemed to hang on him like an old suit of clothes.

In the quiet hours that now came all too seldom his conversation would almost always turn to the hard years he had spent as a child in the working-class town of Muskegon Heights, Michigan. He would talk forlornly of the experience, of the orange house he had lived in as a child, of the tattered baseball jacket that he wore till the stitching came unraveled and hung down on him in loose threads. Poor or rich, a young man growing up in a Pentecostal home could never have known real contentment. There were few, if any, wealthy Pentecostals in those early days, as there were later in the great days of PTL. The way to true faith was arduous, unremitting, a little frightening.

Pentecostalism had existed in one form or another ever since the days of the Apostles. But it took on its starkest form among the poorly educated hill people early in this century, spreading out into the working-class suburbs of the growing midwestern towns and later coming down out of the southern mountains. That was the religion Jim Bakker had known as a child. He had grown up more frightened than poor, so alarmed at the all-seeing and very personal God who supposedly presided over his Sunday school class, and indeed over every facet of his daily life, that he may have had some excuse for growing up with hazy and confused memories of his early years in Muskegon.

His grandfather, old Joe Bakker, had been a truculent and unforgiving evangel of the Pentecostal religion. People remembered him as a young man pedaling his bicycle about the streets of the little Michigan town, distributing biblical tracts and growling out his message of an implacable God wherever he could get a crowd together. He preached in poolrooms, on street corners, and at least once each week at the county jail, bedeviling cigarette smokers and beer drinkers with the promise of an early death and assurances of eternal damnation. Here, then, was the true spirit of the Pentecostalism recognizable to most Americans born in the second quarter of the twentieth century. Young Bakker could remember his grandfather coming home at least once with a swollen black eye, souvenir of a fistfight with an unpenitent prisoner.

His own father was equally devout, if not quite the zealot old Joe Bakker had been. He talked of seeing angels during a trip to Florida, of meeting the ghost of his sister-in-law at his Muskegon home. He was often at PTL in the good days, a quiet, retiring man, himself hardly more than a ghostly presence backstage at PTL or in the atrium at the Heritage Grand, ever tolerant of his son's lies, even when by implication they made him out to be something of a bumbler incapable of providing for his family. Actually the elder Bakker had done quite well for himself. It is true that the early years had been hard: Jim sleeping with two brothers in one of two cramped bedrooms, his sister, Donna, forced to take the sofa, the house heated by a single vent, and no warm water except what they could boil in a pot on their wood-fired stove.

But things were a lot better by the time he hit his teens. Raleigh Bakker was an accomplished mechanic dedicated to his job at a Muskegon piston-ring manufacturing plant. He began making good money during the post–World War II boom and by 1947 was able to move his family into an imposing three-story Dutch colonial that Bakker would later describe as a cement-block monstrosity which his father had mistakenly painted a bright orange. He had written about it in his autobiography, *Move That Mountain,* and others took up the story. The poor boy who had made good despite every hardship, driven by an unnatural yet forgivable compulsion to succeed, at whatever cost, even under the guise of saintly self-indulgence.

An investigator who later looked more closely into the story described something quite different: "The home was hardly so pitiful. What Bakker called cement blocks were decorative stones, textured and beveled. The house had a porch across the front and a gabled roof. At the second story, the stone facing gave way to painted wood shingles. Neighbors and relatives remembered the house painted dark tan, its trim a dark green. Some family friends envied the place." Bakker himself, during a momentary lapse, once boasted that the house was in a suburb where "a number of millionaires had lived."

But mostly he just kept on talking about how that bright orange house and his ragged clothes were the shame of his youth and how he would always persuade the school-bus driver to let him off a block or so from home so that his classmates wouldn't guess the truth about his private life. He needed all that now, maybe even more than he needed the liquor, and could not do without either. Sometimes his aides would send tall, cool drinks onto the set. Other times he would belt down a glass or two while waiting backstage, humming a little hymn of inspiration as he went out and took Tammy's hand for their familiar walk down the center aisle.

Reporters who had known Bakker before the bad days had come, before he had drawn into himself and stopped granting interviews, would continue to speak kindly of the man even after his fall. *Charlotte Observer* columnist Frye Gaillard had seen a Bakker few others had known, and even after all that had happened in that spring of 1987 he still had great respect for the evangelist's "many admirable traits," one above all others: "An innocent childlike faith, utterly sincere, that blended effectively with his considerable talents as a talk-show host." Gaillard seemed less repelled than many of his colleagues by Ankerberg's disclosures and never stopped doubting "the innocence and sincerity of Bakker's faith."

"I liked him," Gaillard told me one afternoon as we sat talking in his editorial office. "I still like him. But clearly he has said many things over the years that are not the truth."

The childhood years Bakker was later to describe as shameful and embarrassing, while his father looked on with a bland smile, were in fact some of his best years. He craved popularity as a high schooler and once admitted that he would do "anything to get it."

He got more of it than could ever be reconciled with the stories of his early life as a tatterdemalion. He enjoyed an enviable status as editor of the school paper and popular sock-hop deejay, already manifesting qualities that one day would become the stock-in-trade of his television show. And he managed all that without straying from the church. Sometimes he would bring girls to preaching service even though he would have to explain that they couldn't wear their makeup. He attended school dances, but nobody ever remembered him dancing. Making a virtue of necessity. Reconciling his religious upbringing with the new rock 'n' roll pop culture. Maybe that was his real talent. The ability to transform himself into a teenage impresario who could technically avoid sin while making it work for him in sensational ways. He had practiced his stage demeanor before a bathroom mirror, worked on his voice with the help of a reel-to-reel tape recorder that set his father back $100, a lot of money in those days.

He had always been a big Elvis fancier, and his slicked-back hair— "Puts Crisco in it," envious rivals would say—apparently went over well with the girls. He always had plenty of them around. Jim Bakker behind the wheel of his father's two-toned blue Cadillac got to be a familiar sight around Muskegon Heights. For a shy young man burdened with the inhibitions of an ignominious childhood he sure had a way about him. Everybody said he threw the best parties in town. Miss Michigan once put in an appearance. And one of his regulars was twenty-year-old Marlene Way, a Muskegon girl who had briefly become famous for her impersonations of Elvis Presley on the "Steve Allen Show." They became friends and maybe a little more than friends and began to see a lot of each other despite the four-year disparity in their ages.

In 1957, as a high school junior, he had concocted a variety show with the Manhattan skyline as background. Everybody figured it was a prelude to a career in show business. But who would have guessed that the Pentecostal religion, unrecognizable as it might have been to old Joe Bakker, would forever remain the chief ingredient in his success?

The way Bakker always told it, everything changed for him one night toward the end of his senior year. He had been out cruising the streets with a blonde named Sandy, his radio tuned to a Fats Domino rendition of "Blueberry Hill," and had just wheeled back into the church driveway when he felt a sudden crunch—sickening, ominous—beneath the front of his car. He had run over a three-year-old named Jimmy Summerfield. The child lay on a cot in the hospital emergency room, his lungs crushed. The doctors held out little hope. As Bakker remembered it, he could not bring himself to get back into his car. He paced the church parking lot, waiting for news, pounding his fists against the brick walls of the sanctuary, praying, weeping, lifting bloody hands to the sky.

Let him live Lord if you will let him live . . .

It was his first miracle; the boy did live, and an immensely relieved Jim Bakker would later tell the story a thousand times: how he had made up his mind on the spot to throw over his carefree ways and devote his life to the ministry.

In this story, as in so much else about Bakker, truth merged conveniently with legend. The accident that had changed his life had actually taken place two years earlier, when he was only a sophomore, and nobody could remember it as the dramatic, life-changing experience of which the evangelist later spoke.

Still, he did go on to study for the ministry, attending North Central Bible College, a Pentecostal outpost in Minneapolis, where he threw in with a crowd of seekers known as the Holy Joes, sometimes joining in fervent all-night prayer sessions in his dormitory's basement and then sleeping through morning classes. It was also at North Central that he met and married a fetching blonde named Tamara Faye LeValley, who had far more reason than he to mourn a demeaning early life of poverty and despair.

Abandoned by her father, she was one of eight children who learned to live not with poverty alone but also with the same austere pieties that had at once haunted and uplifted Jim Bakker's life. A bleak life in a cramped "hillbilly" shack on the Canadian border, no indoor bath, pictures of bearded, fierce uncles glaring down at her from the cold walls—such were the memories of Tammy Faye's youth. A stepfather who worked at a paper mill brought in what money there was, but there was never nearly enough. Never enough money, never enough praying, never enough spiritual torment to satisfy the demands of her faith. She had never even worn lipstick until the day she left home to follow a fiancé to the Bible college where she would later meet Bakker.

Deprived all her life of cosmetics, she now began wearing them in her sleep and would eventually become famous as the most gaudily made-up performer of her day.

There were rules against North Central students marrying while school was in session. With only two months left in her freshman year, Tammy Faye dropped out of school to marry Jim Bakker. Neither ever went back. The newlyweds bought a secondhand Valiant and headed south on a crusade for Jesus, traveling the back roads of the Carolinas and preaching to farmhands and textile workers in down-and-out mill towns disquietingly reminiscent of those they had left behind.

Somehow it always seemed the same—the church, the town—the same gaunt, impoverished congregation—the same clapboard or concrete-block building sitting on makeshift brick piers and lit by a sullen glare of overhead light bulbs—the cigar box that they used as a collection plate always coming back with just enough cash to get them to their next engagement, the next town.

A hard life, but they always found someone to take them in. For four years it went on like that. Sometimes Tammy Faye would have enough to buy lipstick; more often there was not enough to buy groceries. They seemed to be going nowhere when Tammy hit upon the idea of fashioning hand puppets from bubble-bath containers. Her puppets were an immediate hit. So, for once, was Jim Bakker, with his dramatically reworked story of the "miracle" that had saved young Jimmy Summerfield and how the near-tragedy had persuaded him, Bakker, to devote his life to God. The cigar box began to fill; so did the front pews of the broken-down little churches as weeping men and women rushed forward to give their lives to the Lord.

By 1965 Bakker and his wife had worked their way to Portsmouth, Virginia, and were conducting a crusade in the little beach town when they met another struggling preacher by the name of Pat Robertson, who liked to recall in later years that he had started his flourishing Christian Broadcasting Network with a $17 loan. He had wanted it that way even though he had been born to wealth and privilege—to the special kind of privilege that comes from being a Virginian blessed with patrician forebears.

Robertson was the Yale-educated son of a former United States senator and the descendant of two presidents. Except for his born-again faith there was little in his background to have drawn him to the Bakkers. Yet he took a fancy to the pair and offered them jobs as cohosts of a childrens' puppet show on his "700 Club." At first the arrangement seemed to work well. The puppet show was a big success, and the Bakkers had become converts to Robertson's belief that God would shower down Cadillacs and Lincoln Continentals and big, fancy houses, as well as all the necessities of life, on true tongue-speaking believers.

The trouble was that in those days Robertson, like the Bakkers, was more often broke than not. His cable network had begun to flounder, and that was where the teary-eyed husband-and-wife team proved helpful. Bakker would not be bashful about taking credit for an emotional on-camera appeal that brought in $7,000 and kept the bills paid for another month or so.

Not long after that he and the effusive Robertson had a falling out. No one has ever said exactly what happened. But Bakker may have loomed as a growing threat to the founder of the "700 Club," what with the hunger for power he'd never quite been able to hide. Robertson would remember his confrontation with the Bakkers as a moment of high drama. Just as he was on the point of dismissing his puppeteers he heard a booming voice from on high: *Don't fire Jim Bakker!*

Robertson had always heeded such voices and in time would be lavishly repaid—with wealth, power, huge television ratings, and various other emoluments, if not yet with the White House which he now hungered after and which he might have won more readily if he'd stuck with the political orthodoxy to which he was bred. Bakker stayed. And inevitably there was more trouble. This time when Robertson got ready to fire the Bakkers he heard no voices, and the pair was soon back on the streets.

Bakker, working alone for the first and last time, reappeared briefly as host of a religious telecast in California; and one might have thought if he could have worked his magic anywhere it would have been there. In the fanciful land at the end of the West, where some men go to die and others to beg for train fare back home, garish people like the Bakkers sometimes make it big. Not this time. New problems emerged, or maybe more of the same—the old question of too much ambition, too little clout. Anyway, the two were soon back on the road to Carolina, which had always been good to them in its own way.

Who would have guessed how much more rewarding it would be this time? As cohosts of yet another floundering cable station, Channel 36 in Charlotte, the Bakkers again proved that a plethora of tears combined with stories of early poverty and assurances that God had meant for every man to be not necessarily free, but certainly rich, could bring the cash rolling in. The station prospered along with Bakker's new "PTL Club." Fame and personal wealth would quickly follow. Out of his religious telecast would come his own satellite network and more elegant trappings in a restored colonial mansion on Charlotte's Park Avenue. He was definitely on his way up. He installed hot tubs, saunas, an Olympic-sized swimming pool. He had prayed with Jimmy Carter aboard *Air Force One* and would be a featured guest at Ronald Reagan's first inaugural. Like Reagan, he was making the nation feel good about itself—at least that part of it that could stomach his incessant banalities.

By the late seventies it was apparent to Bakker, if not yet to anyone else, that Charlotte was no longer big enough to hold him and his growing evangelical empire. He needed his own town; and he was soon to have it in the form of Heritage USA. But even as the tacky outworks of his theme park began to take shape amid the great forests and on the second-growth timberlands just below the North Carolina line, the rumors had begun—troubling talk of extravagant parties, sordid financial dealings, other women.

From those years dated many of the stories that reached the ears of Ankerberg, Falwell, and the four Assemblies of God presbyters, who immediately took steps to get Bakker stripped of his right to preach under the auspices of their church.

Not many of the people who poured forth the secrets of Bakker's nefarious steam room to the Assemblies of God leaders were anxious to say any more about it publicly, maybe because they'd shared too many intimate adventures there. Others, who had escaped Bakker's snare, were more obliging. Austin Miles, for example. Miles, an old circus hand who never found his true audience until he turned to preaching and began appearing as a guest on the "PTL Club," thought he'd been mixed up in a little of everything until the day he got his first invitation to the steam room.

It was then that he realized he'd spent his more than forty years as an innocent. He was astonished to find Bakker, as he later reported it, "frolicking in the nude" with two male companions. "Absorbed" was the way he described it. Completely, absolutely absorbed. "Dancing around and taking turns lying on the table, massaging each other."

Miles had turned to leave when Bakker grabbed a towel and came running after him with a shout: "Hey, a great show you just did! You'll have to come back!" Miles began to wonder if maybe he'd made a mistake in getting out of the carnival business, which could at least boast the integrity of its own decadence. He had barely exhausted the thought when, as he remembered it, he looked up and saw Tammy Faye coming on the run. She shot right on past him and began pounding madly at the steam room door, yelling for Bakker to stop what he was "doing in there" and to "stop it this minute!"

"Jim Bakker! You come out of there! Do you hear me? I know what you're doing! I know you're in there. Do you think you're fooling anyone? Well, I want you to know right now that you aren't!"

Lurid tales of Bakker's misalliances were soon coming in from all over. We got some of the story from people who, like Miles, were willing to let their names appear in print. As for the rest, how much was rumor and how much was fact we would never know unless by chance it were to come out in court. It never did. Two years later, when Bakker finally went to prison after being convicted on twenty-four counts of financial wrongdoing, the numerous accounts of his sexual excesses figured only incidentally in the prosecution's case. Yet there was a time when those accounts were almost the whole story. The way we got it, the preacher had been sneaking about the back streets of Charlotte in all sorts of guises, wearing blonde wigs and fake boobs and flimsy night things— a fixture in all the homosexual bars, knocking at the doors of all the bawdy houses and massage parlors, hiring consultants to help him set up old-style Roman orgies.

The scandal sheets had quite a run that spring. Their agents drifted in and out of town, pockets bulging with cash, ready to pay for stories well-nigh unobtainable in the more orthodox fashion—to most of us, that is, though not to the high-and-mighty *Washington Post,* which managed to ferret out many of the dirty little details of Bakker's private life much as it had once ferreted out the truth about Nixon and the Watergate crowd. The paper assigned two reporters full-time to the story and reaped a good rich bounty. But even the *Post* would not print everything. The reporting team saved some of its most sordid material for a two-part series that appeared later in *Penthouse.* Consider the case of a masseur named Daniel, who recounted the details of a surprise encounter in Bakker's study:

"He was wearing sweatpants and covered with a sheet . . . I didn't think anything of it. I worked on his back and shoulders, and about fifteen minutes into it, I figured he was falling asleep when his hand brushed my leg.

". . . Within five minutes, I realized he wasn't sleeping. . . . He put his hand on my leg and worked his way up as I massaged him. I freaked out; I acted like I thought he was asleep . . . and left, not really knowing what to think."

By Daniel's account, Bakker kept up the pressure until he got his way, and the two were soon going at it behind the locked doors of his office. It was mostly just "jacking off," the masseur said. "I couldn't do certain things. . . . It lasted four years."

Those were the years when Bakker and his wife began drifting apart. After getting her breasts enlarged and her fat suctioned under a PTL executive insurance plan, Tammy Faye began turning to other men. Her first conquest—never consummated, she kept saying, and we had her solemn, honest-to-God word for it—was a Nashville, Tennessee, record producer named Gary Paxton, an old born-again PTL hand who was fired when Bakker found out about his wife's flirtation.

At one time the future had looked good for Paxton. He had gone west to produce something called "Monster Mash" and had gained a bit of fame singing "Alley Oop" with the Hollywood Argyles. I knew nothing of "Monster Mash" or "Alley Oop," and I had never heard of the Hollywood Argyles. But everybody agreed that he was getting to be a real name in the entertainment world. Why he never made it all the way to the top I don't know, unless it was that old stigma of being born again hanging over him.

Paxton found consolation in PTL and Tammy Faye Bakker. But now we also had his word that they had never consummated their "affair." Was it possible? It had begun as such things often do, as a friendship between wives. In the early days of PTL, Tammy Faye and Paxton's wife had been real chums. They flung all-night parties and went everywhere together. Vacation trips. The races. Big shopping excursions to the K-Mart or Family Dollar Store. The next thing anyone knew, Karen Paxton was filing for divorce and placing the blame on Tammy Faye.

No consummation! Paxton exclaimed. The way he told it, he was only trying to turn Bakker's wife into a world-famous pop singer. But there remains from those days, courtesy of Gary Paxton, at least one published photo of Tammy Faye posing in a seductive negligee. I don't know whether she'd had the photo taken before or after she got her breasts enlarged, but it did nothing to enhance her reputation as the femme fatale of the gospel-singing world.

Bakker kicked Paxton out only to learn almost immediately that his wife had fallen for PTL music director Thurlow Spurr. How far had it gone? No consummation, said Tammy Faye, explaining that Spurr was "just a friend who would listen to me."

Still, it must have gone a lot further with him than with Paxton; she and the maestro were apparently on the point of running off together when Bakker found a shredded letter that alerted him to what was happening. "God told me to look in the garbage can!" Just in time. Tammy Faye's desertion, at which she had hinted in the letter, was coming precisely when it could do him the most harm. His rendezvous with Jessica Hahn now behind him, Bakker had climbed to new heights of religious hucksterism. One clear indication that he had arrived: the engraved invitation he had recently received to Ronald Reagan's 1981 inaugural ball.

Now, as he sat at the kitchen table piecing together the incriminating letter, he could envision—perhaps for the first time—his whole world coming apart. He summoned aides and sent them out looking for his wife. They caught up with her in the parking lot of one of the local K-Marts. Were she and Spurr planning to meet there for their big getaway, as some have said, or was she only trying to squeeze in some last-minute shopping? Talk of divorce was in the air, rumors that Tammy Faye was far gone in her addiction to prescription drugs—that she was tottering on the brink of a psychosis, threatening to leave the show and walk about the streets naked, shouting obscenities. Bakker fired Spurr and packed his wife off to California, where a gang of Christian "therapists" were to have a go at her. No penetration! they concluded. And now we had *their* word for it.

Back in Carolina, she was still petulant and uncooperative. PTL technicians and camera crews had learned to expect—well, they had learned never to know exactly what to expect. For the first time the couple began to travel back and forth from the studio in separate cars, with Tammy screaming and shouting insults at her husband right up until the moment they appeared on camera, smiling and holding hands. "It was a dogfight backstage," recalled one producer. "Tammy would be screaming and yelling about different things. 'I don't want to be on this show! I'd rather be shopping. It's stupid! You're driving me crazy.'"

They were now well into 1987, less than a month from Bakker's fateful meeting with Jerry Falwell in a Palm Springs motel room. Exactly what happened during that encounter would become a hotly disputed topic about which would swirl a whole summer of controversy. For the moment we had only Falwell's version, which quickly became the official version after Bakker refused to defend himself. Carolina didn't see him again for a while. Like a flash he vanished behind the barred walls of his holiday condo and stayed there for more than three months, hunkering down fetal-like (so his wife always described it) and brooding, no doubt, on that most ancient of theological questions: Why must the righteous suffer?

. . .

In the race to piece together all the sordid details of Bakker's downfall, the *Charlotte Observer,* which had set the whole crazy business in motion, had become the next thing to a nonparticipant.

What had happened to the *Observer?*

That was what a lot of people were asking that spring. Me, I didn't think much about it until Kovach—damn him—ordered me to work up a piece of world-class journalism paying "professional tribute" to the paper for its good work in hunting Bakker to earth.

That in itself was bad enough—having to glorify a competing newspaper in print. But it wasn't the worst. Worse still was my discovery that I had been made the chief instrument in a payoff hardly less scandalous than the $265,000 bribe delivered to Jessica Hahn for her silence.

The day before I went up to interview *Observer* editor Rich Oppel, I learned that his paper had joined its voice to the many others busily praising Kovach and his new editorial team as saviors of the *Journal-Constitution,* the South—at least that part of it that Ralph McGill hadn't already saved—and the starving peoples of the Third World. In the *Observer's* account, which dominated the Sunday feature section, I could detect all the familiar echoes: *We're takin' names and kickin' ass. Gonna get us a little respect. So that folks all gonna say: Why them papers has got real world class!*

Now I was to return the favor: my story on the *Observer* in exchange for its story on Kovach. But even that was not quite the worst. The worst of all was the strange reluctance its editors had felt on being dragged into the anti-PTL crusade in the first place. After fighting my way past a surly, overweight deskman who hadn't heard anything about Oppel's pact with Kovach and who kept screaming that the *Observer* couldn't afford to make itself "a part of the story," I learned to my everlasting consternation that the paper had tried every dodge it could think of to stay free of the controversy. Now that it could no longer ignore Bakker's scandalous behavior it seemed far less enchanted with the stories it had printed than with all those it had refused to print for lack of independent confirmation.

Indeed, the editor thought so well of himself that he had worked up a whole long list of such stories. I sat there feeling emasculated and foolish and a little bewildered as he ran through it. But I didn't say anything. For Kovach's sake I knew I'd have to put the best possible face on it. I wasn't certain whether the *Observer* had simply chosen not to compete with the tabloids and the *Washington Post* or whether it was getting beat going and coming and was trying to explain away its lapses in some credible fashion.

I'm still not sure. But after sitting for an hour or more and listening to a lot of high-sounding boardroom talk about journalistic "responsibility" I rather think it was the former. The astounding thing was that the paper had sat on the story for almost four years before being dragged into it by forces quite beyond its control. It just wasn't what the editors considered a suitable subject for "responsible" journalism. Later I was able to get my own independent confirmation of this startling discovery from a former *Observer* reporter named Allen Cowan. Cowan, who had begun poking into PTL affairs in the late seventies, told me he'd decided to leave the paper after being informed that "we were to do no more PTL exposés."

The way Oppel saw it, Bakker's messy sexual indiscretions had nothing to do with the story at all. He had even written a Sunday column about it: "If this newspaper were to set out to give even-handed coverage to the sexual peccadillos of the high and mighty, we would need to get a few more boxes of newsprint each month." Now he was telling me the same thing all over again: PTL had nothing to do with sex. And a preacher's vow to uphold the strictures of Holy Writ had nothing to do with it either. It was simply a question of "stewardship."

So this was what we had come to. Not only were we to be recklessly venturesome, painstaking, resourceful, creative, indefatigable, and all the rest; now we had to be "responsible" as well. It was more than a little disquieting, to tell you the truth. I kept wondering how H. L. Mencken or William Cowper Brann, the Texas "Iconoclast," would have felt about all the ingenious ways the *Observer* had gone about trying not to cover the scandal.

"An unattractive quality of our industry," the editor had written, "is the willingness to suspend normal standards of credibility for charges against public figures, in this case the Bakkers, when they are clearly under siege."

I kept looking at him, trying to take it all in. I guess he just didn't agree with Falwell that preachers of the gospel were obliged to observe more rigid moral standards than movie stars or United States senators or Wall Street stockjobbers. He didn't care anything about the hypocrisy or the gang bangs or all the good times in the steam room at PTL or even about Bakker's supposed dalliance with a woman known only as the "Wilkinson Avenue prostitute." The story had been all over Charlotte television, but the *Observer* had chosen to ignore it. No opportunity for "independent confirmation," Oppel explained.

Even Bakker's rape or seduction by Jessica Hahn—the world would never quite be certain which it was—had nothing to do with it. It was simply a story of "misuse of money and abuse of trust." Bakker had not been a good "steward." In other words, not the blowjob but the $265,000 payoff.

I still didn't say anything. But I suddenly had the uneasy feeling that if the same standards had been applied in the investigation of Gary Hart's affair with South Carolina temptress Donna Rice, the former McGovernite would be well on his way to becoming the next Democratic presidential nominee—a prospect to strike the fainthearted with sheer terror.

The *Miami Herald,* which, like the *Observer,* was a member of the Knight-Ridder chain, had broken the story of Hart's affair only a week or so before I went up to interview Oppel, and the parallels were too obvious to ignore.

I broached the subject delicately, knowing that everything would get back to Kovach.

"Undoubtedly," the editor said, clearing his throat, "there were questions in the way that was handled."

Most astonishing of all was the *Observer*'s stubborn refusal to print the story of Bakker and the hush money scandal even after the editors had it straight from the mouth of Jessica Hahn. Hahn had been calling the paper for weeks, screaming for justice. How long would she wait before she turned to the *New York Times* or *Washington Post* or *National Enquirer?*

"We knew we could very well get beat," Oppel said, "but I felt a responsibility to get Bakker's side of the story." The *Observer* gave Bakker a week to respond, then another week. The ides of March had come and gone. And still nothing from Bakker. The paper gave him yet more time while its lawyers—not its reporters—tried to work something out. Finally the big break came: the preacher was waiting on the phone, ready to deliver his long-rehearsed statement to reporter Charles Shepard. And for this daring display of journalistic enterprise the *Observer* was to win a Pulitzer?

There was more. When the Reverend John Ankerberg, a television minister of undoubted reputation, went on "Larry King Live" to accuse Bakker of every imaginable sort of sexual depravity, the *Observer* printed a brief news item barely mentioning the charges. "We couldn't go beyond that because we couldn't independently substantiate Ankerberg's charges."

When the news of Tammy Faye's affair with Gary Paxton came out, it was the same. "Mere titillation," Oppel said. Again, it wasn't at all clear to him that this little dustup had anything to do with PTL. "Abuse of power and donated monies is the story."

When Jessica Hahn described her experiences in a transcript that cast doubt on Bakker's version of the encounter, *Newsweek* and the wire services quickly picked up the story. Not the *Observer*. No independent confirmation, the editor said.

I sat there with little beads of sweat popping out on my forehead, knowing that somehow I would have to work up a world-class feature article praising the *Observer* for a story that if it could have had everything its own way it would never have printed at all.

On my way to the door I realized with new dread that the arrogant and affected Gary Hartpence might even then have been on his way to becoming our next president if the *Observer* had been in charge of exposing him. Oppel was quite cordial about it all. But I still kept thinking about what Mencken would have said and how close we had come to getting Hart as president and then listening—to make sure I had it right—as Oppel boasted again about all the times he had allowed himself to get beat for lack of independent confirmation and how he would happily never print anything that couldn't be checked and double-checked and checked again with multiple sources and documents.

"Frankly," he said, "I'd rather get beat."

In spite of everything that had come out on Bakker and his crowd, a stubborn remnant of PTL faith partners stuck by their old idol and by the Pentecostal, or "charismatic," creed as he had laid it down—a belief, fundamentally, in the miraculous as a way of life. The partners had drawn new meaning out of scriptural passages that promised believers the power to do marvelous works in the name of the Lord. If they could cast out demons and heal the multitudes with a laying on of the hands and prophesy in an unknown tongue, they could also, in Bakker's philosophy, lay up vast stores of wealth for themselves on earth rather than in Paradise.

Nothing like that could be found in the harsh Calvinistic doctrines brought to Falwell's Virginia by the grim-visaged Scotch-Irish pioneers of prerevolutionary times. Falwell himself was a man of large and generous instincts, at least when the mood was on him, but the theology he had embraced in a first rush of youthful enthusiasm was something else entirely: hard, narrow, unforgiving, joyless. So it was perhaps inevitable that, while the Bakkerites were still recovering from the shock of the sex and blackmail scandal, he would move swiftly to transform PTL into an austere fundamentalist ministry more to his liking. No prophesying in tongues or laying on of the hands.

There was bound to be trouble, but it did not surface all at once. Bakker, still isolated in his Palm Springs condo, was too much an object of ridicule for his sympathizers to gain much support for his cause. Falwell thus had everything his own way for a time. Although the stiffly correct Dortch stayed on as PTL president and talk-show host, a job for which he was imperfectly suited, he had no influence on policy. Falwell and a swarm of dark-browed fundamentalists he had appointed to the reconstituted PTL board of directors were making all the decisions.

With the exception of charismatic believer James G. Watt, who had resigned as Ronald Reagan's secretary of the interior after a prolonged war with environmentalists,* the new directors were a dour bunch indeed. Not a wife swapper among them, as far as we could tell. Most people felt that they could judge the board not so much by Falwell's professed standards of magnanimity as by those of its most notorious member: the Reverend Bailey Smith, who had once asserted that "God Almighty does not hear the prayer of a Jew!" Smith had issued this ringing declaration during the last days of his tenure as president of the Southern Baptist Convention and had thought so well of it, in spite of all the deserved opprobrium it brought on his head, that he had decided to restate the proposition even more forcefully at the 1987 convention: *God Almighty does not hear the prayer of a Jew!*

There was nothing unique in Smith's theology. He came from the purest bloodline of Protestant fundamentalism, and his kindred were everywhere, rising on all fours, monsterlike, in a thousand backcountry pulpits to call down the black thunder of Yahweh on their sweating congregations.

Falwell, a famous Zionist and friend of Jews, had occasionally joked about the remark that had made the name "Bailey Smith" a byword for intolerance. But he had never repudiated it. And now, inexplicably, he had chosen to alienate important segments of the Pentecostal church not only by appointing Smith to his board of directors but also by refusing to appoint anyone except Watt from the other side.

Pulpit thumpers in the boardroom and money launderers onstage. That was the formula that kept Bakker's extraordinarily popular "PTL Club" limping along for a while. But things appeared to be getting a little desperate. The show had turned to round-the-clock telephone marathons in a frenzied effort to raise the money it would have to have to stay on the air. Dortch, the bagman, was always there, pirouetting clumsily in front of the camera, his gleaming white teeth mingled with shards of gold and his great brow glistening wildly in the glow of the klieg lights while, about him, a bevy of fat women belted out gospel tunes. Out would come all those seductive photos of the unfinished twenty-story Heritage Towers. The latest thing in Christian theme-park luxury. Send in your pledge and reserve a package of four days and three nights

---

*Of a commission set up to investigate his coal-leasing policies, Watt had said: "I have every kind of mix you can have . . . a black, a woman, two Jews and a cripple."

in this marvelous edifice each year for the rest of your life. Come one, come all. Rock of Ages. Cleft for me.

All this selling of space that didn't even exist yet, and in fact would never exist during all the months of the ensuing scandal, was an old practice at PTL. Though auditors had yet to find it out, Bakker had long ago oversold space in the existing Heritage Grand Hotel, so much so that people arriving to claim their four days and three nights of unspeakable luxury often found themselves with no place to stay.

"A Ponzi scheme [devised] for pillage and plunder," Norman Roy Grutman would later call it. "The investments sold were five times the lodging space available then or later." In early 1984, on one of the first shows beamed from the Heritage theme park, Bakker had told his audience that he would never be able to accept more than twenty-five thousand membership applications. "That's all the memberships we can have in the Heritage Grand. In two weeks, [the memberships] will be closed." He and his pitchmen sold more than three times that many for the hotel alone, not counting the thousands of others now being sold for the unfinished Heritage Towers.

Only a little more than half the money went into the construction of the hotel. Of the $74 million raised for the Towers, only an estimated 15.4 percent was actually set aside for construction. The rest of the money? Into one of Bakker's suitcases it went, or maybe into some secret bank account. More than one financial officer apparently warned him of the danger. Steve Nelson, PTL's vice president for world outreach, had early become aware of what was happening and, as he would later testify in court, warned Bakker that he could go to jail for his cavalier flouting of the law. But Bakker didn't want to hear anything about that, just as he hadn't wanted to hear anything about the payoffs to Jessica Hahn. His only real concern was whether his rich and diverse talents as a television huckster would ever be adequately rewarded.

Once, for example, after touring Oral Roberts's Tulsa University, Bakker complained that by comparison with the Oklahoma evangelist, he lived much too "shabbily." That, at any rate, is the way his closest personal aide, diamond-bestudded David Taggart, who owned almost as many mink stoles, sporty cars, and big houses as Bakker himself, would later remember it. By Taggart's account, Bakker was constantly whining about his shameful treatment. Why couldn't he make the kind of money

Johnny Carson was making on the "Tonight" show? Didn't he go into as many homes? Was his following any less rabid? It was about this time, long after the Heritage Grand had been overbooked and then some, that an order for the sale of another five hundred partnerships came down. Dortch and the others quickly went to work and raised more than $30 million. It was gone in less than six months, whether for operating expenses or to finance one of Bakker's vacation trips no one was quite certain. In the end, the perfidious preacher would have siphoned off more than $4 million in PTL funds to finance his extravagant living habits.

By the time the scandal broke, stories of people showing up to claim their nonexistent lodging had become commonplace. But they kept coming and kept coming, maybe writing it all down as some sort of mistake or oversight. "God bless you, Jim. We know it won't happen again."

The people who drove long distances to march in the streets for Bakker and to raise a mighty cry against Falwell were mostly big donors who would eventually lose all of what they had put into the ministry and would simply shrug it off as money well spent, whatever Bakker might have done with it. Most of them would never change, not even after court documents proved their hero to have been the most monumental fraud in evangelical history.

Others would not find it so easy to forget or to make their stories heard—pensioners of limited means who had put their life savings into PTL and sometimes couldn't even get up the money to make the long trip into the wilds of upper South Carolina to claim their four days and three nights of vacation time. Some would finally make it only to find that there were no accommodations after all. Like the wife of a disabled coal miner who had spent $1,000 for a "family fun partnership" thinking that it would provide an inexpensive vacation for herself, her husband, and their thirteen children. They finally got there to find that PTL's promise was worth nothing.

In the end, as Dortch would later confess, PTL was looking almost solely to the sale of lifetime partnerships as a means of staying solvent. "To find the funds to operate the ministry this had become the primary source of income," he said, "and it was working." And maybe would have gone on working for quite a while longer if it hadn't been for Jessica Hahn and the big hush-money scandal.

Dortch had spent $2,000 of his own money and later borrowed $10,000 from a fellow employee in an effort to buy off Hahn. The word quickly got back that that kind of money wasn't what she had in mind. Dortch gasped, swallowed hard, and put on his most obliging smile when he realized that it would take more than $250,000 to silence Bakker's accuser. But who around PTL had that kind of ready cash? Nobody, apparently, except Bakker, who didn't want to hear anything about the negotiations, and his old friend Roe Messner, the Kansas contractor and clean-living Pentecostal who had built dozens of futuristic churches around the country as well as most of Heritage USA. Messner was happy to put up the money. "I just didn't want to see the church dragged into anything like that."

Acting on Dortch's instructions, Messner wired the $265,000 to a California trust account set up by a somewhat mysterious character named Paul Roper, Jessica Hahn's only official link with PTL. Roper never identified himself as anything but a "businessman." In this case, his business was to collect a fee, the amount never disclosed, for brokering the payoff. He and Dortch had worked everything out over lunch at a Los Angeles hotel a month or so before Bakker's resignation. In her first year Hahn collected some $20,000 in interest payments. Messner? He was supposed to get his money back by billing PTL for bogus accounts. He always contended that his bills were for work he had either started or completed. Not many of them were ever paid, and his Kansas building firm eventually declared bankruptcy as a result—but Jessica Hahn apparently got most of her $265,000. Hence the cry that PTL funds had gone to buy off Bakker's lover.

Dortch's official explanation, as Roper later outlined it: the money had come from a house Bakker had been forced to sell. The proceeds came to exactly $265,000, and since the evangelist had no other funds to his name (such was Dortch's story), he was unable to agree to a larger settlement.

"I don't want to know," Bakker always said. "And I don't want to hear anything about it."

. . .

The overselling of partnerships would prove to be the crux of the federal case against Bakker. It would also be the crucial factor in PTL's ultimate decision to seek financial protection through federal bankruptcy laws.

But everybody seemed to have forgotten that a great deal of space in the Heritage Towers was sold in much the same way during the first weeks of the Falwell regime.

At the time it looked as though the ministry might be able to survive. Money kept coming in. There was never enough, but there was always hope that contributors would eventually regain their faith in PTL and that the next marathon or the next might conceivably produce enough dollars to keep the ministry functioning at something like its old level of popularity. For those who wanted to pray about it, PTL had provided a direct-dial phone service: Dial the number, friend, and commit yourself to a new life in Christ, and don't forget to send in that pledge. The latest album of Tammy Faye Bakker singing her favorite gospel hits is just one of the many benefits you'll receive. Yessir, friend. Pick up that phone. Get right with the Lord. A PTL prayer partner will be waiting to take your call.

I kept wondering how the prayer partners felt about their old boss's headlong plunge into sexual debauchery. One evening, after a couple of bourbons, I decided to dial the number and find out.

"I'm Sylvia, your prayer partner," said a dulcet voice on the other end. "For whom would you like to pray? Why do you feel that you need prayer?"

I could think of a lot of reasons, but there was no time to get into all that right now. I explained my real business. Perhaps by being plain and straightforward I could get something publishable for the morning editions. What about all this talk of homosexuality and adultery and mate swapping at PTL?

"I just hope it isn't true," Sylvia said.

"But if it is?"

"I'd rather not say."

"Your last name?"

"I'd rather not say. It's not allowed."

I could see that it would take some doing to convince my prayer partner that I really was an honest-to-God, big-name reporter for the *Atlanta Constitution* and that I desperately needed something fresh for a morning update.

"I'm sorry," she kept saying. "We really aren't supposed to talk about that."

Perhaps, then, I could speak to her supervisor.

"I will ask."

She was gone for a good five minutes or longer. When she came back I adopted a saccharine tone full of duplicity, explaining that whatever her suspicions she could be certain that I was only looking out for the good of PTL. What about Bakker, then? Was it indeed possible that he was nothing more than a . . . well, er . . . ah . . . pervert, whoremonger, and frequenter of sleazy massage parlors?

"I'm really sorry," Sylvia said. "But my supervisor says that that information isn't available to us. She suggests that you call our business office on Monday morning."

7

After the going-over Bakker had been getting in the press you'd have thought he would be finished by now. Not so at all. True, Falwell had moved unhesitatingly to tighten his grip on the PTL ministry, throwing out bagman Dortch along with the secretive, highly paid Taggart, both of whom would eventually go to prison, and cutting off blackmail payments to Jessica Hahn. But he never could quite shake off the presence of the skinny little preacher, not even with him holed up all that time in his Palm Springs condo. BAKKER DASHES THROUGH BUSHES TO AVOID REPORTERS, cried one headline out of California.

In late May he came out of his hole long enough to make a sensational appearance on ABC's "Nightline," attacking Falwell as a master of perfidy who had agreed to relinquish his "caretaker" role at PTL after a decent interval and who had now gone back on his word. With Tammy Faye at his side, Bakker scored a major triumph, attracting a 46 percent share of the late-night television audience, largest in the history of the show. Falwell had been watching along with everyone else, and Bakker's performance had given him a rare sleepless night.

So far he'd been able to play the role of statesman. Flying into Charlotte next morning, he realized he would have to move swiftly to rebut Bakker and that this time he couldn't afford to leave anything out. First he summoned his directors, and then the press, matter-of-factly making his case. He had plenty of evidence that Bakker had been routinely lying to him ever since the night he first blubbered out the details of his encounter with Jessica Hahn. The way Falwell got it during their Palm Springs meeting, Bakker had been the near-victim of a rape, escaping Hahn's clutches only because he was "temporarily impotent" and then flinging himself into a shower and exclaiming, "O my God, I've been with a whore!"

The truth as he now understood it was quite different: Bakker had shared Hahn with a fellow preacher and confirmed dissolute named John Wesley Fletcher, who had set up the encounter, and also with a third man, unnamed, who had gone into her steamy boudoir hoping for thirds only to find her "prostrate on the floor and unable to accommodate him."

Not long after Ankerberg's television appearance Falwell and his directors had confronted Bakker with their new findings, only to have the discredited evangelist huffily change the subject, reminding the PTL board that his demands for adequate "severance" had never been met. He had included a list of those demands in a letter of May 6: a $300,000 annual salary for himself, $100,000 for his wife, maid service, a secretary, free phones, two cars, health insurance, permission to move back into PTL's $1 million lakefront "parsonage" at nearby Tega Cay, and round-the-clock security.

Now, on the day after Bakker's "Nightline" triumph, Falwell held up the letter to an auditorium full of reporters, rather gingerly, as though hoping to avoid contamination, and got off one of his more telling lines: "I don't see any repentance there. I see the greed, the self-centeredness, the avarice that brought them down."

There seemed no end to Bakker's excesses. About the time he was submitting his "laundry list" of severance demands, Falwell learned that the former chairman and his wife, in their last full year at PTL, had taken out of the ministry not $1.6 million, as originally reported, but something more like $1.9 million, excluding bonuses, book and tape royalties, and other benefits.

Now Bakker was saying he was all but broke, down to his last $37,000. "I don't know how you spend that much money in a year unless you hire someone to help you do it," said a flabbergasted Falwell.

What it all came down to, as he went on to explain, was this: Bakker was nothing but a greedy little bastard who felt no shame or guilt for his conduct and who still hadn't thrown himself on his knees and asked the Lord Jesus to forgive him his great sin.

And now he wanted to come back into the ministry? Falwell had originally agreed to consider the request, but only if Bakker could get a vote of confidence from the Assemblies of God, the church in whose name he had created PTL, and on the further condition that he had been guilty of no other sexual indiscretions. He had flunked both tests. The Assemblies presbyters had since chucked Bakker out of the church, and Falwell himself had sat at a table with men willing to swear in court that they had been repeatedly harassed by the preacher's sexual advances.

"To say that Jerry Falwell and this board stole PTL on March 17 is like accusing someone of stealing the *Titanic* just after it hit the iceberg."

A picture of Falwell holding up Bakker's severance letter would appear next day on the front page of almost every newspaper in America, along with all the other evidence newly disclosed by the Lynchburg minister. It made no difference. Bakker steadfastly refused to go back into his hole or seek the womblike comfort of earlier days. Faith partners disenchanted with the new regime had seized on Bakker's "Nightline" coup as proof that their hero was about to mount a comeback, and they were convinced now, if they hadn't been convinced before, that he was indubitably the victim of a long-standing conspiracy.

It was about this time that we began to hear the first real murmurings against Falwell. "He's a liar and a thief and he's going to jail," said big, genial Paul Wood, a Georgia partner who'd had a bit of success marketing a citrus-based aerosol fumigant—his own invention—and had given most of the money to PTL.

It was Wood who made me realize that the "conspiracy" was even darker than advertised.

"Falwell and Hahn, they're both in it together," he confided one afternoon. "They're both occultists. Devil worshippers. We're getting it all documented. We'll soon have everything we need to put them away. I've got a lot of names. A lot more stuff coming in."

Nobody paid him much mind. But he was part of a growing contingent of partners that had been carrying on a kind of underground war against Falwell from a rented frame house just outside the gates of Heritage USA. Nobody paid them much mind either. Not at first, anyway. Yet Wood numbered their sympathizers in the hundreds of thousands. Falwell said you could have crammed them all inside a phone booth. Again, that may have been true at first—but no longer. Some were already in the streets, carrying signs or holding prayer rallies to call down death and Hell on the Falwell crowd. Across the roof of the ramshackle operations center hung a banner emblazoned with the words Association of

PTL Partners. By early June it had turned into quite a busy place, with big, shiny out-of-state cars crowding the yard almost every day now and regurgitating fat retirees anxious to add their voices to the protest.

"It's our ministry," said Atlantan Joe Haviland, president of the association. "We paid for it with our donations. We want it back."

That would become the big cry of the summer. "We're really getting to the bottom of this thing now," Paul Wood would say. "We're getting it all down in black and white." Almost every afternoon he would draw me off into a hot airless room at the back of the Partners House and go over it all again: how Falwell was merely a secular humanist in disguise and how he and Jessica Hahn had been conspiring at least since 1980, and probably a long time before that, to steal the PTL cable satellite and turn it over to George Bush and a sophisticated gang of cutthroats known as the Illuminati.

During those same years they had been devising their intricate plot to frame Bakker and had worked it to perfection, thanks to unlimited backing from some of the world's most powerful financiers.

"We've known about Hahn for a long time. We've got people who're willing to testify in court." And that was not all: Falwell himself was not the real source of the plot. A mere tool. A front man. "Maybe he doesn't understand that himself. Because we're dealing with the real big people here. The Illuminati. The assassins."

Then he would lean over the table, his voice taking on a more confidential tone. "We're not ready for the papers yet. But when this thing hits its gonna be real big."

He would always explain how Falwell had first met Hahn at an international convention of witches or something of the sort and how he had been mixed up in the whole nasty business of occultism for many years, he and all his people, and that the "conspiracy" went back a lot farther than any of us could imagine—perhaps even back to the time of the druids and the other mystery religions of prehistory. It was something, all right, and it was leading us straight down the road to Armageddon.

"We're getting real close," he informed me on one occasion. "I could lose my life in this thing."

I looked at him. His voice and his whole manner always seemed infinitely sensible even when he was making no sense at all. He wasn't what you would have expected—not at all like one of those dirty little evangelists shouting at you from the curb or staring at you with feverish eyes from behind the bars of an asylum.

The truth was, as he explained it, that he, too, had once been a skeptic. As shameful as it sounded and as much as he hated to admit it, he had held out for a long time against all the people who had tried to enlighten him about the dark conspiracy that was leading the world to the end time. It took all of the mysterious circumstances surrounding the Heritage takeover to bring him around. And now he was the most uncompromising of believers, though, as I say, without any of that feverish, driven quality you might have expected. At a recent meeting in Atlanta some of his followers had gone even further: Falwell, they insisted, was no longer merely a front man, he was a personal emissary of Lucifer himself, come back to hasten the day of the Great Tribulation and the Last Judgment.

"We've really got the goods on him," Wood said. "We're tracing it all the way back, and we're turning up some really big names. Some of the world's most powerful institutions are involved in this thing. But we aren't ready for the papers yet."

"Big names?"

"Some of the biggest."

"Maybe even the Trilateral Commission."

He looked at me shrewdly, enigmatically, smiling a little as though he was now finally convinced that he had found somebody—a member of the secular press, no less—who understood the darkest, most far-reaching implications of the conspiracy. I had mentioned the Trilaterals only as a joke. But I could see that I had hit him dead center. He half rose out of his seat, his voice growing louder even as it dropped into a kind of stage whisper.

"Now you're getting right in there," he said. He resumed his seat, glancing around significantly, his voice at once hushed and electric. "That's a big part of it. Get the prayers out of the schools. All of it figures in. Even your police forces—they're in it to a T. And your Knights of Columbus and the Masons. If you trace it back far enough you can see how it all ties together."

The way Wood had it figured, it was a whole lot bigger than any one man or institution. Gary Paxton, the Nashville music entrepreneur who had seduced Tammy Faye Bakker into thinking she had a great future as a pop singer, was another part of it. John Wesley Fletcher, the roaming evangelist and Falwell front who had set Jim Bakker up with Jessica Hahn, he was part of it too. But these people were nothing compared with the really big names Paul Wood had been turning up. Pretty soon he would be ready for the papers. Big headlines worldwide as people began to understand for the first time how all-encompassing the conspiracy really was. It was bigger even than the Trilateral Commission or Jesse Helms (yes, the senior senator from North Carolina was part of it too) or the Vatican or the Mafia or the Pentagon or the Jews.

As I sat listening to him, with my eyes beginning to glaze over, I could hear a blur of voices far off in another part of the house, as though from another dimension, not part of us at all, just the far-off talk and me and Paul Wood sitting there in the hot room with the tape recorder going, him leaning over the table again and his whole manner more expansive now as his voice dropped off into its darkest, most conspiratorial tone:

"You're dealing directly with the Illuminati in this thing!"

He rared back and studied me closely, smiling a little as he awaited the impact of his momentous disclosure.

I just sat there. He had spoken before of the Illuminati. But I guess I just didn't get it yet.

I looked at him. "The Illuminati?"

He leaned forward again. "The world's most powerful people, the biggest financiers, the power brokers, the high rollers, the druids."

So it was true: the conspiracy did go back a long way, a lot farther than anyone could possibly have imagined, all the way back to the druids and Stonehenge and the days of human sacrifice.

"The druids," Paul Wood said. "They're still around and they're real big. They had a meeting over at Stonehenge just last year."

I knew that Stonehenge had always been a popular gathering place for modern-day practitioners of witchcraft. But now to find that Falwell was part of it all? There was just no way of getting around it, Wood said—the great Falwell himself right in there among them, submitting to all the arcane and obscene practices that he would have emphatically repudiated in the pulpit of his Thomas Road Baptist Church. Oral sex was a big part of it—or at least the best part, though it was important to remember that mere sensual gratification was secondary to the larger implications of the ritual. I wondered how it happened that *Hustler* had never got hold of the story. I thought of him again as *Hustler* had described him, in the outhouse behind his big Lynchburg home place, copulating with his mother.

"The Stonehenge gathering," I said. "I think it's sort of a periodic ritual—a commemoration. I don't think they actually . . ."

Wood wasn't even listening. "Some of the little people, I mean like your ordinary guy in the Masons or something like that, they don't even realize what they're in. Falwell didn't realize it either, at least not at first. I think he does now—or at least I think it's possible that he does. And I think he could be in real trouble if he doesn't go through with it—I mean, if he doesn't succeed in bringing down Jim Bakker and stealing the PTL satellite for George Bush. A lot of people don't believe it. At first I didn't believe it either. I didn't even want to hear it. I didn't have time for it, but the more I got to looking into it, the more I could see how it was all adding up and where it was leading."

Could it be a mere coincidence that all this was happening at the very moment Pope John Paul II was planning his first-ever visit to South Carolina?

"I thought it was mighty funny," Wood said, "the pope suddenly deciding to come over here at a time like this."

The Vatican had accepted an invitation for the pope to speak later that summer on the campus of the state university, fueling cries of disbelief and outrage among Baptist fundamentalists. In Protestant demonology the pope had often been identified as the Antichrist. And his forthcoming visit, taken together with Falwell's seizure of PTL, could only mean one thing: Roy Grutman had had it all wrong. The last great battle was never to have taken place in Roanoke, Virginia. It was to take place right here amid the pine and stubble fields of the upper South Carolina Piedmont, with Heritage USA itself as the grand prize.

It sounded a lot like all the old fevered prophecies of my fundamentalist youth. Yet there were surprising new elements: the druids, the Mafia, the Masons, Grutman, Falwell, Hahn. I wondered if Wood had got it all mixed up somehow. But he assured me that he had gone back to reading Revelation with a new insight and that all the elements had begun to fit together quite nicely.

I sat there in the hot room with the sweat hanging off me, listening as he went through it one more time. The three and one-half years of the Lesser Tribulation. And then another three and one-half years of the Great Tribulation. Double, double, toil and trouble. The last great battle. Armageddon amid the pine barrens. The heavens raining fire and hail and bitter rain and the rivers turning black in the September sun as the Antichrist shucked off the papal robes in which he had long disguised himself and prepared to lord it over the earth for a little season, setting up an Abomination of Desolation in every town and village and restoring all the ancient rituals of human sacrifice.

"I used to be real naive," Wood said.

"How's that?"

"You know what it says in the Bible—that no man can buy or sell in that day unless he has the Mark of the Beast either in his right hand or on his forehead. But I was real naive about that. I used to think it was a real mark—I mean, a 666 branded into your forehead or the palm of your hand."

"That isn't it, then?"

He leaned closer. "That isn't it at all."

"What, then?"

"Microchips."

"Microchips?"

"Yes. Now you begin to see, don't you?"

"Sure." I didn't see at all.

"Microchips," he said again. "It's all so simple and makes so much sense when you see the logic of it. We've been moving steadily toward something for a long time. You know what the Bible says of the last days: that every man shall take a number and it will be 666. Well, I was real naive about that for a long time, because like I say, I thought it would be a real number, burned into your forehead, like the Bible says, or in your right hand. But, you see, people haven't taken into consideration how far we've come with all this new technology. They didn't realize that it's all gonna be done with microchips. I could see it a long time ago—money going out of style and all the credit cards coming in. All that was part of it. A natural succession. I was really naive."

I sat looking at him, marveling again at the sanity in his voice, his eyes. I guess I had been a little naive too. I had always heard the same thing: that it was to be a big, garish 666 burned into your forehead or right hand. The Mark of the Beast. Your only means of survival in those last hard days. Only a lucky few would be called up to meet the Lord in the Rapture. Everybody else would be left behind to suffer the terrors of the Tribulation. Like millions of others who had hardened their hearts against the blandishments of the Holy Ghost, I had long ago been condemned to this unseemly fate. The Lord had given us every chance; yet we had rejected His repeated offers of redemption as though He were nothing more than just another peddler of shoddy merchandise bought at a slightly disreputable hillside auction. Now we would have to pay.

If you could survive those years without taking the mark, the 666— or, as Wood now explained it, a microchip implant—you could still grope your way into Paradise. That was all but asking the impossible, of course. Without the implant you wouldn't be able to buy food or pay the rent. You wouldn't even be able to visit your local bordello or drink a beer at your corner bar. You wouldn't have anything to throw away on a card game. You wouldn't even be able to pick up the scroungiest sort of whore off the street. *Where's your implant, bub?* Your only chance of survival would be to flee to the hills and plant a victory garden, or live off locusts and wild honey, and hope that somehow the Antichrist's sophisticated spy helicopters wouldn't find you out. And what chance was there of that?

"I was naive as all get-out," Wood said. "And then one day it just hit me. I was in the checkout line at the supermarket—one of those places where they have all those up-to-date scanners. I just kept looking at those scanners, thinking about all this new technology we have. And then it just came to me: it's not gonna be a mark the way people have always thought. You're not gonna have to get a tattoo or anything like that. It's those scanners, I thought. And right then and there is where it came to me: you're gonna have one of those electric-eye chips popped right into your forehead or into your hand and it's gonna program your whole life. It will operate instruments for you and open doors and start your automobiles and nobody will be able to steal anything from you. I was real naive about that—and that's not all . . ."

I kept looking at him, a big, amiable fellow, neither palsied with Saint Vitus's dance nor shot through with the kind of fanaticism ordinarily associated with latter-day religious zealots. Maybe it all made sense in a way. I mean, this was the age of advanced technological wizardry. So there was no real reason why Lucifer and his agents shouldn't have all those computerized gizmos at their disposal.

Death and Hell would always be waiting for you at the end. But life would be good for a while. Taking the implant would make it easy. You could simply wave your hand over the scanner at the checkout counter or bend your noggin to it and out would tumble all the groceries and liquor and lottery tickets and bonus coupons you would need to see you through those last hard days. Anyway, you would have little choice. The Antichrist would have his troops on every corner. Even with all the determination in the world you would scarcely be able to avoid taking the mark. Soon you would be falling down in the street and groveling at his feet like everybody else,

Praise Him!
O praise him
all ye hosts of iniquity
and lost second chances!
Praise ye all the sons of Belial
and kiss the ass of the Antichrist!

"Except that it won't be a man at all," Wood said. "Don't you see? That's the other part of it. That's the part I was coming to."

I had always thought it would be one of those guys the Bible talked about—Gog or Magog or somebody like that, storming down out of the snowy Siberian hinterlands; one of those big, fiercely bearded barbarians with a thick Russian accent and a gaudy blonde always hanging on his arm. Amid his riotous banquets, the like of which even Jim Bakker would never have seen, he and his filthy colleagues would always be plotting the overthrow of Heritage USA and—what I gathered was much the same thing—their final assault on the fortresses of the mighty Yahweh.

"No," said Paul Wood. "Don't you see? That isn't it at all. It's all so simple once you see the logic of it. Because, you see"—another hush as he again glanced portentously about the room—"it's all gonna be handled by microchips, by computers—one of those walking computers you hear about. It's coming and it's coming fast. Don't you see? They've probably got the prototype up at MIT right this minute."

So that was it, then: a walking computer programmed to impose on an unthinking world all the horrible edicts of the Antichrist, implanting the microchips and whiplashing the multitudes into groveling submission.

"We've got a lot of it documented and I've got a lot of names," Wood said. "We've got people all over the country working on it."

I could still hear all those other voices—dim and dreamy and unreal—coming from what seemed a long way off, mingling with the sound of jar flies and the faint, sporadic whine of distant traffic, coming up out of the dead weight of summer itself as Paul Wood sat talking about the great evil of the Falwellian conspiracy and the hard years that were already fast upon us. By this time he had managed even to bring Ted Turner and the Coca-Cola Company and Procter & Gamble into it. They were all a part of the conspiracy. They were all "simultaneous." All in cahoots.

"It's coming fast and we're getting together everything we need to document it. We're putting it together right now. We're gonna have a whole list of names. And you can be sure that right at the top of that list you're gonna see the names of George Bush and Jerry Falwell."

"Where's the list coming from?"

"Out of Texas. It oughta be here any time. When we get it maybe we can publish something. But"—again the hushed voice, the sudden faint show of alarm—"we've got to be real careful right now. A lot of people could get into real trouble over this thing. It could be real dangerous. I'm still missing some pieces, but I'm tracing it all out and it's gonna come right down to George Bush."

He explained that I was the first newsman to know the whole story. I was different from the others, older, probably a lot more trustworthy. He, too, had decided that I was a "great American journalist." I didn't tell him that Falwell had realized it first. That would have ruined everything.

"We just aren't ready yet to spread it all over the papers," he said. "I'm still working on it. But we're gonna have all the names soon. All down in black and white."

He walked me back through the crowded house and out into the hot front yard.

"Like I said, I didn't believe it either at first. But the pieces all fit together too well for this to be only an accident. I'm not out here just witch hunting. I've been tracing this thing down. We're gonna have the documentation and we're gonna have the names."

He took a good long look down the road toward Heritage USA. "Who knows? That stinking little water park down there might change the destiny of this whole country. But we've got to be careful. We're working with a very bitter spiritual thing right here. The Christian people are in total chaos. They don't know how to get together. And like I was telling you, a lot of us could get in trouble over this thing. It could be serious for Falwell too. He might go to jail. Or he might even lose his life."

"You mean they're after Falwell too?"

"That's it. I'm absolutely convinced that if he doesn't succeed in destroying PTL and stealing the satellite he may be in real trouble. He could die of a heart attack or a cerebral hemorrhage or in a car accident— anything. Kennedy was assassinated by the same crowd. You remember how all that was hushed up. They've got ways of taking care of things like that. I could lose my own life too if I go too deep. Because, like I said, we're dealing directly with the Illuminati in this thing. I've got to make absolutely sure that I've got all the documentation."

"I don't mind sitting on it for a while."

"It's gonna get real big before it's over. Real big. But we just can't print anything yet."

"Don't worry."

"I'll let you know. In the meantime . . ."

"Mum's the word."

Not everybody agreed that the grounds of Heritage USA had been chosen as the site for the last great battle between good and evil. I had begun to wonder about it myself. I was a long time getting the documentation Wood had promised—no names, no real line on the Illuminati. But even the people who couldn't agree with Wood about anything else could at least agree that Falwell had to be run out of town. And most of them had no doubt whatsoever that he had been plotting from the very outset to steal the PTL cable satellite, if not for the enslavement of the world and the transfiguration of George Bush, then certainly for himself and the "Old Time Gospel Hour."

Late that spring Falwell brought more maledictions on himself when he condemned Bakker's prosperity gospel as "the most damnable heresy being preached in the world today." Though he had been born to wealth and had created one of the wealthiest congregations in America, something in him and his fundamentalist upbringing recoiled at the *idea* of wealth—of being promised wealth as a condition of your devotion and generosity.

For the Lynchburger there was something mischievous and perhaps even blasphemous in the charismatic belief that the Lord was ready at a moment's notice to ride to the rescue of His besieged congregations like some masked stranger out of the Judaean hills or the towers of Gotham. In fundamentalist lore the gift of "tongues" and the healing art were gifts that the Lord had "withdrawn" after the first age of the Apostles, so that man might find his way by faith alone. This was essentially the doctrine that divided the fundamentalists from the first Pentecostals as well as from charismatics of various other faiths. But where was the evidence that He had actually withdrawn those gifts? The *whys,* as Falwell and other fundamentalists explained it, were buried deep in the complexities of Calvinistic theology and, more to the point, in almost two thousand years of orthodox Christian experience.

Charismatic theologians of a more thoughtful bent were also beginning to question the excesses of their movement. Two years after the fall of Bakker, J. I. Packer, a Canadian theologian, would write in *Christianity Today* that "the charismatic movement appears as a child of our time in its antitraditionalism, its anti-intellectualism, its romantic emotionalism, its desire for thrills and emotional highs, its narcissistic preoccupation with physical health and ease of mind, its preference for folk-type music with poetically uncouth lyrics. In all these respects, the renewal reflects the late twentieth century Western world back at itself."

Packer would also note that a fellow historian, Richard Lovelace, writing in a 1988 issue of the *Journal of the Evangelical Theological Society,* had spoken even more directly of evils much like those that had hastened PTL's plunge into religious debauchery:

"The charismatic renewal continues to express the mystical spirituality of the Puritan and awakening eras, but often without the rational and theological checks against error and credulity maintained by evangelicals. As a consequence, charismatics have some of the problems of the radical spiritualists in the anabaptist and Puritan left wing. Gifts of the spirit are more prominent than the call to sanctification. The charismatic garden has a luxuriant overgrowth of theological weeds, including the health-and-wealth gospel, the most virulent form of the American heresy that Christianity guarantees worldly success. A fuzzy and unstructured ecumenism lives side by side with rampant sectarianism."

Bakker, of course, was neither the first nor the most prominent of the prosperity preachers. His onetime boss, Baptist charismatic Pat Robertson, a newly announced Republican presidential candidate who not long before had "prayed" a hurricane away from his Virginia Beach headquarters, had just as big a following and even more to lose now that the PTL scandal had begun eating away at his political base.

Falwell had nothing to say against Robertson, the patrician evangelist and fellow Virginian with whom he had long been friendly, or against Jimmy Swaggart, another prosperity preacher of sorts, although

I'm sure he had suspected the worst of the Louisianan way before the rest of us learned that he had long been a patron of the seedy New Orleans whorehouse district. To Falwell, the ultimate purveyor of this hellish "slot machine theology," as he described it, wasn't Bakker or Robertson or Swaggart or even the oafish Ernest Angley. It was a flashy black diamond-studded New York television personality named Frederick Eikerenkeotter—Reverend Ike to his followers—who had frequently asserted that "the best thing you can do for the poor is not to be one of them."

By the time Falwell got around to explaining that he hadn't meant to condemn all Bakkerites as heretics nobody was listening. "Farewell, Falwell" went the cry, and every day the clamor grew louder, with Wood warning that we were already in the last days and all the other people at the Partners House shaking their heads a little sadly and saying, "Yep. It's just too bad. The fundamentalists have taken over everything now."

James Watt, the only new PTL board member sympathetic to the charismatics, must have agreed. He had resigned within a month of his appointment, telling reporters that he didn't like it the way the fundamentalists had been meeting behind his back to mull over the Bakker question. Falwell explained that it wasn't like that at all and that Watt was just about the finest individual ever to serve in Reagan's cabinet and that his presence on the PTL board would be profoundly missed.

But he waited all summer before replacing him with another Pentecostal. This time it was Sam Johnson, a thundering orator who had broken with Bakker over PTL spending policies and was therefore a Falwell favorite. The new PTL chairman had already brought Johnson back to replace Bakker as pastor of the Heritage Village church before appointing him to the board. Johnson was the last solid link with the rebellious minority of faith partners and one of the few Pentecostals Falwell ever trusted completely. But as a minority of one, Johnson was unable either to influence board policy or—now that he had thrown in with the hated enemy—to bring about a reconciliation with the growing aggregation of PTL dissidents.

It would be hard to argue that Falwell didn't have the best of the theological argument. Although there was plenty in the New Testament about faith healing and the phenomenon of the Unknown Tongue, you could find hardly a word about worldly prosperity. Like the frantic pulpiteers of my youth, the fundamentalists kept harping on the same grim theme: "What profit, brethren, if a man should gain the whole world yet lose his own soul!"

I couldn't help thinking about all that when I started seeing all those big cars parked in front of the Partners House. Had all of these people signed some sort of Mephistophelean pact in which they had agreed to give up the promise of eternal life in exchange for earthly prosperity?

Maybe so; maybe not. All I knew was that they had come a long way since my youth. I had first known them as an ignorant snake-handling hill-country sect, drifting down into our town by the hundreds after World War II to take jobs in the tobacco and textile factories. Their churches were nothing more than ruinous clapboard affairs or cinder-block buildings hastily flung up in broom-sedge fields along deserted roads outside of town—or less than that, even. They would worship anywhere they could get the like-minded together, in abandoned filling stations or in falling-down tenements or in crummy cold-water flats that had seen better days as whorehouses. Almost nightly their frenzied cries would fill the summer dark as they banged their heads against the walls or flung themselves riotously about the floors in great wild transports of the spirit.

"Ignorant white trash," Mother always said, shuddering when she learned that a newly arrived Holiness couple was about to build a house not far from our own. "Bless my soul. Has it come to this? Are we no longer to be safe in our own neighborhoods?" Then she would drop her voice as though *they* might be listening and say: "Just promise me, Son, that you'll stay on your side of the street and we'll pray to goodness that they'll stay on *theirs*."

Not only were they ignorant, trashy, and loud, they were also doctrinally impure—so we had been taught—and possibly corrupt. We never could decide for sure whether they were going to Heaven, but I stayed on our side of the street all the same, trusting that in time they would give up their disreputable ways and become civilized.

It didn't exactly work out that way. They never did become civilized by any of the standards we had known. But by the time Bakker was getting his start they were certainly prosperous, and their proselytizers were everywhere. Bakker's own denomination, the Assemblies of God, which was also the denomination of Jimmy Swaggart, was the richest and fastest growing in America. Its sanctuaries were in all the best suburbs now, towering over the lesser churches, its membership rolls swollen with converts from many a dying Baptist or Methodist congregation.

But prosperity had not tamed its primal instincts. In the midst of Sunday church service men and women otherwise circumspect would be suddenly and rudely jerked into a new posture—their heads lolling back like dolls' heads on loose swivels and their eyes going all crazy as the Divine Spirit, if that is what it was, moved among them, filling their mouths with an indecipherable and somewhat alarming babble. Learned scholars were said to have investigated this strange phenomenon of the Unknown Tongue. Some had pronounced it akin to the language of the ancient Medes and Persians. Others were just as sure that it was Sanskrit. Still others had argued persuasively that it was a species of medieval Bulgarian or perhaps even a derivative of the ancient Scythian tongue. For all I knew—and no one ever disputed the possibility—it could have been some patois or other known only to the people of glorious, sunken Atlantis or maybe only to the tribes of the African rain forests.

Whatever its origins, whether from planets yet undiscovered or from civilizations long forgotten, it was rapidly becoming popular with a lot of people besides Pentecostals. Doctrines once confined to mountain hollows had begun to spill over old denominational bounds and to invade many a sedate big-city congregation. Whole new sets of believers had sprung up; they met clandestinely at first, in church basements or in private homes, testing their new gift of tongues and indulging in unpublicized orgies of divine healing. I guess it was about this time that they began to call themselves charismatics.

Built on precepts that had gone underground until well after the middle of the twentieth century, the charismatic movement had come of age without our being more than half aware of its existence. And that isn't all. Anyone who had watched Bakker and Swaggart and their imitators at work would have had to agree that it was the biggest thing to hit American Protestantism since the Great Awakening of the early eighteenth century.

But I wondered how many people who'd gone in for this new brand of worship would remember the monumental debt they owed to a man now openly scorned even by their own preachers: the legendary faith healer Oral Roberts, who had emerged from the Oklahoma pine flats in mid-century to become the first of the great prosperity preachers and also the first to turn evangelism into a television spectacular.

. . .

Roberts was still a struggling minister of a parsimonious Holiness con- gregation in Enid, Oklahoma, when he heard a voice from on high: "I wish above all things that thou mayest prosper!" After a month of fasting and prayer he heard another voice: "Stand upon your feet. Go and get in your car. Drive one block and turn right. From this hour your ministry of healing will begin. You will have my power to pray for the sick and to cast out devils."

For the next two decades Oral Roberts toured the country with his sound trucks and his smooth-talking advance men and with what he advertised as "the world's largest gospel tent," saving souls at a rate of about $5 apiece, as he later estimated it. But say what you would about Oral, he had never sought prosperity only for himself. He had never gone in for big cars or more than one luxurious house at a time or lavish vacation trips to exotic Hawaiian spas; he had put most of his money into the university he had built in Tulsa and into his City of Faith Hospital, inspired by the accidental deaths of his daughter and son-in-law. Nor had he ever preached Jesus as an investment in which you could hope to double or triple your return. Best of all, he had never stood with the Bailey Smiths of the world in consigning all unbelievers to everlasting perdition.

This was no way for a man of the gospel to act. And many of the people who owed him the most had never forgiven him, neither for his beliefs nor for his outrageous displays of showmanship. An excerpt from his magazine, *Healing Waters,* describes a characteristic Roberts performance of the vintage years:

He leaped off the platform with the strength of a lion, people started running toward the platform. . . . Cripples were hobbling as fast as possible, the blind were groping their way, mothers with little babies were crying for God's touch on their afflicted bodies, the deaf were brought and while Bro. Roberts touched them or they touched him God's sovereign power swept in. . . . Next morning crutches were lying all around the tent where they had been left.

. . .

By the late sixties it appeared that the great days were over. At a time when thousands of right-thinking, correctly behaved Christians were streaming into the Pentecostal denominations, Brother Roberts joined the Methodist church and faded into respectability. But the old Holy Roller chafed under the new constraints. He longed for the days when sensationalism and controversy were all that made his life worth living and his ministry worthwhile. And in early 1987—strangely, only two months before the eruption of the PTL scandal—he was back in the headlines. He had heard the voice again. "Stand upon your feet. Gird up your loins and demand of the people—money!"

This time the Lord had sent down His orders in the form of a ransom note, confronting the evangelist like a common highwayman and ordering him to fork over $8 million by March 30 or pay with his life. The ransom was to be spent to train physicians for foreign mission fields. But that was an awful lot of cash. Could he raise that much in the short sixty days left to him?

After delivering this news to a stunned television audience he retreated to the privacy of his prayer tower to await results. He eventually got every cent, the last installment of $1.3 million being paid just before deadline by a Florida dog-racing entrepreneur named Jerry Collins.

But that was only the beginning of wonders. Later that spring we learned for the first time that Oral had been blessed from his youth with the power to raise the dead and had exercised it unhesitatingly during the early days of his tent ministry. Satan had taken a special interest in this work and at least twice had tried to strangle him to death. But Oral was tough as an oak knot, and he had come out of those struggles a better man than ever and was now pleased to announce that he would return from the grave in the year 2000 or thereabouts to reign at the side of Jesus in power and great glory.

You had to admire a guy like that. Who else in this turbulent spring of 1987 could possibly have competed with Jim Bakker for headlines without ever once being accused of adultery, wife swapping, sodomy, bestiality, or the like? But I felt ashamed of myself, for though I now realized that Oral Roberts would eventually be honored as one of the greatest of Americans, I also thought back wistfully and a bit guiltily on the days when I'd felt a compelling mission to expose him as a fraud.

· · ·

The year was 1960 and Roberts was at the very peak of his fame and glory and I had just started my first tour of duty with the *Atlanta Constitution*. August came, the season of revivals, and one night we learned that Oral had thrown up his big tent off a busy highway near Marietta, an industrial suburb some twenty-five miles northwest of Atlanta. The way I figured it there was only one explanation for his remarkable success: hidden wires by which he could bring electrical impulses from some far corner of the revival ground to sting mourners into penitence or shock the sick into a sudden show of health.

My job: find the wires.

The tent was already packed when I got there. Onstage stood a large, formidably built woman in a two-piece white suit with a red rose pinned to her bodice, stomping her feet and emitting periodic squeaks of joy as she testified to the healing power of the great evangelist. Somehow I would have to get to the underside of the speaker's platform. I figured I was onto something big when I saw all the security guards standing around—mostly young Holiness preachers recruited from the local churches. In the press of the crowd I was able to work my way past them while, above me, the woman in white howled for Jesus and glory. I had just started looking around under the platform when I heard another voice, just over my shoulder.

"Are you saved, my friend? Have you felt the working of the Lord Jesus in your life?"

It was one of the security guards, a man just my age, no more than twenty-five or twenty-six, his face pinched and fervent, his dark jacket and trousers a bit too stiff and too sharply angled somehow, like one of those old-fashioned zoot suits from World War II days.

I explained that I was a noted reporter from the *Atlanta Constitution* and that I had come out to do color on the big revival.

"The press table is over thataway," he said, motioning with his head and staring at me with a look not quite murderous. He seemed thoroughly unimpressed by my credentials; perhaps he had not been out in the world long enough to understand the importance of a good press. Not that he would have gained anything from it in this case.

I kept playing for time, dismayed that I hadn't found any sign of the wires or electric prods or portable generators.

"I guess I got a little confused," I said.

"The Lord will lead us out of our confusion if only we are willing to confide in Him and trust in His grace and mercy."

You couldn't get anywhere near the press table, so great was the crush of people. I had to go back around front and jostle my way forward among all the other gawkers who had come too late to find seats. The woman onstage had stirred the crowd to a near-frenzy, talking again of the terrible days when she lay at the brink of death. The funeral arrangements had been made, the flowers ordered, the gravesite prepared, and the diggers already standing with the mattocks and shovels in their hands when, by the oddest chance, she had fallen into the hands of the great healer—Roberts himself—with results only too apparent.

Roberts now took the stage and explained in tones almost too understated that he had come again to wrestle with Satan and that, as always, the Lord would give him the victory.

"We're gonna say 'No!' to the Devil tonight. We're gonna say 'No!' to death and Hell!"

The sermon was a mere brief prelude to the healing. The sick had been waiting for a long time. First up the ramp came a woman in a wheelchair, quite old, quite blind, quite arthritic, shot through with an occasional spasmodic jerk.

Oral laid his hands on her. Then he looked away and stepped to the side.

"Let me tell you something, brothers and sisters! Hear me now! This woman has been sent to us tonight as a lesson to unbelievers. But I'm not gonna heal this woman tonight!"

A murmur went through the crowd; then, a heavy silence as the evangelist raised his arm with a mighty shout. "No sir! I'm not gonna heal this woman tonight!"

A long and significant pause as she looked up at him, maybe wondering why she had come all this way.

He moved forward, leaning on the pulpit, his voice dropping an octave as he explained that he was saving the woman "for a higher purpose."

Another pause as he searched the silent crowd. "This woman has been sent to us that we might show, through her, the work of the Holy Spirit in a disbelieving world. THEREFORE . . ."

He paced the stage, waving his mike at the crowd. ". . . THEREFORE, I'm gonna wait and allow the spirit of the Lord to heal this poor woman on national TV! Listen to me now! We're filming our weekly television show right here in Marietta, Georgia, this coming Tuesday night. And this woman is gonna be healed on that show—that His spirit might be made manifest through her—that she might be a token of His redemption and healing power."

Shouts of "That's right, Oral! Amen! Leave her for television!"

"Bless God!"

"Glory!"

"O praise His holy name!"

Next came a gaunt, stoop-shouldered man who looked to be near seventy, mighty spiritless, moving slowly up the ramp. Roberts looked him over and then swept the crowd with his powerful gaze. Again his voice dropped. He was almost apologetic.

"Dear brothers and sisters, I'm not gonna heal this man tonight!"

The man looked up at him with a kind of abject astonishment.

"No, dear brethren! I'm NOT gonna heal this man tonight!"

The evangelist stepped a little away from his victim, not wanting to touch him at all, fearful perhaps that he would accidentally brush against him or something and maybe heal him in spite of all he could do to stop himself.

"Praise God! I'm gonna wait and allow this poor sick man—I'm told it's terminal TB—to be healed on my weekly television show! O praise the name of the Lord! For I say to you, brothers and sisters, that this man has been sent to us for a sign. Look at him, brethren. Look at him, sisters. A sicker man I have never seen. He'll not live out the year. Hallelujah! He'll be gone before the new moon. Except—hear me now!—except that he allow the mighty healing power of the Lord Jesus into his life!"

Tuesday, then.

"Yes, Tuesday! Praise God! Glory!"

The man went on down the other side of the gangway, a tubercular cough racking him unmercifully as he stumbled weakly into the arms of two Holiness preachers. About that time it hit me what the trouble was: the wires weren't working tonight. Or maybe the engineers just hadn't finished getting them installed. Maybe that's what it was. Oral was a slick one, all right. Thinking up all that malarkey about curing those two poor old people on television. But it was only because the wires weren't working.

I went back around to the rear entrance and this time found it blocked by a whole phalanx of Holiness volunteers. I could hear Oral Roberts thundering away on the PA system and the cries of "Amen!" and "Hallelujah!" coming up from the crowd. But I couldn't get anywhere close enough to see how the electrical installation was coming. I envisioned the engineers frantically at work; Oral couldn't afford to put everybody off till Tuesday.

It was then that I got my first look at the other tents—half a dozen of them spread all around the broom-sedge field, inside a roped-off area patrolled by more volunteers. I moved through the rope toward one of the tents and was immediately set upon by the man who had been left to guard the place.

"Are you saved, brother? Are you ill tonight and needing Jesus?"

I explained only that I was a big-name reporter for the *Atlanta Constitution.*

He looked at me strangely. "This tent is for the sick. After the service they'll come in here to be healed. You will see people walk that have never walked before. You will hear shouts of joy from people who at this very moment are deaf and dumb and unable to hear the precious word of the Lord Jesus. Men and women blind from birth will be blessed with the gift of sight. You will see the terminally ill nourished back to health. You will see . . ."

I made as though to enter. He quickly laid his hand on my shoulder, warning me in a voice fraught with meaning that it would be best for me to remain outside unless I was prepared to be emptied of my sin and made whole again. His hand grew more insistent, his voice peremptory.

"This tent is only for the sick."

I got on out of there in a hurry. Start an argument with these guys and you'd be there all night. And I still had plenty to do just trying to get back inside the main tent and complete my investigation of the wiring system. Then I got to thinking that maybe I just ought to go on and get out of there. What good was it anyway? The engineers would have the wires disconnected and the generators all back in the revival truck before I could get the kind of evidence I needed for a big story.

I started for my car and then, thinking better of it, trudged off instead to another of the satellite tents. Empty. I went on in and took a seat in one of the folding chairs near the back, listening to Oral Roberts over the PA amplifier. I was just nodding off—the sound of the revival slowly fading, a sourceless drone coming from way off in the night somewhere—when I felt a sudden violent wrench of my arm.

"What the hell is this, mister? Turn my arm loose!"

It was another volunteer, flashing an eerie smile at me. He wore a blue jacket trimmed in gold braid, a pair of tasseled shoes, and a glittery tie much too wide for the current fashion.

"I would like for you to take another seat," he said, explaining that the row where I was sitting was to be left vacant.

"Why is that?"

"Wait and see."

I told him with a certain amount of savoir faire that I was from the *Atlanta Constitution*.

He looked at me more sharply. "In that case, would you mind waiting outside?"

He glanced at his watch and signaled some of the other volunteers. "You all get ready now. They'll be here most any time."

Then all at once they were upon me, a bunch of spillovers from the main revival tent, men and women, young and old, all crowding through the open flap with sad faces and frightened eyes. These were the people, I later realized, who had gone up to be saved that evening but were still a little confused about everything and so had come here for further indoctrination. I wonder how they feel now, after all these years—after hearing about the old days when Oral Roberts sometimes raised the dead in his big revival tents. Was this one of the times? Perhaps. And me, a chronic hogger of front-page bylines, not even catching on to it— never suspecting a thing until I picked up my own paper almost thirty years later and read the whole wild story of his youthful prodigies.

There was not a little commotion among the volunteer ministers as the newly saved flocked into the tent. The ushers herded their captives to their seats and ordered them to their knees, spacing them by a prearranged plan: every other row to be kept empty so that the preachers could circulate more freely.

Among the last to enter was a dark-haired young woman with her son and daughter. The boy couldn't have been more than five, the girl maybe a year older. They took seats near the rear, crying and shaking all over and finally going to their knees as a dismaying and slightly repugnant character in a baggy suit hovered above them, shouting in a kind of loud, belligerent singsong: "Believeeve in Jeesus! Believeeve in Jeesus!"

He was older than the others, bigger, shaggy haired, belly sagging over his belt, veins bulging grotesquely from his neck as he bellowed his cry of damnation into the ear of the young woman.

"Believeeve in Jeeesus! Believeeve in Jeeesus! O believeeve in the name of the precious Lord Jeesus that thou mightst be spared an eternity of grief and wailing . . ."

It went on like that for some time. I watched him from the corner, hating him with the hatred of the righteous: his thick jowls, his bulbous lips splotched with purple. He was at least six-four. He'd probably been a drunk or a professional wrestler in his youth. But I figured I could handle him all right, even if I had been away from the weights for a while. He kept circling around, like a clumsy panther, his voice loud and grating, his mouth right up in the woman's ear, as though he were blowing in it as well as yelling in it.

"Believeeve in Jeesus! Believeeve, I say. Believeeve in His holy name!"

By this time the crowded revival ground had begun to empty of cars— headlamps flaring in and out of the tent opening, the repetitive screech of rubber on gravel, a thickening sound of traffic out on the big four-lane leading back to Atlanta.

Time for me to get back to the office if I was going to make deadline. I took one more look at the frantic scene and headed for the exit, moving warily past the huge, crumpled preacher as he drummed out his furious tale of imminent damnation. I'd just worked my way into the aisle and had started to duck through the opening of the tent when his beefy hand suddenly shot out and caught me by the bicep—a bit too roughly, I thought. He drew me toward him, having mistaken me for one of the penitents, staring me down and still chanting maniacally as he rose once more to his full height.

"Believeeve in Jeeesus! Believe, brother, that thou mayest . . ."

I flung him away. "Hands to yourself, mister! Can't you see that you've got the wrong man?"

I wasn't looking for trouble. I just wanted to get on out of there. He came toward me again, grabbing my arm and screaming in my face. The same mad cry of damnation. "Belieeeve in Jeeesus! Belieeeve in Jeeesus!" I gave him another shove, whacking him a good one in the midriff and spinning him around a couple of times.

"Damn you, mister! Damn you! Keep your hands where they belong, goddammit! And leave that woman alone! Leave all these people alone!"

He just kept right on spinning—a slow, cumbersome whirl that carried him all the way to the front of the tent, his voice never changing at all. "Belieeeve, I say. Belieeeve in Jeeesus!"

Then I saw the others: three of them coming toward me with their arms swinging at their sides, my antagonist a little behind them, bellowing out the same unrelenting refrain. They closed in on me without a word—no apologies, no explanations—moving me briskly toward the tent flap and bumping me on out into the dark.

"Why, you bastards!"

I swung on one of the men—missed. He came forward a couple of steps. I thumped the butt of a Camel contemptuously at his feet. I could tell he wasn't all that crazy about starting a fight. It would have ruined the Christian atmosphere of the place. Besides, he couldn't have known how out of shape I was.

I guess I was banking on that in a way—him not wanting to start a fight, I mean—because I didn't have time for any real trouble. I was already flat up against deadline and still facing the long ride back to Atlanta. They stood looking at me, thin and mean. Sure, another time and I could have taken them easy. But not now and not on their own ground. They would simply have ganged up on me, pounded me into the dirt, and then, when they got around to telling it later, they would swear up and down that they needed only one guy to put me out of commission. And him with one hand tied behind his back. I moved on off through the dark, feeling their eyes on me, hearing the sobs and moans of the redeemed coming from inside the indoctrination tent.

When I got to the car—more trouble. A big cop stood tapping his nightstick against a No Parking sign I'd chosen to ignore.

"What the hell is this, fella? Can't you read?"

"I'm from the *Atlanta Constitution*."

"That explains it."

I lit a cigarette with the ultimate in savoir faire and decided my best bet was to take him into my confidence. I blew a bit of smoke in his face, directed his attention to the main revival tent, and alerted him to my worst suspicions: electric wires, portable generators, all the rest.

I watched him as he wrote out the parking ticket. "I don't guess you've noticed anything suspicious—no shady characters lurking about, anything like that . . ."

He didn't say anything.

"Well, I figure it doesn't hurt to inquire. You just never know with some of these guys around."

He slapped the ticket into my hand. I looked at it as he went off into the dark. The bastard. Nailing me for a trivial parking infraction without taking any account at all of who the real lawbreakers were. I still couldn't figure out how Oral had pulled it off. No wires, no electric prods. I figured I must have overlooked something—but what? That Oral was a smooth one, all right. He'd fooled the newspapers, the cops, everybody. And now I was the one with the ticket—and trying to figure out how to make deadline while Oral was sitting off in some hotel room somewhere with a big cigar and a pint of cheap Communion wine, laughing with the boys about the real slick little deal he'd pulled off on all those Christian yokels down in Marietta.

At least that was the way I looked at it then. Naturally, things are a little different now. You have to understand that that was before I realized he was able to raise the dead and that on at least two occasions he'd put Lucifer down for the count and that he would be coming back someday to reign at the side of Jesus in power and great glory.

Part Two

THE RETURN

The summons comes again, at first light: "Jim and Tammy are back in Tega Cay!"

And then the mad scramble as you climb out of bed, groggy after another sleepless night, looking for the tranquilizers, the misplaced travel bag (yes, you were sure you'd put it here somewhere so you'd be sure and have it handy the next time you started out), the TV blaring as you try to catch up: how Bakker and his wife had unexpectedly grabbed a plane out of LA and flown back overnight to the Tega Cay lakefront retreat that had been their home during the years when they had rivaled Donahue as the biggest draw on daytime television.

You are still trying to straighten it all out and not getting very far as you grab the handbag, the attaché case, the tape recorder, the note-pads and pencils, the paperback copies of Dostoyevsky and *The Essential Erasmus* and *Gnosticism and You* (always a good idea to take some of the good stuff, even when you figured there would be no time to get into it); and then out of the house feeling vaguely warm from the pills and hoping you can somehow make it to the airport in time for your 7:35 flight. Your wife speeds you frantically along the interstate, her voice coming from a great distance and your own voice coming from way down inside you somewhere,

. . . by God they'll pay this time they'll pay for sure those bastards de-stroying your life just when it was getting started again phoning you in the middle of the goddamn night OK so it wasn't the middle of the night so what's the difference anyway rousing you out of a rare sound sleep for some goddamn idiotic half-assed chase along roads that go plunging heedlessly and forever off into the maw of unripe morning *Smile pretty mister you hear me goddammit smile* rousing you out of bed out of the still-drunken night for a fevered rush off into sunlight and forever beyond sunlight forever thy will be done Amen rousing you out of what could have been the first decent sleep . . .

The sun comes straight at you now, splintering the windshield, your eyes, your whole being as you glare fixedly at the concrete, trying against all odds to stave off an inexorable seizure of narcolepsy.

At the airport you stumble through security, arguing with the glassy-eyed guard who insists that you break down your computer ("They puts bombs in them things nowadays, fella!") and then snarling back at him as you rush headlong half stumbling plunging madly toward the gate *bye honey bye now be careful,* the big jet already revving up as you climb aboard and blindly feel your way to your seat.

"Good morning, sir. A very good morning to you."

You are almost alone in first class. The editors haven't figured that out yet: how you can pay only a little more for first class and get almost twice as many frequent flyer miles even if you're going no farther than Charlotte. Eighteen minutes in the air. The round-trip would get me another three thousand extra miles. Some laugh on Kovach and his crowd if they ever found out.

The flight attendant is anxious to accommodate. "What can I get for you, sir? We have a variety of very nice juices."

You take the orange juice, knowing bourbon on the rocks would not look right at 7:35 A.M. or is it only 6:35 you have half forgot? You drift off for maybe half the eighteen-minute flight to Charlotte. You stagger out now, having drunk the orange juice, wondering what you had left behind this time and congratulating yourself on all those hard-earned frequent flyer miles that would help get you to London or Istanbul one of these days if you could survive PTL and the Antichrist and the druids and the Mark of the Beast and the nonsensical editors who'd never been out on a big story and could hardly even envision the complications and hardships and *goddammit you'd left the Erasmus on the plane you should have known it you should have guessed*

You grab a copy of the *Charlotte Observer* as you rush to flag a bus to the rental car lot. The story adds little to what you have heard on television. You will have to wait until next day's edition to get the whole sickening account, the candid shots of Tammy signing autographs and

Jim Bakker browsing thoughtfully through the Book of Job as the plane launches into flight.

"Let the day perish wherein I was born and the night in which it was said, There is a man child conceived."

You would look at the photographs in disbelief, remembering all the stories and rumors, all the talk of those midnight visits to Charlotte's brothels and massage parlors, the thin man in blond wig and silk stockings, giggling behind his veil. Was it really Bakker? The Assemblies of God apparently had no doubt, having banned him forever from their pulpits after hearing a tale that the world at large had heard only in part.

Now he was flying back, a man suddenly devoid of empire, without a church or even so much as a paper certifying him to preach. Down to his last $37,000 too, despite all the talk of the more than $2 million in salary and bonuses he had collected the year before, plus another $300,000 or so in the first three months of 1987.

"Let it not come into the number of months. . . . For the thing which I greatly feared is come upon me . . ."

Then he would be off the plane, smiling again, cheerfully greeting a crowd of sycophants at Douglas International Airport; and Tammy Faye flinging herself to the ground and kissing the good earth in front of their Tega Cay parsonage and leaving a pink flush of cosmetics there long after she and her husband had disappeared inside.

"Yes, yes, so good to be back; yes, we're home now, home at last."

Yet it is such a dreary place, all in all, the upper South Carolina Piedmont. The pine barrens and waste places, the shameful towers of Heritage USA rising just ahead as you drive again down the familiar tar-patched road past the Partners House and the once-gaudy billboard from which the pastel-tinted faces of Jim and Tammy Bakker had been summarily banished. On orders from Falwell. The old warthog. One of God's bullies, Paul Wood called him.

This time you do not turn in at the gate. Your destination lies south toward Lake Wylie and the palatial waterside dwelling peremptorily reclaimed by the Bakkers. Will Falwell evict them and risk making new enemies among the faith partners? No one can say. A tough character, Falwell. He won't give up easily.

You stop at a gift shop to ask directions. On a rack just inside the door you see the latest in Tega Cay high fashion: silk gowns, leather skirts, and the special for the day: T-shirts splotched with a kaleidoscope of bright colors and a smudge of heavily mascaraed eyes, with, on the back, the words I Bumped into Tammy Faye on My Way to the Mall.

"Would you like one?" says the woman behind the counter. "I'm sure we have your size. They're just out. Looks like its going to be a real popular item."

The barricade has been long in place by the time you get to the Bakker compound—and no place to park on the crowded hillside that runs up to where the reporters are waiting. Some of the big names are there. *Newsweek, Time,* the *Washington Post,* all the networks. But mostly we are a faceless and abject lot. Some have been there since 2:00 A.M., within minutes after word had come that Jim and Tammy were flying back from LA. Others are arriving all the time, hanging over the sawbucks, anxious, waiting.

Beyond the barricade a steep, narrow street pokes its way straight down to the water. You can't see the parsonage. It lies well off to the right, hidden behind a thick stand of oak and beech. The word is out, however: the Bakkers are enjoying a late morning in bed and a leisurely breakfast. Perhaps later there will be a press conference.

"Anybody know when?"

"Could be any time," the Associated Press says. "Could be a lot later. You never know with Bakker."

"The little bastard."

"Yeah. Fuck him. That's what I say. But we're stuck here. Hell, you don't dare leave unless you've got some relief. Sort of like a death watch."

"I guess in a way that's what it is."

"Yeah," says the AP. "Maybe. Lots of people saying Bakker may still come out on top in this thing. Looks like its gonna be a long wait, though. Our bureau down in Columbia is talking about sending in a trailer. Cots. Hot food. The works. So we'll have somebody fresh all the time and won't miss anything. First we gotta try and gauge how long he's gonna stay holed up down there."

"The little bastard."

"Yeah. That's what I say. Fuck him."

The mayor of Tega Cay has closed the street to newsmen and curiosity seekers, which is taking a lot on himself, seeing as how it is a public thoroughfare. Once you have confirmed that the mayor has gone beyond his prerogative you move on past the barricade, knowing there will be trouble. Enterprise journalism—imaginative, challenging, obtrusive, insulting. All in the best tradition of the profession. Or, as Brice always said, "Good old-fashioned, obnoxious American journalism." Last thing he told you after he'd waked you up that morning. " 'Course, I guess you oughta try to stay out of jail if you can."

You try the maneuver three times before noon. Each time chief security officer Don Hardister comes out. Soon he will defect to the new regime, but for the moment he is like everybody else: waiting to see if Bakker can muster enough strength for a comeback. He is amiable at first, explaining that, unfortunately, there are to be no interviews this morning. The next time he is wary, a bit defiant, and the third time quite angry, waving us back, warning that there will be trouble.

"No interviews! No interviews! How many times I got to tell you?"

"When exactly?"

"Maybe by two o'clock."

So you climb the hill again and stand morosely by the sawbucks, the sun really coming down hard now, more reporters arriving all the time, another TV camera crew dragging itself up from the main road. Nobody takes lunch; too big a risk. The great fear is that Bakker will appear unannounced at any moment. How would you fake it to your editors if you came back and found that you'd missed the story? You pace the ground, hunting for shade, swapping small talk with the *Fort Mill Herald* and the *Greenville News* and the *Washington Post*. You could as easily have left the big Russian Dostoyevsky on the plane with Erasmus. There will be no getting into him today. Not that it makes a great deal of difference. Who cares any more about the great evil that lies at the core of our existence? Metaphysical questions raised by Dostoyevsky and his kind can't stand up in the face of an exciting, fast-breaking news story like PTL.

But look at it another way: PTL derives from the same dark inner longings that gave rise to *The Brothers Karamazov* or *Crime and Punishment*. How would Dostoyevsky have handled the story? Or for that matter Poe or Faulkner?

Two o'clock.

No Bakkers.

Moments later a man in a white Seville comes up the long drive from the parsonage—no one had seen him go in—and halts outside the sawbucks to engage reporters in an extended conversation. A pleasant chap named William Thompson. An entrepreneur from Greenville, South Carolina. Says he's been down to talk to the Bakkers about setting up a television ministry that would have a whole new kind of appeal. He has even picked out a name: the Total Life Center, with headquarters in a plush resort complex on Hilton Head. Sounds like exactly the right sort of place for the sybaritic Bakkers to make a fresh start.

But there is nothing to it. "They didn't talk," Hardister says. "He left a proposal. Jim may look at it later."

A neighbor and longtime friend of the troubled pair, PTL gospel singer Vestal Goodman, also goes down for a visit and comes back to report that "Bakker is beautiful."

Then she collapses into sobs and convulsions, looking frail and vulnerable all of a sudden in spite of her great bulk, steadying herself against the sawbucks as she shouts imprecations against Falwell.

"He's stolen the ministry! He's stolen it all! He's stolen everything we've ever worked for! There's nothing left now!"

Blubbering, she staggers down the path toward her house and tumbles sideways into a clump of bushes. Two reporters help her up.

"We're not through yet! You'll see! He's not going to take everything we've built here and treat us like dirt and get away with it!"

Two-thirty.

No Bakkers.

Three-fifteen.

"When's the press conference?"

"They'll be here any time now."

Then comes astonishing news: the Bakkers have fled! The word is that they've departed by boat across Lake Wylie for parts unknown. What follows is even more astonishing: they have descended triumphantly on the grounds of Heritage USA, greeted by hundreds of screaming loyalists. "Welcome home, Jim! Welcome back, Tammy!" Could this be the first step in the takeover? They mingle briefly with a crowd in front of the Heritage Grand and then they are off again.

"Come back, Jim! Come back!"

Only later do we learn that it was all prearranged. In the meantime I am left with nothing for deadline. All the good enterprise journalism of the morning hours seems wasted now. How am I supposed to tell my editors that I have been played for a sucker? Root, hog, or die. I explain over the phone how the other reporters ran me down and left me half crippled. I am only limping now: a busted knee and a sprained ankle and my arms skinned all the way to my elbows and my best seersucker suit ruined, to say nothing of the emotional trauma that has forced me to overdose on gin and Xanax.

"We'll have to go with the wires," my editor says.

"Hurts like crazy, Brice."

"Call us when you have something."

And so back to the barricades, the dark coming on fast now, the other newspeople beginning to pack up and drift away. Maybe this would be my chance to redeem myself. If I could stay out there long enough and keep close watch I might be able to get a glimpse of something none of the others had yet seen: Jim Bakker reverting, vampirelike, to the nocturnal habits that had guided him through his PTL years. I could hang back at a safe distance and maybe even pursue him to one of his old haunts. "Hey, girls, Jim's back. Call the boys." His second triumphant return of the day and, for me, big headlines in the morning editions:

BAKKER FOUND DISGUISED AS WOMAN

Former PTL Chairman Explains
He Was En Route to a Masquerade

"I am not a homosexual," he says indignantly.

10

Two days after the Bakkers flew in from Palm Springs, Falwell's PTL was frantically petitioning for financial protection under Chapter 11 of the federal bankruptcy code. When his aides summoned us for a press conference that Friday afternoon, everybody knew what was coming. Attorney Grutman would explain that PTL had exhausted every financial resource and had been forced quite against its will to seek refuge under the bankruptcy laws. But we knew the truth: the Falwell people were afraid of Jim Bakker. His reappearance at Heritage USA had brought too many people into the streets. By the weekend, barring federal legal protection, there was no way of predicting what might happen.

Worse, Grutman had chosen that moment of all others to squash me like a piss-ant on national television.

We went back a long way, Roy and I—all the way back to the big 1984 *Hustler* trial, where I had disgustingly betrayed my lack of sympathy for the obscene effusions of Mr. Sleaze. Which was why Grutman had rung me with his March "exclusive." It turned out to be nothing, but he still remembered me fondly, if somewhat incorrectly, as a fellow traveler of the fundamentalists. Next (I had been sure of it for some time) would come an invitation to visit his $3 million New York estate. Don't bother to call. Just drop in any time.

Now, suddenly, he turned on me with a venomous sneer. "Your paper has been invariably hostile to us, sir!"

He had begun calmly enough, explaining that PTL was flat broke and had been unable to find creditors willing to take a chance on its future. "We were totally pinned down. We had no free assets that could possibly have been posted as collateral and there were other creditors ahead."

All lies. Or at least not the whole truth, not exactly as he had stated it. From a conversation I'd had the week before I knew that there'd been at least one internationally backed investor willing to loan the ministry up to $50 million long before anything had been said about bankruptcy.

Brent Butts, a financial broker based in Marietta, Georgia, had floated the deal at a secret meeting in Savannah and then complained to the *Journal-Constitution* when the Falwell people refused to return his phone calls.

Everybody knew that Bakker somehow figured in PTL's decision to petition for financial reorganization. Yet there seemed no way of getting around Grutman's ponderous rationale until I hit upon the idea of bringing up the Butts deal.

Grutman turned to me with a look of offended dignity. "Let me assure you, sir, that at such times as these all manner of trolls, pecksniffs, and hobgoblins come out of the financial woodwork to . . ."

When I assured him that it wasn't trolls or hobgoblins, he flared again, his voice rising, the veins in his neck throbbing like a metronome.

"You're invariably hostile to us, sir! I can tell you, sir, that we will *not* be duped simply because there are those who think that we are *in extremis,* that we are without resources . . ."

"You have said you are broke."

"Short term, sir! The long-term assets of PTL are incalculable! PTL possesses resources vastly in excess of whatever known liabilities it has at the present time. Nor is it devoid of the capability of paying creditors whatever its just debts or obligations may be. It is simply that by reason of the chaotic mismanagement of the previous administration we cannot simultaneously gratify the financial expectations of the institutions that have imposed cash demands on PTL that cannot be sustained absent the protection of the federal court."

There was no way of getting around his monumental perversity, and we could never have induced him to confess the truth—that Bakker's return had indeed thrown him and his colleagues into "extremis." But there was more to it than that. Grutman had developed an enduring hatred for the *Journal-Constitution* after the paper printed an article questioning the ethical standards of Jerry Nims, the millionaire Atlanta businessman and Falwell associate who had been appointed to untangle the PTL financial mess and who had accompanied Grutman to the press conference that afternoon.

Nims had made his millions as a promoter of various ingenious financial schemes and had also spent a large part of his career fending off legal challenges. The most serious recent allegation against him was that he had fraudulently put himself forward as coinventor of something called the 3-D Nimslo camera. The real inventor was a Chinese technician named Allen Kwak Wah Lo. When the device proved a marketing flop, Nims dumped his stock in a hurry-up offshore deal that netted him $6.9 million and cost other shareholders dearly. Such were the charges.

After Grutman descended on the *Journal-Constitution* and threatened to call down thunder, the editors, as usual, cravenly backed off. The article, as it finally appeared, had little bite. But Grutman cherished old grudges the way some men cherish old wine or priceless antiques. As we exchanged parries, his voice took on an ever more threatening tone, as though, like the great Owen Glendower, he would at any moment call demons "from the vasty deep." (But would they come when he *did* call for them?)

Nims, not liking the drift of the exchange, leaned over and calmed the attorney with a timely whisper; and no bad thing either, for even as he did so I was musing on my likely fate. I remembered how Grutman was said to have once impaled a courtroom foe with a withering quotation from Walter Raleigh's prosecutor, Sir Edmund Coke—"Thou, sir, art the very spider of hell!"—and wondered if I was to suffer the same indignity. But it was all right. When I got home, everybody said, "Hey, you looked real good on TV. When you gonna get your own show?"

11

How to get the Bakkers out of the house. That was the big question. The talk among the faith partners was that Jim and Tammy had a legitimate claim to the parsonage and would be able to make it stand up in court.

"All we want to see is the deed," Nims kept saying. "All we're asking them to do is show us a little sheet of paper."

There was no sheet of paper, only the word of Bakker's old board of directors—now defunct—that even though the house had been purchased in the name of PTL the intent was clear: no one other than Bakker was ever to own the place. Now he had come back to stake his claim, not merely because he believed the house to be his—if, in fact, he believed that at all—but mainly because it would have been exceedingly awkward for the Falwell people to throw him out.

He would draw it out as long as possible, conferring with lawyers and old confidants, hoping above all else that the cops would eventually show up with an eviction notice so that he would have it to wave at his growing throng of supporters.

"See. They're throwing us out. They've painted over our billboard, deep-sixed our albums and books, and now they're throwing us out of the house! And, furthermore, I am not a homosexual!" And then the chant coming up from the crowd:

"See. We told you. He is *not* a homosexual! And now they're throwing him out. What're we gonna do about it!"

Maybe a lot; maybe nothing at all. By now the rumble against Falwell had grown loud and ugly and unremitting. Every day there was a new stir in the streets, more people coming in from all over the country, automobiles sporting license tags from New York, Maine, Ohio, Nebraska, and points west. Sometimes visitors speaking a foreign language would appear—or was it only another species of the Unknown Tongue?

People who had never even seen each other would gather in small angry groups to sing hymns, chant prayers, be healed, and curse Jerry Falwell. Long days would grow into long, fevered nights as Paul Wood mustered his forces for the last great battle between good and evil. Men who at one moment had been standing around talking about crops and the weather would suddenly fall under the ineffable spell of the spirit and begin to cry out in loud, indecipherable voices that whooshed violently up into the sunset. Women talking about vacation plans or the toilet training of children would fall victim to the same mad impulse, flinging themselves crazily about, like bacchanals consumed by an unslakable holy thirst.

So it would go. Paul Wood was always there to provide direction, summoning the faith partners to prayer, launching into fulminations against the Great Beast of the Apocalypse that was about to come into our lives, and explaining how the International Society of Druids, Incorporated—Jerry Falwell, ambassador at large—had spent years plotting to steal Heritage USA and was even at this moment on the verge of triumph.

"Are we gonna let 'em do it?"

"No, praise God! No!"

Sometimes as you drove along the road at dusk you would hear a low, almost piteous moan coming up from the crowd, other times a shrill, harpylike shriek. "Farewell, Falwell! Farewell, Falwell!" The worshippers would circle mysteriously about, as in a childhood game of pop goes the weasel, or go snaking off in a long line across the grassless front yard, sinuously waving their arms and hips while emitting a single loud rancorous unchanging cry:

"Farewell, Falwell! Farewell, Falwell!"

.   .   .

The dock was clear and the sun coming down hard across the water when the boat dropped anchor. There was no stir about the house, no noise, no sign of a uniformed guard—nothing, in short, to prevent me from undertaking the most daring enterprise of my fading journalistic career.

"An amphibious assault on Bakker's rear flank" was what a fellow reporter, Raad Cawthon, had called it over drinks the night before. Cawthon was one of our best; he had flown in from Atlanta to provide backup coverage after I had inexplicably failed to head off Bakker at the Heritage Grand.

The idea of "taking Bakker by water" had come up over dinner as we sat pondering the latest edicts from our editors. Everything had gone crazy in Atlanta. Excuses and more excuses. To hear them tell it, that was all they'd been getting. Tight security. Big cops. And they were tired of hearing it. They wanted something firsthand from Bakker and they wanted it in one powerful big hurry, preferably in time for the Sunday editions. That left us only a day to complete this mighty task.

"What're you guys doing anyway? Looks like you've signed up to be a regular part of the PTL party. Up there just playing with your dicks. Is that it? What'd ya think we're paying you for?"

One thing they were not paying us for was overtime. A fine Saturday morning like this and here I was mounting an assault on Bakker's rear flank when I had promised to be home in time to help with the fencing. Overtime? In four years I'd got hardly a cent, and no compensatory time except on those rare occasions when I'd grown desperate enough to threaten the *Journal-Constitution* scofflaws with physical violence or legal action.

"Shit," my editor would always say. "Don't you know that Reagan has suspended the wage-and-hour law?"

Anyway, there was no time to think about that now. "A waterside assault," Cawthon had said as he launched into his fifth Scotch. "We'll be on him before he can even think about calling the guards."

"I expect they'll be watching the water too."

"Maybe not. You never know about Bakker. Whim and caprice. That's his whole *modus operandi*. You can't tell how it might hit him. He might take it as a providential sign and decide that now's the time to do the big interview. Or he might decide to do it on a lark." Cawthon sipped his Scotch and smoothed his blond mustache. "You just never can tell about Bakker."

It had sounded like a better idea over liquor and cigars the night before than it sounded on this hot, glaring June morning. Finding a yachtsman who knew the whereabouts of Bakker's digs or had the time to waste on such an expedition was the big problem. We had spent almost two

115

THE RETURN

hours making the rounds of the Lake Wylie marinas and were about ready to give it up when we lucked into Pink Slaughter. An amiable gent of about fifty, lean, with thinning hair, excited about the prospect of seeing Bakker up close. He had always wanted to be a part of history. Besides, he said, it would give him "somethin' to tell the grandkids." If he were ever to have any, that is, which he had come to doubt, because his own kids, well, they were already "growed," and it didn't seem to him, truthfully speaking, that they had much interest "in getting themselves hitched up and all tied down."

We settled on $30 as a fair price. A bit exorbitant, given Pink's great personal interest in being part of the expedition. An eyewitness to history, so to speak. But it was all going on the expense account anyway. Cawthon and I flipped coins. I got the call and climbed aboard while Cawthon went back to guard the barricade. I wasn't exactly sure who was the winner and who the loser. But it would be all the better for me. If the backdoor assault were to work, I'd have all the glory. Nobody would have to know it was Cawthon's idea.

JIM BAKKER TALKS ABOUT HIS FIRST TIME

Ace *Journal-Constitution* Reporter Scoops All Rivals. Discredited Evangelist Discloses Intimate Details of His Sexual Acrobatics with Tammy Faye and Others, Vowing That He Will Recapture His PTL Empire and Hand Falwell over to the Illuminati.

Maybe I could even start thinking about a Pulitzer. This time the editors would be forced to wire congratulations. Pink Slaughter leaned far to port as he drifted into anchor. "Betcha the thirty you owe me they ain't even up yet. Still lyin' up there in the bed screwin.' Betcha he's had it six times since daylight."

I looked at him, then back at the dock. Maybe it would work out exactly as we had planned. Just the sort of thing that might appeal to the dirty little sodomite. Whim and caprice. His whole *modus operandi!* I could imagine that at any moment he and his wife would look up from their breakfast drinks—probably gin and tonic at this hour—and see me standing out on the dock. Maybe they would take me for an interested buyer—interested enough to pay the $1.3 million they said the house was worth, and to do so without even seeing the deed. Close the deal right there on the wharf. On the other hand, if things went badly I could always feign disorientation, pretending that I'd been let off at the wrong landing.

The guard was on me the minute I hit the dock. I had no idea where he'd been hiding. He was pleasant enough, yet all menace inside.

I glared at him arrogantly and flashed my credentials, thinking that maybe I could carry it off with a Grutman-like pomposity. "My card, sir!" I explained that I was a citizen of "no mean city" and represented a paper that, as he had doubtless heard, "Covers Dixie Like the Dew." What better forum for Bakker to elaborate on his plot to recapture PTL?

"Besides, it's not even his house," I said.

"I got my orders."

I was not sure how much would satisfy Kovach. Don't push it to the point of criminality. Still, they would want a full accounting if we didn't get something in the paper by Sunday morning. The loveliest weekend of the spring and everybody else in creation at home with the kids. "Just try to stay out of jail," my editor had said. If I failed? I wasn't even sure the paper would send an attorney.

"Thirty days. And break them big ones into little ones, mister."

The guard closed in on me with his fetid breath and backed me toward the water. I squared up to him, wondering how far to carry it. "My card, sir!" But I knew it was no good. My astrological transits were all wrong for this kind of exploit. I had known that for weeks; so will anybody else who has been thus far attentive. It will therefore surprise no one to hear that as I turned to hotfoot it back to the boat I slipped on something at the edge of the dock and pitched headlong into the water.

It hadn't turned out anything like Pink Slaughter expected. But he gave me a hand anyway.

"We ain't supposed to let nobody near the place," the guard said, not even bothering not to laugh. "I got my orders."

I sat there dripping like a wasted mackerel. Cawthon and his big ideas. Slaughter lifted anchor and swung away from the dock, grumbling something to the effect that I sure hadn't got me much of a story.

We drifted silently toward a tree-studded bank where I would be able to sit for a while and dry myself. Slaughter looked at me as though I had let him down miserably. He was probably thinking I wasn't very good at my job. Letting a smelly security guard push me around like that. A whole Saturday morning wasted, with him sitting out there watching me make a fool of myself when he could have better spent the time getting his boat cleaned out for his big Saturday afternoon outing. A big cookout with grilled steaks and great tubs of cold beer and a lot of laughs.

No doubt he'd been counting on the adventure at Bakker's wharf to make the day a real success. Now he'd have to spend all his time explaining why he hadn't had a chance to clean his boat up good and proper. But at least my cowardly retreat from the dock and subsequent plunge into the water would give him and his guests plenty to laugh about. He couldn't exactly count the day a total loss. Even if he hadn't had a chance to witness any of the boisterous orgiastic rites he'd been hearing so much about from PTL insiders.

We drifted toward the dock, sunny now beneath the tall, bare trunks of the pines. From there it would be only a short walk back up to the barricade. Slaughter dropped anchor while I climbed out.

"Sure was hopin' I'd get me a look at that little fucker. It woulda been one for the scrapbooks. Like being an actual part of history."

I explained that it had been a big gamble and that, all in all, the result was about what I had expected. I gave him the wet thirty.

He looked at me again. The disappointment in his eyes had quite plainly turned to contempt. He lifted anchor and drifted a ways before engaging the engine.

"Too bad it didn't work out," he said.

"Just part of the job."

. . .

I went up the hill toward the barricade, wondering how I would explain everything to Cawthon. Thirty bucks for nothing. I stepped out of the trees and in front of a sporty late-model Mazda that had just turned in from the main road. Two guys looking for the "show."

"They got started yet?" said one, grinning broadly and a bit lasciviously as he hung out the window. "I reckon they're doing it with the shades up. Hahahahahaaa!"

"Straight ahead," I told him. "You with the press?"

He was a cherubic and slightly overweight thirty-five, already drunk and planning to get a lot drunker even though it was not yet noon.

"Yeah," he said. "We was just having a little drink and figured since we was in the neighborhood we might as well go up and see the show. Besides, looka here at what I got."

He hung it out the window. A T-shirt smudged back and front like a rag that a painter had been using to clean his hands, the same shirt I had seen at the gift shop my first morning in Tega Cay.

"See what it says here. 'I Bumped into Tammy Faye on My Way to the Mall.' I ask you now, Ain't that one for the books?"

"They say it's really selling well."

"Say, buddy, hop in and we'll give you a ride. You look like you know the ropes. Maybe you can get us on the inside."

"Pretty hard to do. Well-nigh impossible, I would say."

"Is that right? You mean, you can't get to 'em at all? Shit, we was hoping to shoot us a squirrel."

"Not much chance of that. Nice shirt, though."

"Hahahahahaa! Ain't that a blister, though? Might as well try her on, I reckon."

I watched him as he did so. He looked back at me drunkenly and foolishly with the sloppy T-shirt hanging off him.

"They got another item up there you might like," I said.

"Yeah? What's that?"

"A good special on the Tammy Faye dolls," I said. "Eight hundred and fifty dollars. But they're going fast."

He looked at me with new interest. "One of those gizmos that you can blow up and it works like a real woman. Is that it?" He looked at his partner. "What'dya think, Jack?"

"Whorehouse'ud be cheaper," Jack said.

"No, man, that's just a one-time deal. Shit, you can take those dolls anywhere. Motels. Camping trips. Throw 'em in the trunk and then when you feel like having some fun, out she comes and you go to it. No big bills for food and liquor. A lot better than a one-time deal with some floozy in a cathouse. No worries about disease. Why, shit, Jack, they say some of them dolls is so real you can even smell the perfume. Real hair, too. Even under the armpits. They get it off dead folks. Hahahahaha! Ain't that a blister! And here's the kicker: they've even got some of them dolls wired up so that they'll talk dirty to you. Hahahahahahahahahahaaa! 'Course, you gotta remember to wind 'em up each time you go to get a piece. What d'ya say, Jack? Think we oughta check it out? Yessir, I'll bet that Tammy Faye doll is one more good piece."

"You're crazy, Alvin. You know that? Just plumb ever-lovin' crazy. And why don't you take off that ridiculous-looking shirt? I wouldn't be caught wiping my ass with that rag."

"I thought we came down here to get laid."

"By a goddamn balloon? You slimy little pervert. Anyhow, they ain't got any kind of dolls up there like you're talking about."

"Naw," I said. "It's just a keepsake. A memento. Nothing like what you've got in mind. Money goes to feed the poor, train the handicapped, counsel unwed mothers."

"All that money for something that won't even give you a hot time?"

"A lot of people want 'em. You might check Perry's Jewelry Emporium. Like I say, they're going pretty fast. But you could still get one on special order."

The Mazda scooted on up the hill, flinging up a spray of fine gravel and leaving faint tire tracks in the hot asphalt.

Alvin stuck his head out the window and looked back. "Shit, Mac. All that money for a goddamn doll that won't even give you a blowjob? 'Course, now, in a way, I can see where it might make a difference if the money all goes to a good cause."

"Yeah, foreign missions. All kinds of religious stuff. It's not like people aren't getting anything for their money."

12

It went on like that for another week. More long days of waiting. Life's precious moments gathering at your feet like little puddles of sun. Evenings when the Bakkers came up the drive in their midnight blue Mercedes was about the only time we ever saw them. They would be sitting in the backseat behind the tinted glass like a pair of fancy-dress ducks: Tammy bespangled with jewels, laden with makeup, opening her window slightly and dangling a limp, velvet-gloved hand toward us like a movie star arriving for opening night at Hollywood and Vine. Bakker beside her, grinning, slightly effeminate, never opening his own window or saying anything; and the rest of us hovering about the car screaming maniacally while the security guards removed the sawbucks.

Then would come the long chase through the twilight to wherever they were going for dinner. They would vanish into a back room somewhere or behind an imposing array of bodyguards while we stood there smoking cigarettes and wishing it would all be over so we could go back to the hotel for a drink.

Once, just at noon, I returned from a brief and frantic lunch—having wondered every minute if I were missing the story that would end my career—to find the reporters and television cameramen bunched against the barricade with new intensity, all gazing down the steep lane into the thickly wooded hollow. Not knowing what I was about to see, I was understandably in a particular big hurry to see it.

"What is it?" I asked one of the newsmen.

"Shhhh," he said, hushing me with his finger. "It's the Bakkers."

I gathered that they'd appeared briefly at the bottom of the drive and then vanished into a grove of trees opposite the house. None of the cameramen had got off a shot. But that was all right. Their prey would have to come back by the same route. Hence all the anxious preparation. The TV people stood focusing and refocusing their lenses, hanging over the sawbucks, stooped, silent, waiting.

Having found out what I was about to see and knowing that it was nothing, I rushed even more frantically to see it, moving directly into the path of the TV cameras, whereupon there fell on me such a flood of oaths and screams that I temporarily lost my balance and skidded halfway down the hill on the loose gravel. I had to feel my way back up the edge of the drive. But I was still in front of the cameras.

"Hey!" yells one of the cameramen. "Down in front!" And then another: "What the hell is this, goddammit!"

"Outa the way, mister! We had an arrangement!"

I stood doing a little dance on the slippery gravel, defiantly waving my notepad.

"Down in front! Down in front!"

"By God!"

The war between newspaper reporters and television people went back a long way, not often flaring into open hostility, as it had at the moment—a conflict more grumbled about than fought to a conclusion. But as a Hemingway hero said of World War I, even when he wasn't at the front, "the war was always there."

"Just hold it right where you're at, mister!"

The young man who spoke lurched from behind the sawbucks with a defiance born of sheer desperation. In another mood I might have been sympathetic with his plight. What if by some quirk he were to miss getting a shot of the Bakkers when they again passed across the clearing? How would he explain it to the producers of his evening telecast? He had me on the downside of the hill. A blondish, big-shouldered youth. I would've been mighty easy work for a guy like that. It was like being back in the schoolyard—or maybe as though I'd wandered by accident onto a dangerous side street of an unfamiliar city.

"We gonna whup yo ass, Red!"

"Name's not Red."

"Your name's whatever we goddamn well say it is."

"Ain't Red."

"Don't hit the old guy," someone yelled.

"Just let it alone," I yelled back, forgetting momentarily that I was the old guy.

"You stay outa my picture or you'll damn well pay. You hear me, Red?"

"Me and you," I said. "Any time. Any place." I watched him as he took out his appointment book. Looked like he had a pretty full schedule that day.

"Just let it go, Ray," said his companion. "It's nothing. From the angle they're coming, the old guy won't hurt us any."

We were merely a sideshow in the larger history of the moment. "Cut it out, you guys! The Bakkers are coming!" We could hear them now: voices from deep in the woods, footsteps and ribald laughter, a muted far-off roll of kettledrums.

A dramatic hush fell along the barricade. The voices grew louder, the hush more expectant as the notorious couple strode into view.

Snap! Click! Flash!

The cameramen had only the barest instant in which to record this tremendous scene. The impact now bore in on us more fully.

"I've been to the mountain!" one of the TV people yells.

"The highlight of my career," yells another, flinging his cap into the air. "What a thing to have something like that to add to your résumé!"

.   .   .

Toward evening, with the barricade still jammed, there was another crisis. The chauffeur-driven Mercedes suddenly appeared, moving slowly up the drive. Just for a moment we could see them, the gloriously arrayed Tammy Faye and the boyish Bakker, looking out at us, as through a glass, darkly. We crowded about, shouting questions. Would they be taking the house? Where was their deed? When would they make their big move against PTL? What had their lawyers said?

They smiled dimly through the tinted glass as the Mercedes rumbled into the road. We turned in a panic and went rushing off to our own cars, ready to fling off in mad pursuit. All for nothing, as it turned out. This time the Bakkers were only out to visit neighbors, three doors away. Off went the TV people, lumbering along with their cumbersome cameras, stumbling, bumping into trees, parked cars, and each other, yelling and fighting for equilibrium like frantic moon walkers tangled amid their gargantuan life-support systems out in the middle of space somewhere.

The rest of us, the newspaper people—the only authentic journalists there—were forced as always to fight against impossible odds for our rightful position. I hobbled along, trying to keep up, the arthritis flaring up again in my bad knee.

"This all seems a bit ridiculous," I told *USA Today*.

He looked at me uncomprehendingly and rushed off to join the others. Not surprising, I guess. This was more in his line, all this chasing after peckersniffs and hobgoblins. A reporter from the *Charlotte Observer* seemed to assent. Like everybody else on his staff he apparently had wearied of the story now that the paper had its Pulitzer locked up.

"Quite absurd, really," I said. "I think the profession had more dignity before television got into it."

He wasn't sure. "Remember *Front Page?*"

"Sure. The Ben Hecht play."

"Absolutely brilliant farce. Right on the money. Probably the best thing ever written on the absurdities of the newspaper game. But just think about it a minute: the reality may be even worse. Look at all these guys. All these pack journalists you see around here. Everybody afraid he'll miss the big story if he relies on his own instinct—tries to do his own thing—or dares turn his face away even for one minute from those goddamn sawhorses. And look at those bastards in Washington. Nothing more than lackeys for the administration. Whichever administration happens to be in power. Even the big-name columnists. And you call that dignity?"

"I guess you're right. Maybe there never was any dignity in it."

No dignity, no integrity. But I should have realized that before anyone else. How could I have worked for Kovach and his crowd for almost a year and still retain any respect for our craft? "Yeah, I'm really afraid we make ourselves look awfully foolish at times."

We plodded along and were soon up with all the others, crowding the porch and fighting for position, shouting questions and demanding satisfaction from a man we'd never even seen, the best of us being shunted aside, as always, in favor of the TV cameras.

The war was always there. This time it ended abruptly when a police car, its blue light flashing, careened into the yard. With an insensitivity beyond belief, the owner of the house, a man whose name I hadn't caught, had gone behind our backs and placed a call to Tega Cay police headquarters.

"You all just move along now," said the cop in the driver's seat. "Ever'thing's off-limits 'cept that street out there. By order of the mayor."

A shower had come up. We moved slowly back across the wet grass and into the road, the *Observer* and I still lagging behind, the blue light spraying across us like deadly smoke.

"You're right," I said. "There just never was any dignity in it."

So it was back to the barricade for another long night of waiting— me and the other authentic journalists squatting on the gravel and asphalt with our notepads, leaping up at the approach of every automobile or unidentified pedestrian, always waiting for the Bakkers to come out: the hand at the window, the bracelets, the diamonds, the smiles blurred behind tinted glass.

I had not seen my adversary again. Maybe I had gained a sort of respect by standing up to the guy. Or maybe everybody had found out I was the one who had stood up to Grutman on national television. In some such manner you would amuse yourself, thinking of ways to exaggerate your importance as you squatted by the sawbucks and stared down the long drive at the hole in the trees, waiting for whatever you were supposed to be waiting for. On this night you would wait until long after the others had left, knowing that if perchance Bakker were to slip out for a midnight visit to a massage parlor and somebody else found out about it you'd never be able to explain why you weren't there to report the story.

"Goddammit," one of Kovach's enforcers would say. "What about the wig and the silk stockings and the false titties? You mean you didn't see nothing?"

The next day the death watch finally paid off—after a fashion. Late that afternoon Tammy Faye, alone in the backseat of the Mercedes, came crashing through the barricade—off to buy cosmetics at the K-Mart.

Snap! Click! Flash!

Another moment of stunned silence and then a great caterwauling of laughter, caps flung high in the air, a shout: "Back to the mountaintop! Praise God, I have seen the glory!"

So it went, on into the sunset and beyond, long nights at the sawbucks and more long days in the sun, while Bakker contemplated his next move. What could it be exactly? We had no idea how he was spending his time. Did he sit there for long hours hovering over the Book of

Job, trying to reconcile its fateful message with his gospel of prosperity? Or was he still looking for ways to pervert the austere words of Jesus into a doctrine more palatable to his followers?

I am come that ye might have life and have it more abundantly

Perhaps he had decided to cast himself in the role of England's Henry IV, who had returned from untimely exile to seize the throne from a vacillating Richard II. Like the great Bolingbroke, Bakker had hoped to strike a lofty and dignified pose, distancing himself from the "common-hackneyed" multitudes. He would stir only as a comet, to be wondered at, "that men would tell their children, 'This is he!' Others would say, 'Where? Which is Bolingbroke?' "

Falwell, however, was refusing to play the frivolous Richard. So we could only guess what it all might mean. All we knew for certain was that there was now a mighty stir in the streets by hundreds of angry faith partners, who had come to believe with a conviction beyond all reason or debate that their hero had been the victim of a conspiracy long in the making: defrauded, hogtied, and finally raped by the godless Hahn.

Beyond that, we knew only that the Bakkers would fight to recover their lost kingdom by whatever means at their command. How or when we had no clue. Mostly it was just a question of waiting them out, the TV people standing hanging over the sawbucks in the sun, and the rest of us—the authentic journalists—squatting on the gravel and asphalt, staring, anxious, waiting. *For my kingdom is not of this earth nor my words to the mighty*

Let there be a stir in the trees, however faint, and we would at once be at our posts, the cameras pointed down the long drive at the hole in the trees and the rest of us with notepads and pencils held in breathless expectancy—the "war" surfacing again as we jostled for position.

"Get the hell outa the way, you guys!"

"Down in front! Down in front!"

We sho gonna whup yo ass, Red!

. . .

"I wake up every morning wishing they had just killed me, because I know what it's like now: I know what it's like to be hunted to earth like a little scared animal and running all the time, and not even being able to get in your car and go anywhere because of all those awful cameras pressing against your windows. I just hope Jerry Falwell never has to suffer what he has made us suffer. I just hope he and his family never have to go through what they've forced us to go through."

She had come up the drive alone and on foot. Another hot June afternoon as we crowded around her with notepads and cameras.

I know what it's like now we're just tired of all that running Jim and I like little scared rabbits all the time running

She was crying again, the rouge and mascara dripping down her cheeks, the blue eye shadow all melted. She seemed a little drunk. She stood tottering on the uneven ground, flicking her eyelashes and daubing her face with a handkerchief. Just like all those times on TV when she'd stood begging for money—the anxious look giving way to a mask of tears, and her face all rubbery with the crying as she pled with her viewers to double their contributions and then double them again. Because there was nothing left now. Nothing. "We've put our last dime into this ministry. Everything!"

No shame, everybody said. She has no shame, because even as the mail sacks filled with money they would be off again to California or Gatlinburg or the Florida Gold Coast, leaving Dortch or another of the lesser names to sit in as host of the "PTL Club."

It was like revisiting all the old shows as we stood there on the hot graveled drive listening to her lugubrious tale of duplicity, theft, and satanic intrigue. How much better for everyone, she kept saying, if Falwell had simply gone on and put a bullet in them. "I wish he'd just gone on and killed me. Jim wishes it too." Yes. It would certainly have been much more thoughtful of him, much more kindly and decent if he'd simply dug their graves on that warm evening back in March and shot them over into it; and then casually blown the smoke off the barrel of his six-shooter and gazed at the sky for a moment and said, "Sun'll be up directly. Some of you men grab the shovels."

"All this running," she said, "this constant running. Never knowing who'll be after you next. I'm just so tired of it. Jim's tired of it too."

And another thing: they were broke again. Nobody believed it. Yet it was true. Down to their last $37,000 and Jerry Falwell lying to the whole world about the more than $2 million they'd received just the year before in salary and bonuses.

Somebody reminded her that the figures had come from licensed auditors. Did she now deny that they'd got the money?

She daubed her face amid more tears. "Everybody keeps saying we've got all this money, but if we've got it I don't know where it is, because we've got only $37,000 left. I just wish he'd gone on and put a bullet in us; that's what I wish."

Falwell had even sent her dogs to the pound and sold her little boy's car—that special little toy car his father had given him for Christmas. "Our little boy came to us crying and saying, 'Daddy, why'd they have to go and sell my car?' Because he's only eleven and doesn't understand people being cruel to each other."

Falwell had not stopped there. The big bully had sold their air-conditioned doghouse too, along with most of their imitation antique furniture and their wall hangings and their expensive *objets d'art* and all the other elegant piles of PTL refuse—the gaudy and shameless accumulation of more than ten years of riotous living.

He had done the deed at a big PTL auction back in May. I had been there that morning—another incomparable spring day insidiously filched from my life—in the big barn of a building that served each Sunday as the Heritage Village interdenominational church.

Thousands had crowded in from all over the country to gaze at the clutter: powerboats, ornate desks, gilt-laden French provincial dressing tables. And big pier mirrors. Frederick Remington bronze castings, Chippendale couches, overstuffed wing chairs, crystal chandeliers, tasseled lamps, jade whatnots, figurines emblazoned with cupids and water nymphs and leering satyrs. Furs, stoles, stockings, silk robes, fluffy night things still smelling of *kolnish wasser*. A 1928 Franklin automobile that had sat for years on Main Street USA in the Heritage Village shopping complex. (Dortch had posed for pictures there on the day I interviewed him, way back before the fall.) A gold-and-copper-plated giraffe. Another $600 for a bauble that Bakker had used as a paperweight. What was it? Jasper? Carnelian? Isinglass?

No matter.

"Sold to the lady in the pink pullover and white carnation!"

An excellent price for the bauble; not bad for the Franklin. But the auctioneer had thought the giraffe was worth at least $6,000.

"A steal," said the man who bought it. He was a retired textile executive from Charlotte. He stood looking at me in the hot May sun, cigarette smoke flaring from his nostrils. "A real steal," he said. He would use it to decorate his Rhode Island condo. "Folks'll always be wanting to know where it came from, and I'll say, 'Well, do you remember all that mess that was in the papers about PTL?' And they'll say, 'Sure, we remember that.' And I'll say, 'Well, that's where it came from.'"

God's bullies had sold all her stuff. Yet who was to say it was theirs? "Decidedly not theirs," Mark DeMoss said later. "I have the invoices. It all belonged to PTL."

Actually, nobody cared about any of it except the air-conditioned dog-house. That was what most of them had come for: to see PTL sell the doghouse. It brought $4,500. And it wasn't as though it was much of a doghouse, after all. Just some plywood nailed together with two-by-fours and a Montgomery Ward air-conditioning unit stuck in the side. No windows or built-in comfort stations. But the new owner, a forty-seven-year-old Californian named Jerry Crawford, seemed pleased with it just as it was. The reporters swarmed about him, engulfing him madly to find out what he was planning to do with his acquisition. By then he was on top of it, dancing around, the cameras grinding away, the reporters shouting questions and him saying, no, it really wasn't worth all that much if you just counted up the plywood and the nails and the two-by-fours and the air-conditioning unit.

"But I don't make business decisions when I give to Jesus!"

He wasn't planning to keep it, anyway. The Lord had told him to donate it back to the ministry so that the auctioneers could sell it again. The next time it brought only $600; and maybe it wasn't worth that either, certainly not to Tammy Faye's dog Snuggles.

"He wouldn't stay in it," PTL's public relations director, Neil Eskelin, confided. "Snuggles didn't care for the air conditioning."

Not content with auctioning her doghouse and selling her little boy's car, Falwell had gone on to do something that no man of ordinary decency would have thought of doing: he had buried all her old phono-graph records and cassette tapes. There were hundreds of them, maybe thousands, all left over from the days when she was singing regularly for the "PTL Club." Her best friends had told her about it—how Falwell had hauled all of those tapes and records out of the PTL warehouse and buried them in a big hole in the ground.

He wasn't even tactful about it. He just got on the bulldozer and went out in the woods and dug the hole and pushed all those big crates full of records over into it and then drove off chortling like crazy. Some of her friends had gone down there and dug them out. Most of the boxes hadn't even been opened, and now they were all crushed to pieces and covered with dirt. It was the saddest thing she could possibly think of. She just couldn't understand why he wanted to haul them all off in the woods and bury them like that when he could easily have given them to someone who would have appreciated good old-fashioned gospel music that came straight from the heart.

Then she was gone, betrayed again by her trickle-down pancake makeup. I turned to get a head start on the crowd, anxious to make deadline; but again the younger reporters trampled me into the dirt, scurrying around and over me as they raced for their cars. *Newsweek* shouldered me aside and left me for dead in a prickly pyracantha. I still might have made it if I hadn't crashed into a guardrail on my way back to the hotel. Easily a thousand dollars worth of damage or more. The insurance would pay. But what was I to do about another car? By that time I was well past deadline. I would get little sympathy. Editors had a hard time understanding all the little things that could happen to you when you were out on assignment; they didn't know how it felt to be doing all that running or to be trampled underfoot and hunted to earth all the time like a poor little scared animal.

I could hear Kovach's chief enforcer, Corleone himself, screaming at my editor as I tried to explain it.

"Fuck him!" he was saying. "That trifling moronic son of a bitch hit a goddamn guardrail we'll nail his ass to the wall fuck him where's the goddamn story?"

It had come roaring in hours before over the wires of the Associated Press and United Press International. Staff and wire reports. That's the way our story would read the next day after I had added the little I could legitimately produce as my own. And Corleone shouting crazily as he careened around the newsroom, jabbing the air with his fingers: *Fuck him! Not even a goddamn byline to show for it and him out there a whole stinking week out there at the fucking barricades the goddamn fucking son of a bitch fuck him!*

It was no excuse that the wire version had also been good enough for the *Observer*. None of it mattered because the *Constitution* was stuck up there at the barricade with an old guy too old to come to God or even to meet a deadline, so that now the company would just have to find a place for him on the desk somewhere maybe off in some lousy corner where he wouldn't be getting in everybody's way just give him an old guy's job like they always gave the old guys when they pulled them off the street . . .

Fuck him!

All that day it was the same. When the subeditors gathered that afternoon to swap ideas for Sunday's combined edition, Corleone, as I later learned, kept squirming in his chair and leaping about the room and jabbing the air and shouting, "Fuck him! Fuck him!"

The conversation turned to the Iran-Contra scandal and to the pending congressional investigation of the affair.

"Fuck him!"

The discussion moved on to the riots in Korea and the Middle East.

But the only thing the terminator Corleone was thinking about was the old guy up at the PTL barricade and how in the hell could we be a world-class newspaper if we couldn't even learn how to meet a deadline?

There was talk of Julian Bond, the former civil rights leader who'd been implicated in a big cocaine-snorting story.

The terminator kept jabbing the air, sweeping papers, notepads, and a water glass onto the floor.

"Fuck him, I say! Listen to me, goddammit! Guy like that calls himself a reporter and couldn't even find a Jew in Hymietown!"

Maybe if I had been there and hadn't had to get all this secondhand, I would have figured that my future at the *Journal-Constitution* was less than secure. Many of my friends had been forced out by the new regime; others were waiting for the bad news. I had been a little harder to reach, being way up in North Carolina. But now that I had been run over by *Newsweek* and had come near to totaling a rental car on an I-77 exit ramp everything had changed.

That evening two other reporters were on a plane, winging their way from Atlanta to Charlotte. OK. So that's the way it is now: he's just an old guy almost fifty-three years old, too old to make it in the big leagues anymore. Like a sore-armed pitcher. Farm him out to the minors. How would he like it in Far Lake, Nevada? Or maybe up the road a ways in Alpharetta? Cox Enterprises, Incorporated, had a string of papers all around the country. Strictly minor league. But maybe if he shows he's still got the stuff we can bring him back up.

At nine o'clock a disarming blonde reporter named Kathy and a summer intern named Alex joined me for drinks and a $200 meal at the Radisson. They would soon find out what it was like living the big life and covering PTL. We would hit all the best restaurants and lounges. Before it was over we would spend almost $15,000—maybe more— some of it still unaccounted for, because whatever else you might say about Corleone you had to admit that he didn't mind spending the boss's money. Maybe he would take a different view when he found out how the Cox people felt about big-spending editors. They were a traditionally niggardly bunch, and nobody survived under them for long without understanding that they wanted you to compete with the best as long as you didn't overspend your budget.

Alex was there with a tape recorder, mostly to stand watch over the barricade. Kathy was only twenty-eight, shapely, a daunting blue-eyed temptress. Were my astrological transits about to betray me again? I could suddenly imagine myself among the legions of PTL greasers who had gone before me—little blisters of sweat popping out on my forehead and my teeth all white and glittery as I went panting feverishly after a younger woman.

13

Paul Wood walks fast down the narrow sand-clay road through the tall stand of pines, his massive frame quivering with excitement as he shoots a glance first into one part of the woods, now into another, looking for the ravine or gully or whatever it was that was sure to contain the vast inventory of phonograph records, cassette tapes, and at least three tractors Falwell had stolen from the PTL warehouse.

I'm not sure how Wood found out about the tractors. Apparently somebody who worked at the warehouse had tipped him off. Anyway, it was the first big break in his long, tireless struggle to bring Falwell down.

His mission had taken on new urgency after Tammy Faye Bakker's hysterical outburst at the Tega Cay barricade—the first "independent corroboration," as he described it, that Falwell was nothing but a dirty double-dealing agent for the Illuminati. And now we were off on a mad quest for the refuse dump that was supposed to yield up the darkest secrets of the conspiracy. If only Wood could figure out which road to take.

He kept plunging half-blindly about the countryside, into the pine thickets and out again, not knowing exactly what he would find, not even certain that he was on the right trail.

"I've just got that feeling," he said. "It's like you can smell it—like you're right on top of it without being able to see it."

The search would eventually lead back to the PTL landfill, where the first incriminating cache of records, tapes, and inspirational tracts had been found. But first there was the more important business of the missing tractors. The way Wood figured it, the cagey Falwell would never have been so careless as to hide the really big items on the Heritage grounds. And sure enough, a second tipster had informed him that somebody had seen a suspicious-looking ten-ton dump truck coming out of a side road just that morning half a mile east of the theme park.

A dirt lane led from the road far back into the forest, and Wood's ever-reliable intuition had told him that he would find the tractors down there somewhere. And if we could find the tractors, the Lord only knew what else we might find: luxury yachts, powerboats, airplanes, bulldozers, air-conditioned doghouses, priceless furnishings from ancient Byzantine monasteries—plenty of everything to put Falwell away for a long, long time.

I was still a little rocky from all the after-dinner brandies of the previous evening and wasn't sure at first exactly what Wood was getting at. Why would Falwell steal his own inventory? What would he have to gain? Wood seemed startled by my naiveté; he looked at me condescendingly and explained that that was the preacher's way of "cooking the books"—making it appear to federal authorities that the Bakker crowd had been guilty of all sorts of sinister financial manipulations, when, in truth, he had engineered the whole nasty plot himself.

It was only part of a move, he went on to explain, as he had dozens of times before, to turn the country over to George Bush and the Trilateral Commission. He reminded me again that Falwell and Jessica Hahn had been up to their necks in the whole nasty business for more years than anyone could possibly imagine. An ideal setup for them both: Hahn would have her big monetary payoff and a reputation as one of the nation's most seductive courtesans (as soon as she could get her nose fixed and her breasts enlarged), and Falwell would have the PTL satellite network to add to his booming evangelical empire or, as an alternative, to place at the disposal of the Bush people.

Too many brandies, too little sleep, not enough Xanax. The seductress from Atlanta and I had been out since early that morning. She had phoned right after sunup, scared that we would miss something and that Corleone, the Black Bart of the newsroom, would "have our ass." Now it looked as though he would have it for sure. Because we sure hadn't found anything to justify a whole morning chasing around in the wilderness. Like a lunatic bunch of peckersniffs on the prowl. But we still had plenty of time left. Maybe it would all work out.

The trouble had begun when I called my editor and said something in passing about Wood's latest conspiracy theories.

"Hold the phone," he said.

Moments later he was back on the line with near-panic in his voice.

"Pursue the Bush angle!"

"What?"

"Pursue the Bush angle!"

"It was only a joke."

"Corleone thinks we ought to pursue it."

So we got out on the scent in a powerful big hurry, me in a suit too hot for the hot day, and Kathy in her best dress and a fresh pair of panty hose that kept getting snagged on the briars.

"What'd'ya think?" she said.

"I say we're fucking lost."

"Exactly as I figured. Listen, I'm gonna get outa here. We aren't gonna find anything out here that's gonna put Falwell in jail."

Wood, preoccupied, seemed to hear nothing. He just kept darting off into the timber and shouting back assurances that the payoff could come at any moment. Was it possible that the three tractors had really been stolen? "Mum's the word," he said. "Just keep everything close to your vest and we'll have everything documented and you'll have the biggest story of your lives."

But now deadline was approaching and there was new reason for concern.

Pursue the Bush angle!

"Oh my God in heaven," Kathy said. "This is nothing but a lot of bullshit. We're never gonna get anything in time for deadline. Boy, are we gonna catch hell this time. Brand-new suit, brand-new pair of hose. All ruined. You think that damned Corleone cares about that? What a sweetie he is! He's sure gonna have our ass this time."

He had probably been waiting for our call all morning, hanging over the phone with maniacal screams and curses.

Fuck them! Fuck them both!

Wood went up all the side roads and down along all the ravines. "Look at this," he would say, leaning over for a moment to examine some obscure clue that would have been lost to a less zealous eye. Once, he spotted fresh tracks and leapt up with a bound. "Not more than an hour old! Somebody's been through here just this morning!"

Off he went, wildly, triumphantly, because he could see now where the tracks were going: straight out the road toward another distant stand of timber, toward the secret ravine, the cache of stolen goods that would provide him with everything he needed to present to a grand jury. We raced to catch up. We were deep in the forest now, plunging this way and that, the limbs whacking at us like crazy and my seersucker hanging limply about me and Kathy alternately laughing and cursing amid the brambles.

"Jesus, there goes another pair of hose."

How would I explain all this in my memoirs? Wood just kept right on going, never even looking back and still talking—during those times when I could keep up with him—about Falwell's carefully orchestrated plot to throw PTL into bankruptcy as a first step toward seizing all its assets for his own use.

"Let me tell you," he said. "When you go into bankruptcy you're as good as saying that you've failed—that you've done everything you can to raise the money and that it just isn't there. So if Falwell thinks he's failed, what's he sticking around for? Don't you see? If that's the way it is, there's bound to be some kind of gain in his heart. And I'll tell you what it is: it's that closed-circuit television network touching fifteen million people. And it's the names of all those PTL contributors: that partners' list that he's already stolen, and when he pays his $70 million* he'll still have $100 million left over, and he'll be able to put anybody in the presidency that he wants in it."

It didn't make any sense, of course, the idea of Bush locking himself into a fundamentalist constituency and then losing the middle ground. But we kept pressing on ahead, pursuing the Bush angle, my whole being shot through with the pangs of last night's debauchery and Kathy tearing her hose again and getting cockleburs in her best skirt.

*Estimated worth of PTL at the time Chapter 11 financial protection was sought.

"Jesus, where the hell are we now? I'm burning up. I sure wish I had a beer."

We had come out into a clearing, and Wood moved on off into the sunlight with a mighty stride, leaving us in yet another wild panic to catch up. "I just feel we're right on top of it," he shouted. And then, as we came up beside him, he took up in mid-sentence his previous thought: ". . . that stolen partners' list, that's what Falwell was after. And those fifteen million voters out there. If Bush gets the nomination—well, I guess you can see how important that satellite will be to him after that."

He plunged straight ahead, his feet crunching emphatically in the dirt, a big, obliging man whose thought that he was "really onto something this time" had infused him with the strength of ten.

We had come to a fork in the road. He stopped for a moment, looking around. He must have taken a wrong turn somewhere.

"Now what?" Kathy wanted to know. "You think he knows where we are or that we'll ever lay our eyes on even one of those idiotic tractors?"

Three horseback riders came along. Wood eagerly seized one of the bridles. "You all see anything of a big dump truck down this way? Maybe in the last couple of hours or so?"

Not a thing. Sorry. The riders clomped on off, and Wood lurched off toward an even more distant stand of timber, following what appeared to be the more recently traveled of the two paths. We were a long way from anything now, scouring a barren and desolate stretch of land that would have inspired a brooding Poe with desperate thoughts about the fate of man.

I still wasn't sure how Bush fit into it at all. But we had gone about as far as we could in pursuing that angle. We would have to figure out some way to explain it to our editors. They probably had the headline already written:

PTL SCANDAL TO BOOST BUSH

We turned back to where we had seen the riders and halted while Wood pondered his next move. He looked around thoughtfully for a moment and then shot down the second of the two forks, the one that looked as if it hadn't had any traffic for a year or more.

"It's got to be this way. We've looked everywhere else."

This time we waited him out. "Yell if you find anything."

"It's our ass now," Kathy said.

Back came the shout of discovery even sooner than I'd expected. We went rushing off to investigate. "Look at this," he said, bending over and peering at a mound of freshly raised dirt. The dirt had been scattered here and there, all around, leading off into the woods. "Now that's right interesting, isn't it? Why would they spread it out like that unless they didn't want you poking around down in here?" Wood leapt to his feet and rushed off to follow the suspicious-looking trail of dirt, with us again frantically trying to catch up.

"What are they trying to hide?" he said. "That's what I want to know. *What are they trying to hide?*"

Off we went, into a deeper and darker part of the forest, fighting for breath and sanity, the land pocked with deep gullies and leaf-choked hollows, any one of which could have been the incriminating PTL burial ground. None were. We kept going. "I'm telling you," Kathy said. "It's damn well gonna be our ass." We had come out at last into a freshly plowed field from which, just ahead, we could see the towers of Heritage USA.

But still no El Dorado of hidden garbage. We retraced our steps as best we could and came back out into the lane. Wood walked more slowly now, back up the long road in the sun, trying to figure out where he had gone wrong, wondering if he had been right on top of it and had overlooked some clue that would have given the whole dastardly game away.

"Now what?" Kathy said. "What does it matter anyway? We've missed our last deadline now."

It was past noon when we got back to the Heritage grounds. We drove past the entrance booth *God loves you He really does* and under a high-arched gate at the top of the grade and swung west toward the official PTL landfill, where we should have gone to start with, where the other reporters had already been. Given our luck, the news would already be going out over the wires. Well, maybe Kathy was right: the people taking names and kicking ass would never let us get away with this one.

Wood bristled with new excitement as we sped toward the great mountain of refuse. I knew now how Moses must have felt when he first laid eyes on Mount Sinai. Wood bounded out of the car, stopping only long enough to feel the hood of a bulldozer that stood near the deep gorge.

"Still warm!" he shouted. "Couldn't've been more'n an hour since they buried the last load."

Again we raced to catch up, but he was already too far ahead.

"This is it! I can feel it! We're here! We're right on top of it!"

We came boiling up to the precipice just as he gave a mad scramble down into the thick of all that junk, his foot striking a piece of glass or something and flipping him bottom side up on a bed of inner tubes. Could just as easily have been glass. A sign that the Lord meant to keep him alive at least long enough to expose Falwell's unspeakable duplicity.

He was up in the same instant, clutching at roots, outcroppings of rocks, boxes crammed with fragments of electrical wiring and plumbing parts and the odds and ends of old motors and just anything else you could think of. "I can smell it! It's all here! It's like a graveyard! We're right on top of it!" Not only could he smell it, he had found it now, or part of it—the corner of a box that did appear to contain some of the missing loot. When he dragged it out and snatched off the top I could read one of the labels: *The PTL Musical Family.*

"Look at that," he said. "Brand spanking new. And Falwell kept saying it was all just a lot of surplus inventory—a bunch of old records all warped and cracked and not any good for anything. Boy, what a liar."

He dragged the box out from beneath the rubble and then another just like it and came stumbling, half-falling, back up over all the refuse with an inner tube hanging around his neck like an aloha wreath.

"It's here. It's all here. Falwell's going to jail."

"What about the tractors?"

"They're down there, all right."

"You mean you saw them?"

"Not exactly. But they're there, all right. We'll have to get a court order or something to go through all this stuff and dig them out."

He came up out of the pit looking happier than I had ever seen him, dragging the crates over to his car and locking them in the trunk. He turned to us with a smile of huge satisfaction as he went over to feel the hood of the bulldozer again.

"If we'd come out here a little earlier we'd probably have caught them in the act. But one way or another we're gonna come back in here and dig all that stuff up. There's no telling what we'll find when we get to digging. All those PTL Bibles that have been missing—somebody told us they were down there, and I expect it's the truth. And anyhow, if there's nothing down there I want somebody to *show* me there's nothing down there."

He had forgotten about the inner tube. He took it off and examined it closely for a moment, as though it were another crucial piece of evidence, and then tossed it absentmindedly into the backseat.

"Imagine Falwell thinking he could get away with a stunt like that. Just discards, he says—old warped records that weren't any good for anything. Well, we've got him where we want him now. Yessir, that big crazy pile of garbage back there, that's the very thing that's gonna put that ol' boy away for a mighty long time."

14

Wood never did get the court order. By the next afternoon—Friday—events had built to such a fevered pitch that there was no longer any time to think about digging up all that garbage. We'd just got the startling news that Melvin Belli, the notorious publicity-seeking lawyer from San Francisco, was in town, being chauffeured about in a block-long Cadillac limousine, handing out copies of his autobiography, and proclaiming in the face of all conceivable logic that he was getting ready to restore PTL to its founder.

The fat man came into Tega Cay in the full glory of his years. An entrance worthy of emperors, dictators, and papal emissaries. "But Lord," wrote one reporter, "it's hard to be humble when your name is Melvin Belli."

Privately, we all said, "That doddering old ambulance-chasing fool!"

All except Kathy, who said she had finagled a dinner invitation with Belli—or "Belly," as she liked to call him—through one of Bakker's lawyers, a man she had known when she was working the backwoods of the North Carolina mountains for the *Asheville Citizen*.

I knew, of course, that it was a trick—that the interview had probably been set up by the Illuminati long before the PTL scandal even broke, simply to prove that I didn't have it anymore. The same as when Hahn and Falwell had conspired against Bakker when he was still a nobody.

"I got a date with Belly," she said. "What am I gonna ask him? C'mon. You gotta help me out."

"He's an old guy, even older than I am. What good is he anyway?"

"Ahahahahahahhaaaaa!"

It wouldn't do him any good to offer her money. She had plenty of that through an inheritance and had gone into newspapering only because she was looking for a career full of adventure and excitement. It had worked out well for her. She had a gift for transforming even the routine into the very essence of high drama. And we were forever racing to Tega Cay and back to Charlotte and to various motels in between, looking for the latest in PTL dirt. She had never expected anything like this, though: an exclusive interview with the most famous ambulance chaser in the land.

I knew it would make me look bad to the editors in Atlanta. But how could I compete with Kathy? Ten times the looker that Hahn ever was. I knew how Bakker felt now: tricked by old friends and trusted former associates. Editors with whom I had once enjoyed respect had brought me down. Like Bakker, I was to be merely one more innocent victim of the Great Tribulation. But how did Belli figure into it? What secrets would that quivering Vesuvius be willing to betray for a chance to get her into bed? You could bet he would be willing to give up plenty. And I could read all about it on the front page of the Sunday *Journal* and *Constitution*.

Somehow I didn't feel resentment. I didn't feel anything. I just didn't care about it anymore. I just wanted to have all of it behind me and to lose myself, Jim Bakker style, amid the deep-carpeted bars and bordellos of metropolitan Charlotte, with tall drinks of gin and plenty of tranquilizers always near at hand.

But did Belli actually have a case?

No one knew for sure, not even the *New York Times* or the *Washington Post* or the pushy BBC news team that had arrived from London the day before and started ordering everybody around. Paul Wood had spotted the Britons before I did and was immediately suspicious. He knew they had come from the land of the druids and the Illuminati and could not rule out the possibility that there was some sinister design in their visit.

There were four of them: an unctuous public affairs anchorman, a nasty-tempered little blonde who introduced herself as "the producer," and two nondescript cameramen. I had first seen them at the Partners House, talking to Wood. The blonde seemed to be in charge. She was a hard article, for sure. To Wood she says: "Well, old top, what do you have for us? Shall we be going? I believe you know where the evidence is buried."

Wood nodded.

"Well, then, let's be out and going, shall we?"

Wood was cannier than we thought. He wasn't about to give anything away, certainly not to people who for all he knew might be on a speaking acquaintance with some of the top people among the Illuminati. He played the shrewd dissembler when she asked him about the garbage dump and its news potential in the international market.

"I believe we threw 'em right off the scent," he confided later.

I had to agree. But the Britons, damn them, went on out and found the garbage pit anyway and, as I later learned, had spent most of the morning out there, cameras grinding away, while we were off on a fruitless chase in distant woods.

. . .

But the weekend didn't belong to BBC or to Falwell or even to the Bakkers. It belonged almost solely to the old fat guy Melvin Belli, who liked to call himself the "king of torts" and who attempted to strike something of a debonair pose as he strutted, huffing and blowing, around the grounds of Heritage USA.

The king of torts to everybody else, maybe, but to Kathy he was just plain old "Belly."

"You think he knows anything about those idiotic tractors?"

"Maybe there aren't any tractors."

"Maybe. Maybe not. But I just know we're gonna stand around and let ourselves get scooped on something like that. And by a bunch of British reporters at that. Jesus! Wait'll Atlanta reads about George Bush and all those tractors in the *London Times*. Then you can damn well know it's gonna be our ass for sure. There won't be any need for either of us to set foot in the newsroom again."

. . .

Bakker had come out of his fetal position long enough to join his new attorney at the Tega Cay barricade. There had been good news for the discredited preacher that week: a support group known as Bring-Back-the-Bakkers had set up shop in a nearby Holiday Inn and installed a hokey toll number that would allow disillusioned partners to vent their feelings of outrage in return for Tammy Faye's taped version of Falwell's "hostile takeover." Now, with no less an eminence than Melvin Belli hinting at some sort of monstrous cover-up, things were really beginning to look good.

"Why," said Belli, "we have letters showing that Mr. Foulwell has long coveted the ministry here. I'm sure he'll be happy to cooperate with us when he sees the evidence."

"It would be well if we could see the letters," someone said.

"All in good time, my good man. All in good time."

Belli sneered at "Foulwell" as a conniving old "warthog" and pretended never to have heard of Roy Grutman. "Sounds like he ought to be playing right tackle for the Packers," he said, ostentatiously stifling a laugh.

The old guy had long ago seen his best years, but he was still one of the biggest names in American jurisprudence. Why, then, had he decided to come to the rescue of Jim and Tammy Bakker? Almost no one except Bakker's fanatical followers and the lawyers already working for him believed that he had much of a case. So if there were no damages to be collected and if Bakker was down to his last $37,000, as he kept saying, who was going to pay the bill? It was bound to be a whopper. Belli was as proud of his outsized fees as he was of the more than $100 million in personal injury awards he'd won during his fifty-four-year career. "I'm the king," he kept saying. "The king of torts." A cannon atop his San Francisco law office bellowed forth the news of every victory. Now, as incredible as it sounded, he was telling us that he was about to score a triumph that would throw all the others into eclipse.

Was it possible that Falwell had been hiding something after all?

"I can assure you," Belli snorted, "that Jim Bakker will very shortly be back in charge of this ministry."

.   .   .

Belli or no Belli, I was finally getting the day off I'd been promised for more than a month. A chance to relax and celebrate Father's Day with the family. My friend Kathy, the lovely, big-breasted seductress with enough energy to fuel a nonstop freight, would get all the bylines and win all the acclaim. But that was all right. I just didn't want to be a part of any more big stories. I didn't want to have to think about digging up all that garbage out of the PTL landfill or even how I'd handle it if she decided to make herself available for a romantic intrigue.

"Jesus," she said as I was checking out of the hotel. "You can't leave now. What if this whole thing just breaks wide open? What do I tell Atlanta? What if Paul Wood really turns up something on those tractors? That would be just my luck, to get caught here with a story like that and nobody to cover my backside."

SMILE
PRETTY
AND SAY
JESUS

"I don't think I'd worry about those tractors."

"They say BBC's already got to Belly. And we won't even know what they got out of him unless we catch an overnight to London. I just wish I knew whether Falwell would really do something like that."

"What?"

"Steal all those frigging tractors."

"Well, let's just hope BBC doesn't know about it."

"Maybe Belly does."

"You could ask him over dinner."

"I hope he doesn't think I'm just trying to be a wiseass."

· · ·

The phone was already ringing when I got back to the farm. My wife handed me the receiver. It was Kathy.

"These frigging editors are after our ass."

She'd got almost nothing out of Belli. Only that in his dubious opinion Falwell was truly an "evil man."

"I don't guess we can print that," she said.

But that wasn't why she had called. She had discovered that Falwell's long-standing connection with the druids and Illuminati had suddenly stirred an intense interest in the *Constitution* newsroom. And the editors wanted something in a hurry.

There'd been a big meeting that evening at one of the Pentecostal churches in Atlanta and Paul Wood had been there, creating widespread consternation with the news that we were even now in the latter days and that Jerry Falwell had conspired down through the ages to steal PTL and turn it over to George Bush and company. This was a bigger story than the young reporter who'd been assigned to cover the event was prepared to handle.

"People keep asking me how much we can print," Kathy said.

"What do you mean? I thought we finally convinced them there was nothing to the Bush angle."

"They aren't interested in that anymore. The big thing now is that everybody is going around calling Falwell a druid. Can we print that? What's a druid anyway? Why do I keep thinking they live in trees?"

"That's dryads. Dryads live in trees. But I think druids worshipped trees or something. So maybe it's all part of the same thing."

"Dryads! Of course! We used to read about them in English lit. But is it OK to call Falwell a druid? It was said at a public meeting. Who were the druids?"

"A priestly caste in Celtic England. Associated with witchcraft. Stamped out by the Christians."

I was happy for a chance to pose as a learned antiquarian. Perhaps it would serve as a passable substitute for youthful vitality.

"What does that mean?" she said. "Does that mean Falwell isn't even a Christian? I guess that would be news to a lot of people. But I don't guess we could print that either. Do you really think he could be mixed up with those Illuminati people? Paul Wood claims that Falwell is their chief ambassador or something. And the people in the newsroom are all in a twidget to find out what it's all about."

"Tell them it's nothing. Tell them it isn't about anything."

"I don't think they'll listen. They're saying he's in with Satan and the pope and everybody you can think of. Ahaahahahahhahaha! Falwell dwells in trees. Can we print that?"

"That he dwells in trees?"

"Calling him a druid . . ."

"I don't think Falwell cares if we call him a druid."

"Well, it *was* said at a public meeting. But I still don't think we can call somebody something like that without getting reaction."

. . .

Midnight and another frantic call from Atlanta.

"You been in touch with Falwell?" my editor says.

"This was supposed to be my weekend off."

"They're saying he's in with the druids. Do you know anything about that?"

"It's nothing."

"It appears to be tied up with the George Bush thing. Did you ever get anything on that?"

"It was all a joke. The druids are all a joke. Everything about this whole story is a joke."

"Well, it looks like they're going to go with it."

"They're gonna call Falwell a druid?"

"They're quoting people as saying he's tied up with Satan. Or maybe that he *is* Satan. Anyway, see what you can get out of Falwell. Try to work on the conspiracy angle. Has Belli got anything on him? Ask Falwell if he's planning to resign."

"Sure."

Arguments were pointless. Kovach and his crowd had never been able to rid themselves of the assumption that Falwell was forever sitting by his answering machine with his eyelids propped open, waiting for my late-night telephone calls. So I went through it all again, futilely dialing his unlisted number in Lynchburg and getting the usual recorded message before reporting back to Atlanta.

"Can't raise anyone."

Brice grunted with disbelief. "We still gotta have reaction. We gotta have something."

Goddammit shut up do you hear me shut your goddamn fucking mouth goddammit

.   .   .

A mist was coming off the mountain as I drove back into Lynchburg next morning, my Hertz rent-a-car blending anonymously with a slowly thickening mass of going-to-church traffic. Forget Father's Day with the kids. Forget all the promises and big plans. Once more into the breach damn you once more and smile pretty damn you smile ha ha ha Falwell lives in trees spindly-legged dryad with the big gut but what else could you expect of somebody who would screw his own mother in an outhouse? Ha ha ha. Probably the offshoot of some incestuous union himself *I'm telling you mister you'd better smile goddammit* you with your nose up the ass of the Antichrist and close up the wall with our English dead!

All roads lead to the big pulpit where Falwell, as imperturbable as ever, is well into a sermon extolling the dubious virtues of Abraham the patriarch. The Associated Press, Scripps Howard, BBC—they are all there, waiting to pepper the mighty Falwell with questions for which even he will have no answers. Just the facts, Falwell. Time to come clean. We know about you and your mother. Now tell us about the tractors. That's right. Just tell us all about the missing inventory and we'll ask the DA to go easy on you.

I guess the other reporters were a little surprised to see him there at all, what with Belli on the prowl and threatening to expose him at any moment as the world's most egregious fraud. You might have thought he would have jumped at almost any excuse to avoid looking his congregation in the eye that day and to avoid taking questions from a skeptical press. You could almost guess what he was thinking: *finished for sure and no way out this time forgive me O Lord forgive thy unworthy servant and I will give back every dime and every gold-plated bathroom fixture every vibrator and dildo and aphrodisiac and all three tractors . . .*

But he never did give way to his real feelings, if that is what they were. The story of Abraham, a man with no guts, no backbone, and his son Isaac had absorbed him so completely that anybody seeing him for the first time would never have guessed that such a thing as PTL or Melvin Belli had ever come into his life.

I took my place in the congregation, hoping to remain unobtrusive. But I was in a half-empty pew right down front and at once caught the attention of the entire congregation. I could feel all the eyes on me, the alien knowing smiles, the questioning stares. *Are you saved stranger do you know God?* And as always there was someone to slap a hymnbook into my hand, just so I would have it handy for the next song. And sing, damn you, sing!

I just sat there, ignoring the hymnal, fidgety and angry and disgusted and for that matter a little disappointed in the sermon. I had never been able to work up much sympathy for Abraham and was sorry that Falwell had dredged up the tired old yarn of Isaac's sacrifice for his annual Father's Day sermon. Abraham, the perfect father, mankind's ultimate exemplar of faith and righteousness. But was it really so? What, in fact, could you say about that sort of faith? And how could you make him out as anything other than a bloodthirsty barbarian? Faith to move mountains. Faith to make mountains stand still. Give me Sarah's healthy skepticism any day. Laughs right in the face of the Lord when He tells her she is about to give birth again. Ninety-nine years old and then some, and you say I'm gonna have pleasure again, I'm gonna give birth to another child? Ahahhahhaaahahhaaa! No faith, no respect. But that didn't prevent the birth of Isaac, and it didn't stop the bum Abraham from going out one fine summer morning with every intention of slitting his throat. Just because he'd heard a bunch of crazy voices in his head.

Kill the boy cut his goddamn throat we don't need him anymore

So it was a little hard sometimes to figure his big reputation. Yet every ear pricks up and every nerve grows taut as Falwell builds to an eloquent climax, making the patriarch into some sort of archetypal folk hero while pointedly ignoring all of his glaring character flaws.

I got to the pulpit just in time to get the jump on BBC. One man against a network. BBC fought back gamely. The tall, goofy-looking anchorman sidled up to me and smiled condescendingly.

"I say, old man, if you wouldn't mind, we really do need to speak to him first. We are on something of a tight schedule, I'm afraid."

"Rough for everybody," I said, holding my place.

"I say, old chap, this will hardly do, will it?"

I could see there was going to be trouble. A nod from the anchorman brought the nasty little blonde rushing forward. She again introduced herself as "the producer."

"We've already met."

"Quite. I do hope you won't mind terribly if we proceed as planned."

The two technicians dragged their cameras up, aimed their lights and reflectors at the chair where Falwell would be sitting, and gently elbowed me aside, not as though they expected me to cause any trouble but simply as though they were not even bothering to recognize my just claim to preeminence. It was flat-out war again. The war of the barricades bursting out anew in the most famous pulpit in America. I turned on them with a withering blast of invective—*Goddammit I do mind terribly do you hear me goddammit!*—that could easily have got us into next day's headlines:

BLOODY FEUD ERUPTS AT THOMAS ROAD.
REPORTER MAULED.
BBC CAMERA TEAM JAILED.

Falwell came up. We shook hands. He hadn't heard any of the cursing. Or maybe he was only playing the diplomat. He sure wouldn't want any of those kind of headlines. He'd had enough of those already. He was magnanimous and friendly and still putting up a brave front in the face of Belli's threats.

"Well, the Bakkers are going to need a good lawyer," he said, rumbling with the same dark throaty laughter that had long menaced abortionists, antiprayer zealots, and ACLU radicals. "I'm surprised they haven't had one before now. But how are they going to pay him? My word, Melvin Belli won't work for $37,000."

Maybe he was right. Belli did not even last out the weekend. Either he'd found out that the Bakkers really were down to their last $37,000, with no means of raising more, or that they didn't have much of a case after all. Whichever it was, he hit the road without taking time to hold a farewell press conference or even so much as to issue a face-saving declaration. We last caught sight of him as he flung angrily off the set of a nationally televised newscast, having been thoroughly bested in a rancorous face-to-face debate with the Amazing Roy Grutman.

"This was nothing but a despicable trap!" he said as he roared out of sight. And later he said: "I had the word of the producers that this was supposed to be an interview, not a debate. I was supposed to have a chance to tell my side of the story without being rudely and gratuitously interrupted by unimportant little people out to make a name for themselves."

As summer came on, word drifted back that he was still in charge of the case. But I guess that was mostly for show. The story was that he had chosen a coterie of lawyers from places like Charlotte and Rock Hill and Columbia, where PTL bankruptcy proceedings were now under way, to look after the countless petty details that were beneath his magisterial dignity.

Maybe it was true that he still had a hand in the affair. I don't know. All I can say for sure is that we never heard from him again. Months later we read about him entertaining the Bakkers aboard his luxury yacht in San Francisco Bay, but that was about as close as he ever again came to associating himself directly with the two hustlers. When Bakker was finally brought to trial, more than a year later, Belli's brief connection with the defrocked minister had been forgotten by just about everyone.

During all this time lights burned late at the Partners House as volunteers stuffed envelopes, distributed Farewell Falwell bumper stickers, and plotted their next move to bring down the hated regime. The partners' association had supposedly collected quite a bit of money for Bakker's defense, though no one would say how much, and Paul Wood was always on hand to keep me abreast of his great work in exposing the Falwell conspiracy.

Like Nathan Bedford Forrest at Shiloh or Chickamauga, Wood was ever in the front of the battle, talking darkly of all the incriminating evidence he was soon to let loose on the world and organizing turbulent prayer rallies in which he managed to rouse his followers to the very pitch of insurrection. He never did find the missing tractors, maybe only because the other officers of the association had decided that there wasn't much percentage in asking the court to let them dig up the landfill.

I guess they figured it would look pretty silly if they were to dig up all that refuse and then discover that there were no tractors down there after all. But Wood still had the discarded phonograph records and cassette tapes and a growing dossier of highly classified material, none of which I had ever seen, to help him make his case against Falwell. His agents, it seemed, had turned up quite a bit of new dirt on the Lynchburger. They had even learned, he confided one afternoon, that Falwell might have Jewish blood.

"How would that play, do you think, if we found out Falwell was a Jew?"

"I'd say that it would make quite a headline."

"Well, we aren't quite ready to go public yet."

I was never sure how that odd little notion fit into the larger conspiracy. It was getting a little hard to keep everything straight. Sometimes the Vatican seemed to be in charge, other times the Illuminati or the Trilateral Commission. I hadn't found out exactly how the druids were supposed to fit into it either. But I guess it was all pretty incestuous when you came right down to it, with officers of one group sharing membership on all the other boards and everything getting all tangled up and crazy like the inner workings of the numbers racket or of some big international oil cartel.

I would sit there in the hot room listening to all the gloomy talk, the heavy silence of the afternoon looming ominously about me and a sound of muffled voices coming from way off in another part of the house, urgent, unremitting, like frantic voices beneath a waterfall; and Wood's own voice also seeming to come from afar as he reviewed one more time all the ins and outs of the plot: the microchip implants and the seven years of Tribulation and the coming of the Great Beast of the Apocalypse.

Falwell, he always explained, was not the Beast, only a forerunner, a stooge, a big fat nobody in the larger scheme of things, acting on instructions from other men—faceless powermongers sitting around long, varnished tables in outsized offices in a thousand unnamed cities. When he had completed his assigned task, which was to steal the PTL satellite for George Bush and Ted Turner and other such white trash, he would be unceremoniously shunted aside and very likely led away in chains.

As I say, nothing was ever very clear. But what was clear, if anything was, was that the terrible years being ushered in by Falwell were a mere prelude to the Second Coming. Soon, now, the redeemed were to be caught up in the Rapture, with the heavens splitting open and the angels singing *Gloria in Excelsis* and the rest of us fleeing before Him like locusts before a typhoon and then being left to experience the dubious mercies of the Antichrist and his walking computer. But where did the Beast come in? Wood would leave all that for another day.

Sitting listening to him as he talked about all that, I would try again to imagine what it would be like in those last hard days: the Antichrist striding about the broad boulevards of Heritage USA in all of his papal finery while the Great Whore of the Apocalypse (alias Jessica Hahn with her nose fixed) rode lustily at his side, mounted on a white stallion, whip-lashing the servile multitudes until the streets overflowed with blood, and bearing aloft a huge, garish banner that said I AM THE MOTHER OF HARLOTS AND ABOMINATIONS OF THE EARTH.

Nothing would have any meaning for them anymore. Woe to the earth and all the inhabitants thereof! Our cities would be a confused mass of smoking rubble and dry streambeds would overflow with rivers of blood and concentration camps would spring up from one end of the land to the other and every morning you would get up to find some dramatic new announcement posted on the walls of your prison. FAL-WELL ASSASSINATED! DILLINGER ALIVE!

HITLER FOUND IN SARDINIA

Ex-Nazi Chancellor Tends His Victory Garden
While Devoting Last Years to Charitable Works

"Some of my best friends are Jews," he says.

I would be sitting in the hot, dim room thinking about all that—
how difficult it would be to live in that far-off time—when Wood's voice
would suddenly bring me up short:

"No! Don't you see? It's all coming together for us in this generation,
in our own time . . ."

Yes. It was always so easy to forget that part of it on these peaceful
summer afternoons. He would inevitably have to remind me that the
fateful day was even now fast upon us. No man knoweth the day or the
hour. Yet it was not nearly so difficult to foresee the end as it had been
before the great age of microchip technology. It could come, in fact, at
almost any moment, perhaps even as early as next week.

"That's when we're having our big Fourth of July rally," he told me
one afternoon, leaning over the table with a self-congratulatory air.

He had been planning the event for weeks. It was to be the climactic
event of the summer, if not of recorded history. On that date partners by
the thousands were to descend on Heritage USA. They would come from
every state in the nation and from a dozen foreign countries to join in
a gigantic protest against the Falwell regime. The day would begin with
a march from the Partners House to a rallying point inside the Heritage
grounds and would end in, or rather could end in . . . war!

"We're prepared for it. If that's what they want, they can sure have it."

Men specially trained in the tactics of guerrilla warfare would seize all
the vital supply points and corridors of power, reducing Falwell, Nims,
Grutman, and the rest of their gang to the common lot of refugees, with
nothing left to them but mad, panicky flight and prayerful entreaties for
safe passage into some zone of neutrality. But who could remain neutral
in such a war? Where was safety? Where was escape?

"I think we've got 'em right where we want 'em now," Wood said,
grinning.

The Independence Day march did not turn out to be the opening engagement in the war of Armageddon. It did not even start out to be much of a protest march. Paul Wood had talked of attracting up to 25,000 or 50,000 or maybe even 100,000 people to the rally; he got only about 350 at the most exaggerated count—and not a trained guerrilla fighter in the bunch. Maybe it was only because a holiday was a bad time to start a war, but Wood and his tacticians did not let that stop them from making the most of it. After a round of speeches inside the gates of the theme park the mob marched on to the hotel, where they enjoyed a piece of unexpected good luck.

"There's Falwell!" someone shouted. And then the chant set up—"Farewell, Foulwell! Farewell, Foulwell!"—as the crowd went crashing through a barrier of security guards and surged into the lobby. "Cheater! Thief! Liar! Satan!" One of the demonstrators, a woman, almost got her hands on Falwell's throat, but the warthog once again proved too slippery for his detractors. The security guards came in a hurry, whisking him onto an elevator and off to safety in the upper reaches of the building. When would the protesters ever have another chance like that? Why, they could easily have choked the bastard to death right there at the scene of his triumph.

"We almost had him," said an exhausted Paul Wood. "But we'll get him yet!"

The great pity of it was that Wood himself had been unable to share in this small parcel of glory; he had been stampeded by his own people, left scrambling to his feet way back in the crowd somewhere while Falwell stood chortling down at them through the see-through elevator.

But this was no time to mourn a missed opportunity; Wood was already planning his next big rally. Target date: Labor Day.

"You'll see a crowd in here like you've never seen before. What hurt us this time, we didn't have enough time to get the word out. But it'll be different come Labor Day. And we'll have everything documented against him by then."

That wasn't to say he wouldn't have a lot of other surprises for the preacher in the meantime. One morning an impulse which he later realized had come straight from the Lord led him to the auditorium where the "PTL Club" was airing. Falwell was making one of his periodic appearances as host of the show and had chosen to spend his time talking about the tangled legal problems that had complicated PTL's struggle to free itself from debt.

One of the main questions that had emerged from the bankruptcy hearings in Columbia was whether the partners' donations had invested them with ownership rights in the ministry. Falwell's lawyers cited legal precedents to the effect that charitable contributions of this kind could not be counted as investments in the real sense. Lawyers hired by the partners cited precedents making the opposite case. The truth was that there seemed to be very little precedent to support either argument, and the court was still a long way from deciding the issue.

Falwell had left the stage in the midst of the discussion and had gone out to mingle with a mostly friendly audience when Wood leapt from his seat and charged forward, waving his Partner's Bible like a rod of judgment and shouting, "Falwell, you're a liar and a cheat! And I'm telling you right now, in the name of Jesus, to let my people go!"

Falwell quickly signaled for the music to begin, though not before some of Wood's little speech went out over the air. Having had his say, the gallant partner turned and left the auditorium before the security guards could get to him, exulting in the great rush of applause that accompanied his departure.

But was the applause for Wood or for Falwell? No one could say for sure. Most people figured it was for Falwell and his smooth handling of a bad situation. But try and tell that to Wood and the fervent apostles who had supported his desperate maneuver to instigate a rising of the PTL masses.

"They're for me!" he said moments later as he stood outside the building glorying in his triumph. "They're a hundred percent for me!"

How to build on the advantage? That was what he had to keep asking himself. Falwell would never be so foolish as to provide him with another opportunity of that kind.

"You see, he still doesn't understand that PTL is a charismatic church —not a fundamentalist church. In our church the spirit of God is the prevalent speaker. And the [will] of God overrules the preacher and moves upon a willing vessel."

That is what had happened to him in the auditorium. He had gone there only to plot strategy. Then the big wind of the spirit had come out of nowhere and he had become a willing vessel in the hands of the Lord. The same as on the day of Pentecost. And there was no turning back now.

"Did you hear that applause? I'm telling you, they're a hundred percent for me!"

Wood excitedly promised more action before the morning was out. But I didn't have time to wait for the rest of it. I had to rush off and dictate a couple of quick paragraphs to the people in Atlanta.

"He says there'll be a lot more later," I told my editor.

"This is nothing but horseshit anyway," he said ingratiatingly.

When I hung up the phone an old man who neglected to give me his name came up and angrily accosted me. He had been eavesdropping and had overheard everything. "Rude to eavesdrop," says I. He didn't bother to apologize. He explained that he was a Bakkerite who had been converted to Falwell's way of thinking and that it was people like me who were ruining everything.

I left the convert standing there babbling insanely and shaking his fist at me, blaming me for everything that had gone wrong at PTL during the last four and a half months and for conspiring to provoke Wood's outburst. Just to embarrass the ministry.

"I was there," he shouted. "Listen to me, you good-for-nothing snoop! We were applauding Falwell, not that guy. It's guys like you that're trying to tear everything down." He came along the hall, still shrieking at me, and had begun to draw a crowd. "We know your kind! By God, we're gonna see that you don't get away with it this time . . ."

I raced back to the auditorium and got there just as Vestal Goodman, the onetime PTL singing star with the operatic build, and a coterie of angry hangers-on were joining the protest against Falwell. They had tried to force their way into the auditorium by way of the Hall of Faith and were thrown back by the ushers, and now Mrs. Goodman stood screaming and crying in the wide foyer, talking again about how Bakker was "lovely and sinless and beautiful and clean as a pebble from a mountain brook" and how the old warthog Falwell had stolen their ministry and thrown them out like old dogs to wither and starve in a godless, cold world. Why, she wanted to know, do the wicked prosper?

"But they were applauding me," Wood kept trying to explain. He was afraid that she didn't understand clearly the great success the faith partners had enjoyed that morning or that he was the author of it. Maybe he did not always feel that he was getting all the support and acclaim he deserved. Maybe he would have liked for the others to understand that he had been singled out to lead the fight against the usurpers of Bakker's regime. But he never complained and never ceased believing that every momentary setback—and it had been a long time since he'd had anything he could legitimately call a victory—was simply new evidence that the unsettling prophecies of Revelation were rapidly coming to pass. "All those people in there. Did you hear them? All that applause? I tell you, they're all for us now. The people who've been trying to steal this ministry from us, they're finished now for sure!"

Before the day was out the Falwell regime had sworn out a warrant for Wood and banned him from the grounds. But he was right back the next day, holding a prayer rally in the lobby of the Heritage Grand. The security guards flashed the warrant and swooped down on him.

"Wish you could've seen them drag me outa that lobby. Like I was nothing but a big sack of potatoes. Wrenched my neck too. Pretty bad. I think I've got pretty good grounds for a lawsuit."

But that was all right too. One more strong hint that the "spirit of the Lord" had again intervened in his behalf. He had happily posted his $2,000 bond and later took me aside to explain how Falwell had finally overplayed his hand—how the partners now had the means, thanks to the bullying tactics of the PTL door guards, for dragging Falwell into court and forcing him to answer for his "lies."

"Can't believe he'd risk perjuring himself once we get him on that witness stand and start firing all those questions at him. Yep. It's gonna be mighty hard for him to get out of this one."

. . . .

Before Wood could bring Falwell to justice he found himself in the dock, charged with assault and battery by a woman he later identified as a "Falwell plant."

I had seen her one afternoon at the Partners House. She had come up to me without an introduction, thinking I was someone she had met at church.

"You are Baptist, aren't you?"

"I left the church at an early age."

"Where could I have seen you, then?"

"TV perhaps?"

"Do you have your own show?"

"I only make guest appearances."

She was blonde and freshly tanned and tall and quite slender, no more than thirty-five or thirty-six, wearing a loose-fitting beige halter and matching shorts. Not bad. But there was no time to think about that. She led me off into a side room heavy with the stink of day-old garbage and spoke in a conspiratorial whisper, explaining that she had spent a lot of time at PTL and had talked to the people there and found that they were "all for Falwell."

"You see, that's why they attacked me. I was the only one who would speak up for Falwell."

"Attacked? Where?"

"Here. They were having a prayer service outside and one of their people attacked me. A big, graying, fleshy sort of fellow. I've sworn out a warrant."

For some reason I didn't recognize Paul Wood in her description even though it fit him exactly. He had come into the room once while we were there. She shot a quick, furtive look at him, and he at her. Neither spoke. Later, when he drew me off to explain that the woman had come there on orders from Falwell and the Illuminati, I still didn't suspect him as her supposed assailant. Even after he told me one afternoon that he was being tried next day on an assault charge—"Things are kinda compounding themselves, aren't they?"—I still didn't realize until I got to the courtroom that his accuser was the same woman who had approached me at the Partners House.

This time she was curt, even a bit hostile, looking at me suspiciously and pretending to remember nothing of our previous conversation. On the witness stand she seemed rattled and incoherent. Her story was that Wood had slapped her around pretty good in the name of the Father, the Son, and the Holy Ghost. Because of the unclean spirits.

Unclean spirits?

Yes, unclean spirits. Demons. That was it, of course. Why else would he have beaten her up? It could only have been a case of demonic possession. Otherwise she wouldn't have been talking so crazy and taking up for Falwell as though he were a man of sense and integrity. Or pretending she had remembered me from church. And Wood naturally would have felt compelled to play the exorcist. It all made perfectly good sense in a way, even if he wouldn't own up to it on the stand. Kick hell out of her. That was the only way to handle demons: rough.

The court did not find in favor of demonic possession, but it did find in favor of Paul Wood, leaving him free to resume his war with the Falwell gang.

"We've got him behind the eight ball now for sure. He can lie and go to jail for perjury or tell the truth and still go to jail. We've got him right where we want him now."

.   .   .

The *Journal-Constitution* was no help. It never did get around to printing the truth about the microchips or the druids or the Illuminati or the Great Beast of the Apocalypse. Not that I should have expected anything else. I had learned a long time ago that the best stories never got into the paper. Like the night I had been held captive in the Heritage Grand, not by the PTL people but by my own editors, who had suddenly decided that I had been having too much of a good time and spending way too much money at those big hotels in Charlotte.

"What is it with you and these expense accounts?" my editor wanted to know. "Eleven thousand dollars in one month. One goddamn month. How'd you manage it? PTL must be really driving up the market for women and liquor."

I explained that there had to be some kind of mix-up. Me spend that kind of money? "C'mon, Brice. You know me."

"Eleven thousand dollars and some cents. Every last dime right here on your company credit card."

"We were flying around a lot. It adds up. But I still say there's gotta be a mix-up somewhere."

"One meal after the other: $125, $150."

Naturally I tried to blame everything on Kathy, who had come up there with only $100 in cash and had been ordered by her own editor to put everything on my account.

But there it was. An incredible sum. Never to this day properly accounted for. It was about that time that my editor decided I was to move out of the Charlotte motels and into the iniquitous Heritage Grand, where you could get bargain rates now that the specter of bankruptcy was hanging over the place.

I stayed one night, the only drunk man in the entire place, from all I had been led to believe. I'd had to sneak the liquor in and lock the door. I'd been there only once before: on an April afternoon when in an hour of desperation I'd had to rent a room just to get my story written in time for deadline. The place was everything I remembered: gaudy, tacky, full of phony gilt-edged furniture. On a table by the bed lay a card that said Matthew 7:12. Nothing else. Just the verse from the Bible. I reminded myself to look it up later and then forgot all about it.

Somehow, after a couple of drinks, I fell under the illusion that the whole place had been built out of cardboard. I must have been right. I had hardly lain down after drinking more than was good for me and then taking tranquilizers to ward off the certain hangover when I felt the bed go down with a crash. I lay there for a long time without believing I had really fallen and then lay there a lot longer not only believing it but also, and more importantly, that demonic influences called forth long ago by Bakker and his crowd were almost certainly responsible. How many times in how many lands would I tell the story without finding anyone who wouldn't call me a liar?

I lay there all night amid the wreckage, waking early with a headache and a siege of heart palpitations. More Xanax. I slept again and didn't wake until almost noon, and maybe wouldn't have waked up then except for the pounding at the door. Some guy out there swearing up and down that I had broken the Golden Rule or something, and I knew it was true and only wondered how he had tracked me down and what was to be the penalty. Where was Falwell? Maybe he would speak for me.

I just lay there in the wreckage, thinking maybe the guy would go away after a moment. Instead I heard a key in the latch. I struggled to climb out of the broken railings just as a young man wearing a blue suit with gold tassels tore into the room and threatened to summon the security guards. He looked like the little guy in all the old Philip Morris ads.

"The goddamn bed fell down," I explained.

"Our beds don't fall down without a reason."

"Listen to me, ace. I'm telling you that this bed fell down and that it fell down with no reason at all. Wait'll this hits the papers. And people see what they're getting for their donations."

"You've been drinking, haven't you, mister? Don't you know that no drinking is allowed in this hotel?"

"Not a drop." I had forgotten that the empty bottle of George Dickel was sitting on the telephone table just above me.

"Checkout time was ten. Didn't you know that? We like to think that all our customers will adhere to minimum standards of decency. That's why we leave the card. Just as a gentle reminder. We don't like to be pushy or overbearing."

"I can see that. But what're you supposed to do when the furniture is all falling apart—when the whole place is falling apart?"

"You must have had some kind of fight in here last night, mister. Or maybe the D.T.'s. We've been warned about people like you, but most people obey the rules and don't tear up things. Usually it's enough simply to leave the card."

I finally realized what card he was talking about. The one on which I had left the empty bottle of whisky. I picked it up and remembered it from the night before. Matthew 7:12.

"I'm afraid I don't know the verse."

"That's why we make sure there is a Partners Bible in every room—for those few who do not know."

"I don't get it." I groggily thumbed through my Partners Bible until I found the verse: "Therefore all things whatsoever ye would that men should do to you, do ye even so to them: for this is the law and the prophets."

I looked at him, wondering if he were under the domination of unclean spirits and already beyond redemption, his brain eaten away by an insidious and irreversible rot.

"The Golden Rule. I don't get it."

"Yes. The Golden Rule. It's just a nice way of reminding people to observe the proper checkout hour, to let them know that other people may be waiting to move in. You see, our maids need to get in and clean up so that the next guests will be able to get into their room at the proper hour. It looks as though you have left us with a special problem."

"The bed is nothing. I can tell you right now that this is only a prelude

to what you can expect: this whole tawdry mess is going to crash right
to the ground one day, because anybody can see that it isn't anything but
painted cardboard and is being held up by nothing more than thought
waves and invisible laser beams left over from the great days before the
continent of Atlantis sank beneath the sea. But you won't forever escape
the inevitable, and you can see it coming now, the great fall, as prophe-

sied of old, and you can damn well be sure that an awful lot of people
are going to be hurt by a lot more than falling beds. You'll wish to God

you had listened to me then."

"I think you're still drunk, mister. And I'm telling you for the last time

that our beds don't fall down without a reason."

.   .   .

I wrote it all up for next day's edition. Naturally the paper didn't print a
word. "It's written in somewhat overly dramatic fashion," my editor said.

"I should have known better than to put the drama in it."

"You will have it for your memoirs."

Well, maybe it didn't matter anymore what the *Journal-Constitution*
decided to print or decided not to print. Most of the real fighting was
over now. Where thrones and kingdoms once seemed to hang in the balance, everything had now reduced itself to a nasty little squabble over
legal technicalities in the musty confines of a Columbia courtroom.

But on the surface, at least, life at the theme park was still good.
Falwell had got the better of his critics for at least a day by taking a
memorable plunge—fully clothed—down the Heritage Park water slide.
He stood at the top for a moment muttering either the Lord's Prayer or
the Twenty-third Psalm, depending on whether you wanted to believe
Time or *Newsweek*. Then down he came, a distance of 163 feet (*Time*)
or maybe only 60 feet (*Newsweek*). It was his way of thanking the Lord
and PTL faith partners who had abandoned Bakker for agreeing to con-
tribute $1,000 apiece to the failed PTL ministry by Labor Day. A $22
million August "miracle."

"I'd do it all over again for another $22 million," Falwell said. Was it
really $22 million or only $20 million, as *Time* insisted? Or the far less
significant sum of only $1 million, as reported by *Newsweek*?

Nobody except Falwell ever seemed quite sure. Anyway, there hadn't
been many miracles since then. And one afternoon not long after that—
we were well into September now—I went back to Main Street USA

for what I was sure would be the last time. Gold-toothed Christians still swarmed the water park and crowded the lobby of the Heritage Grand, where the full, lush sunlight of late summer streamed through the atrium down across the high dais where a tuxedoed pianist sat playing "Believe me if all those endearing young charms." Yes, life in that little part of the world was still the good thing it had always been. Parties and group sings and prayer sessions and hallelujahs and a belief everywhere that the good times could never end. Like the nightly revels in ancient Rome as Alaric and his Gothic hordes sat encamped beneath the city walls.

In the cobbled mall shoppers still scurried about, looking for bargains and iniquitous relationships. Business had never been better. "But it still isn't the same," said Millie Freeman, manager of Tammy Faye's Cosmetics Shop. I couldn't understand why. The shop was still getting $9 for a bottle of Tammy Faye face masque and $4 for a pair of Tammy Faye panty hose—and the place was constantly crowded with buyers who figured most of the items were a bargain at almost any price.

"It just isn't the same at all," Ms. Freeman sniffed.

"Why?"

"Don't you know?"

"Not exactly," I said, lying.

"Because Jim and Tammy aren't here!"

The only other difference I could see was that all the Tammy Faye designer dolls—labeled "Forgiven" and selling for $850 apiece earlier that summer—were gone now and no one was planning to stock them anymore. But the JB Wiener Wagon and Der Bakker's Bakkery were still there. And the Heavenly Fudge Shoppe. The next thing to sin. I suddenly realized that after all the times I had visited the mall I had never yet tasted a piece of Bakker's decadent fudge.

I went in and looked nervously around. It was like visiting a brothel for the first time. A matronly woman in a white apron came toward me, her whole being invading me with her eyes, smiling her lascivious smile as she uncovered first the plain fudge and then the fudge with almonds and then the fudge with pecans and then the fudge packed full of squishy cream and then the butterscotch, plain and nut-laden. Wide is the gate and broad is the way that leadeth to destruction.

I took the fudge with almonds and went out. It was strange eating the candy and knowing that it was probably the last time I would ever see the place. The fudge was good while it lasted. But it left me feeling truly remorseful; I felt that I had been guilty of some sort of betrayal. I could only hope that it would work itself out. Maybe it would be OK after a couple of days. Nobody would have to know the truth.

At the Partners House Paul Wood was still building his case against Falwell, undeterred by the plain fact that his activities had begun to embarrass his fellow insurgents. Partners president Joe Strickland took the position that Armageddon was not at hand and that the Illuminati, whoever they were, had not conspired with Falwell and Jessica Hahn to bring down PTL. It was hard on Strickland having to explain all that to his old friend.

"Paul's sort of gone off on a tangent," he told me one afternoon. "We've had to ask him not to speak for the association anymore."

Might as well ask Bakker to stop proclaiming his innocence. Wood went right on speaking his mind anyway, more confident than ever that his great work in bringing down Falwell was ripe unto harvest. The documentation he had promised was all neatly packaged and would be "ready for the papers" almost any day now. And then he would see Falwell in court.

"He thinks he's got trouble now. Wait till he sees the rest of this stuff we've got on him." He followed me outside, grinning broadly and expounding on all the new developments that were about to make his conspiracy theories a reality. "I can tell you right now that Falwell is finished for sure this time."

"You sure you aren't ready to go public? Just about everybody has heard the story by now anyway."

"Not quite yet. But it won't be long. That old boy will be mighty lucky to get out of this thing with no more than two or three counts of perjury hanging over him. Yessir, I'd sure like to hear him try and talk himself outa this one."

Part Three

POWER IN
THE BLOOD

17

My keeper has given it out that I am none too well. Naturally I have not told him everything. He comes twice a day now, an old man in a white coat, with a handlebar mustache curling down absurdly around his mouth. He speaks with a heavy Viennese accent and tells me that in his youth he studied with the great Carl Jung. He has dealt with many strange and difficult cases, but my explanation of the Jim Bakker phenomenon, he says, is something unique in his experience—altogether *de trop.*

Even the little I have told him of the scandal—of Bakker and his improbable wife—he dismisses with a condescending shrug. "Mere grotesquerie," he says, though he confesses that he finds much amusement in my bizarre sense of humor.

I explain again that it is no delusion and that I am prepared to document everything with newspaper clippings.

"*Nein, nein,*" he says, not impolitely. "If such a pair had existed, surely I would have heard. *Jawohl!*"

"Ah, but it is true. Every word."

"Hahahaha."

At last he stifles his laughter, not being much given to it anyway, in an effort to seem more caring and professional. He sniffs the dead air and explains in an almost confidential tone that I am a mere "persona" no longer willing to face the dreadful commonplaces of everyday life. He argues convincingly that I have dredged up this whole nasty business of the PTL scandal from the dark, crowded wastelands of the id and have seized upon my delusion—for surely it is only that and nothing more—as a kind of mechanism to compensate for my feelings of panic and angst and insufficiency. He leans forward again, peering at me strangely, and I am suddenly beset by the odd sensation that he is himself the Great Beast of the Apocalypse, preparing to implant a microchip in my forehead.

"Wait, goddammit! No!"

"You must rest," he says with maddening calm. "Try to understand that your delusions are mere archetypes of the unconscious. If you persist in this manner you will persuade even those who care for you that you are, shall we say, insufficient to bear up under the stresses of everyday life."

I reply with some heat that I am in no way insufficient and that PTL is far from being a mere archetype or compensatory mechanism. Where has he been, anyway? Don't the Viennese read the papers? In the face of such skepticism and bland mockery it is hardly surprising that I have turned ever more heavily to drink and meditation. I sit now in a spacious, heavily carpeted room with a picture window that runs the entire length of the east wall and looks out past a long row of beach cottages toward the Atlantic. The ocean is calm now, and the Virginia resort town, emptied of its summer guests, lies indolently under a warm October sun. Here at last I am alone and can feel free and have found a security I have seldom found in any other part of the world. Nothing can reach me now, not the druids or death or Hell or even the Trilateral Commission.

It is here, at the meditation center, with the sun coming off the water, that the doctor comes to talk of my inadequacy. He studies me closely with his monocle and then with sudden élan rares back and laughs the good hearty laugh of a Viennese who has just downed his third glass of $500 *Trockenbeerenauslese*. Even so, as I say, it is apparent that he is not a man much given to laughter.

At first I half welcomed his visits. But gradually I came to realize that he is like all the others who had doubted that I was once a "great American journalist"—Falwell's own words!—or that I was far and away the most logical candidate to succeed Bakker as permanent host of the "PTL Club." Falwell himself had it in his power to appoint me. Why he failed to do so remains a mystery and is possibly the most scandalous and perverse aspect of the whole PTL controversy. Quite inconceivable, no matter how you care to look at it. Had we not hit it off well right from the beginning? Did I not take up for him at the *Hustler* trial, and have I not long refused to expose him as a mere front for the Illuminati even though Paul Wood has repeatedly offered to provide me with all the documentation I would need to support my case?

I keep thinking of what Bakker had at the height of his power: the gold-plated bathroom fixtures, the vibrating chairs and massage rooms, steam baths smelling of rose water and all the spices of the Orient, seductively decorous saunas and jacuzzis, great banqueting tables laden with the finest smoked meats and imported wines, direct and immediate access to all of the world's most famous Spanish fly markets, women to suit his every whim, curly-haired masseurs when no woman would quite do. He had merely to lift his hand and in would come whores from all the slums of Charlotte, female mud wrestlers still dripping with the residue of their profession, veiled houris from the most exotic of Middle Eastern bazaars.

And it could all have been mine except, of course, for the masseurs, if Falwell hadn't overlooked the obvious. He had experimented with one candidate after another all summer long while passing up an opportunity to hire the one man capable of rescuing PTL from financial disaster and bringing back its great days of lust and depravity. What did it matter if I was past fifty? Jimmy Swaggart was just as old when he went sniffing after prospects in the New Orleans whorehouse district. Age is no barrier to a good, rich life of sin and greed. I could have had the best of everything—diamond bracelets dangling from every appendage, liveried servants at my disposal twenty-four hours a day, bands of reporters clamoring for interviews, an obsequious retinue of publicists, ass kissers, and clinging women . . .

How could Falwell have been so perverse as to deny me my big chance?

I say nothing of this to my keeper. He has grown quite suspicious of late. Every time I speak he seems only that much more confirmed in his belief that I am a mere persona, an undifferentiated self that has fallen victim to a powerful surge of dark and phantasmagoric archetypes from the deepest recesses of the id. He looks at me again, acknowledging with a certain awkward show of indulgence that I have indeed had "some difficult times" and that therefore I must follow his directions implicitly.

I call for madder music and for stronger wine. The apple tree, the singing, and the gold. But he only looks at me with that infuriating and unwavering Teutonic gaze. Presently he extracts from his pocket a Valium tablet that burgeons suddenly into a grotesquely bloated cantaloupe with nipples. The immemorial mammalian archetype. I realize with a mounting sense of panic that I am about to be swallowed by the pill rather than the other way around.

No damn you No!

. . .

Dark comes in fast over an angry sea. I am fully awake now and seem to have been so for some little time. The next day the sea is still restless, the cold sunlight shining with an almost eerie brilliance into every corner of the meditation room. Sometimes, sitting here, I find myself longing for almost anyone—Jungian, preacher, or long-haired Beatnik off the street—who would hear my tale with sympathy and understanding. Yet no one other than the occasional tour group ever comes, smiling benignly and indulgently and perhaps with some slight show of concern as it passes quietly in front of the window and back out into the hall.

It is still storming as my wife and I pack to leave. If the keeper I had envisioned for myself—how authentic it all seemed at the time!—had been there, I'm sure he would have been almost too anxious to sign the release papers. In the end, no doubt, I would have found him less than sympathetic. "Perhaps I need a little more time to regain my strength," I might have explained, whereupon he would have turned on me with an unaccustomed show of impatience, scowling from behind his absurd mustache and insipid monocle.

"Nicht verstehe!"

I would explain again that the great day of Tribulation was at hand and that even now the forces of good and evil were mustering for the battle that would settle for all time the destiny of mankind. Smile pretty and say Jesus! And kiss again the ass of the Antichrist!

"Verschwinde, dummkopf! Verschwinde!"

On the long trip back to Carolina I can feel the fury of the mighty Atlantic building again inside me, flooding up out of the forlorn and murky country of the id, sneaking past the ever-watchful Guardian of the Threshold and alerting me to the turbulence that forever lies waiting around the next curve, beyond the next patch of woods, at my very door. I am in no way surprised to hear the phone ringing insistently as I walk into the house or to see the light on my recorder blinking with a plethora of unanswered messages.

I grab the phone with another sudden rise of panic. Even before I can get the receiver to my ear I hear the familiar snarling voice:

"Falwell has quit, goddammit! We need an exclusive!"

Time, like an ever-rolling stream, bears all her sons away. October again and you are back in Lynchburg for your last interview with Jerry Falwell, being dragged wantonly about the once-familiar streets and made to howl like Gogol's mad king of Spain as you prepare for one final desperate assault on the impregnable bastions of the "Old Time Gospel Hour."

Sorry fella ain't nobody comes in here without he's wearing a badge

You are thrown out of the place just like old times and told to come back at a more propitious hour. Time on your hands. Walk the streets again. Pray for deliverance. Your way lies down through the town and out along the steep bluff of the river and across the viaduct and on up for a short distance into Amherst County and then back again, the clear river sparkling in the afternoon sun, the hills above you blazing away with the glorious implacable fires of late October.

You hoped all would go routinely for once. You are tired of it all now. Everybody is tired of it.

Sorry fella sorry

And so back into town again, the strains of the old gospel hymn drumming away inside your head, a haunting and unrelenting refrain. *Time, like an ever-rolling stream . . .* You walk back along Main Street and then up Church past the stone building that had once housed the town's two dailies and finally up to Court Street by way of Monument Terrace, a lavishly decorated stone-and-marble stairway built in the high style of the Italian Renaissance.

Sorry not this time buster but smile goddamn you smile

Now you are high above the town and the river. The street more familiar than any of the others, for it had been your home briefly in those shabby last days before the once-elegant townhouses started coming down. It was already far gone in decay by then, but it had been the Rivermont Avenue of its day. Home of the Quality. And in your own day some of the old mood of that time still hung over the street, as though trapped irrevocably in the stone itself or in the lavish, decorous smell of the fading roses in the garden below your window.

Now, with the October day fast going, the mood comes again, old mad echoes snatched from the forgotten air: a sound of horsedrawn carriages rumbling up the dirt streets for the big weekend levees of antebellum times, light-hearted girls in hoopskirts bantering merrily as they reconnoiter in richly paneled rooms hung with damask tapestries and crystal chandeliers, their planter husbands sampling sweetmeats from tables set for dinner or strutting in white-suited splendor about the wrought-iron balconies and plotting the final overthrow of Yankeedom, oblivious to and maybe even a little impatient of those other voices that drift up from the rose gardens and courtyards:

> Old James River is deep and wide,
> Gonna find freedom on the other side . . .

. . .

Jerry Falwell, menace to some, messiah to others, sat late in his office on that October evening, talking again of his six-month plunge into the miasma of PTL. He had resigned as a protest against the bankruptcy court's summary rejection of his plan for rescuing the ministry from insolvency. Now he was home again, cheerfully slogging his way through sixteen- and eighteen-hour days. I had caught him at the end of such a day. He looked older now and more exhausted, greatly changed from what he had been in those first weeks after he'd thrown out the lifeline to PTL, yet plainly relieved to have the whole sordid ordeal behind him, even if his worst expectations had now been realized.

Was he ready to admit that he had made a terrible mistake? His "no" did not sound altogether convincing. Then, aroused, he leaned forward and talked more earnestly about the "positive benefits" that had flowed from the debacle. New friendships. Shared experiences in the faith. A rapprochement of sorts with Pentecostals whose precepts of divine healing he did not share. And best of all, however badly things had turned out, the knowledge that he had been part of "God's housecleaning." He paused only a moment before reminding me that even now the crooked way would be made straight and the dark way plain.

He had been the first to call PTL "our Watergate" and to predict that it would mean jail for a lot of people besides Bakker.

"Yet I think you know, as I have said from the start, that that is not what I wanted to see come out of this. It is not what I want now. I wish there were some other way."

The news of Falwell's resignation had fallen abruptly on an unsuspecting world. For weeks PTL had been off the front pages. The fitful clamors of the summer had given over into the orderly and boring business of a Chapter 11 financial reorganization proceeding. All that was left now was a mere haggling over detail—and who was to say when it might end? It could go on for months, perhaps for years: an arcane ritual over which a gaggle of attorneys, executors, and auditors would preside like augurs over the entrails of a goat, uttering mystical incantations and waving wands stuffed with incense.

Back in March almost no one had doubted that Falwell would emerge from the PTL adventure stronger than ever. But recent headlines had told a different story:

FALWELL, PTL LEADERS WALK OUT

Now, on what was left of this fine October afternoon, it was Falwell's turn to talk of conspiracy. Such had been the common theme of the summer: Falwell's satanic plot to "steal" the PTL satellite dish. But now, for the first time, we had what seemed like a sure-enough conspiracy on our hands, and it was all directed at Falwell and his people, not at Jim Bakker. The plot, if that indeed is what it was, had been mounted by principal PTL creditor Roe Messner, the Kansas contractor and stiffly correct Pentecostal who had built most of Heritage USA on what had been called a "handshake agreement." Messner's grievance: no money for all that work he had done out at the theme park. Could he trust Falwell to pay off? Could he trust the court to honor his $14 million claim when he didn't have the first piece of tangible legal evidence to back it up?

A tough question and maybe much too important to be left to the ordinary processes of justice. Maybe it was then that somebody first began to suspect a plot. Messner was saying nothing publicly. But we began to hear quite a lot out of suspected coconspirator Billy Robinson, a Columbia, South Carolina, attorney newly appointed as PTL examiner, a role theoretically demanding the highest degree of disinterestedness.

But maybe not in Robinson's case. Belli's good-old-boy surrogates had worked furtively and with good effect to get their man designated as examiner. "The appointment of Mr. Robinson was perhaps the most important strategic move made by the Bakkers' legal team," said the *National Law Journal* in an article which the Falwell people believed offered firm support for their position. "Mr. [Ryan] Hovis, acting as the Bakkers' lead counsel, boxed the PTL attorneys in a corner by suggesting Mr. Robinson as the examiner; he knew that Judge Reynolds held Mr. Robinson in especially high regard and was unlikely to turn him down."

Robinson never for a moment pretended to be impartial. Instead, he began making all sorts of unfounded statements attacking Falwell's plan as a ruse to deny the creditors everything that was coming to them. The idea, said Falwell, was to discredit the plan so thoroughly that the court would be forced to demand an alternative. Which was exactly how it had fallen out.

Maybe the old judge presiding at the bankruptcy hearings had been a part of the conspiracy; maybe he hadn't. Falwell would talk of him only as a good man who had been "hoodwinked" by Messner and a conniving band of South Carolina lawyers hired earlier that year as stand-ins for the great Melvin Belli, whose hasty and unexplained disappearance from Tega Cay after being briefly exposed to the Bakkers had become a standing joke among PTL watchers.

At first everything had been going exactly as Falwell had planned it. Even the court appeared to be on his side. Then everything had suddenly fallen apart. No one could say how or when it happened. But by the end of the summer his attorneys had sensed a change. They had grown wary of the old judge and began to move into his presence like soldiers entering a minefield. They worked all summer and into the fall on a complicated reorganization plan that was due by October 1. They barely met the deadline—and to what purpose? Less than a week later the judge pronounced it dead, pompously echoing Billy Robinson's complaint that the financial interests of PTL's unsecured creditors and its 120,000 lifetime partners had not been properly taken into account.

Since I was not in Fort Mill on that last day I did not have to sit there and watch the great Falwell all choked and broken, brought low not by the people who had marched and clamored against him all summer but—if what he said was true—by far more subtle foes.

"A tragedy," he said as he summoned his last PTL press conference and talked movingly of the judge's surprising turnabout. "An open invitation for Jim Bakker to come back and take over this ministry." Could it happen? "Indeed," he said. "It can and probably will. Barring a miracle of God, Mr. Bakker, probably within the next six months, will be sitting here running this ministry."

He was wrong about that; the little preacher would go to jail instead. But he was not wrong about the conspiracy. A disgruntled faith partner's taped conversation with Messner had provided all the evidence Falwell and his attorneys would ever need to prove that there had been a plot afoot. Yet for some mysterious reason the court refused to accept the tape as a valid legal document, evidence in itself that something was strangely amiss. Robinson, meantime, was refusing to meet with reporters or even to take their phone calls. Was he unsure of his own research, unsure of Bakker? Had he looked too closely at the financial transactions that had brought the preacher down? We never knew for sure. Because Robinson wasn't talking.

The faith partners felt that they were getting an equally rotten deal from the Messner-Hovis-Robinson cartel and would soon file suit against the whole crowd, even though many of them were by no means ready to give up their deeply held conviction that if there was a conspiracy afoot, it was all Falwell's doing. For months he had been saying he wanted neither profit nor glory from the ministry. But how could one be sure? There was a lot of the circus entrepreneur in Falwell, a lot of what he had most admired in his father. "The P. T. Barnum of Lynchburg," Falwell had once called him. Was it true, then? Had he, in fact, undertaken the PTL rescue mission as a kind of high-stakes shell game? And was he walking out only because he had been unable to pull it off?

Even the people who had come to admire Falwell, after hating him all these years for his politics and theology—that is, the reporters themselves—were never quite sure of his intentions. Maybe the old judge felt the same way. When Falwell's negotiators had gone to see him for the last time, he had spoken plainly. The way Falwell would remember it was this: "He told our people, 'Don't worry about Falwell. He's not going anywhere.' I guess he thought we were bluffing."

He and his board walked out the same day. "It hurts," he said. "It is painful. I'm not a quitter. But I leave here today never to return."

The hardline Bakkerites still refused to believe he had given up his fight to steal the ministry. This was just one more devious turn in a plan that had been many years in the making. Others—a very few—had come to face the truth: that Bakker was nothing less than the double-dealing egomaniac described by Falwell as "perhaps the greatest scab and cancer on Christianity in 2,000 years of church history."

· · ·

Two weeks after Falwell's resignation a faith partner named Deborah Watkins, owner of the incriminating tape that implicated Messner in all sorts of embarrassing illegalities, filed a $190 million damage suit against the ministry, charging the Kansas contractor and his cohorts, Robinson included, with a conspiracy to restore Bakker as PTL chairman.

She and her own building-contractor husband had put more than $5,000 into PTL, and for a long time she had defended Bakker as an innocent who had fallen prey to the machinations of the Lynchburg ministry. By early August she had broken with her hero, even though she was a long way from conceding that Falwell, Nims, Grutman, and company represented much of an improvement. One afternoon toward the end of the month, having read up on the law, the thirty-eight-year-old brunette charged into bankruptcy court and attempted to get herself installed as trustee for the failed ministry.

"Who's your attorney?" the judge wanted to know.

"God is my attorney."

The judge threw her out. "God does not like what happened in that courtroom today," she later told a crowd of reporters. What we didn't know was that the evidence against Messner and his confederates was already in Deborah's hands. We wouldn't find out anything about that until much later, after she'd decided to release to a select few the cassette tape on which the builder had confessed that examiner Robinson was working underhandedly to destroy Falwell. She had made the recording one night when Messner rang her to explore the ever-weighty question of Bakker's prospective return to PTL. How would he be received? How much money would he and Tammy be able to raise?

"The sky's the limit," Deborah told him, still believing it at the time. "But it's going to be useless if we don't get rid of this Falwell bunch first."

"That's true," Messner said. "That's very true. We've got to get rid of this bunch first."

The Lynchburger would have to go, and, the way she saw it, so would Robinson, a mere "dingdong" who'd posed as an ally of the partners and then turned around and "sold out to Falwell entirely."

Not at all, Messner explained. The truth was that Robinson had been "working behind the scenes" to get Falwell thrown out.

"We've been having private meetings," he said. "We've had four of them over the last thirty days, one each Wednesday, and [Robinson] is not for Falwell . . . and . . . just believe me, he's working behind the scenes for us."

"It's like a Howard Hughes thing," Deborah told him. "If he's for us, why can't he say he's for us?"

Now that she had the tape, a hot property to be sure, she hardly knew what to do with it. Turn it over to Falwell? Out of the question. The Lord, however, had other ideas. "Give the tape to Falwell," He told her. *And do it now.* The way she explained it at her lakefront home in Conyers, Georgia, one bright autumn morning was that God had chosen her—much as he had chosen the prophetess Deborah of the Old Testament—to rip the scales from the eyes of the people "who are blinded as I once was."

It didn't work out exactly as she had planned. Bakkerites like Paul Wood, now an affable Atlanta car salesman, would simply add her to the vast throng of demonic beings whose sole mission in life was to steal the PTL satellite and put George Bush into the White House and bring the Illuminati into power throughout the whole length and breadth of the world. Nor did it appear that the tape was likely to put anyone in jail. When Falwell's attorneys tried to get it introduced into evidence, the old judge balked.

He did not say why. A later inquiry elicited the unenlightening observation from Court Clerk George Cauthen that the judge was under no obligation to explain anything to anybody unless someone chose "to make an issue of it."

· · ·

Nobody ever did. Maybe because it just wasn't worth it anymore.

"We didn't mind fighting Bakker, Messner, Melvin Belli, the lunatic fringe, the dissident partners, the thieves, thugs, and perverts," Falwell said as I sat talking with him on that last evening in his office. "But we didn't want to fight the court. We didn't have time for that."

All he wanted now was to put the whole nasty business behind him, to leave the grounds of Heritage USA "never to return." While Bakker was still waiting in vain for the phone call that would put him back in charge of the ministry, Falwell was flying home to Lynchburg.

"Home at last and home to stay," he told a welcoming crowd of parishioners that afternoon at the airport. "If Billy Graham, Pat Robertson, and Pope John Paul II all get in trouble on the same day, they need not call Lynchburg."

For Falwell it was the rarest of homecomings. In all his years of flying about the country and flailing away at the godless deities of "secular humanism," it was the first time he had come home to find a crowd awaiting: students and faculty members from Liberty University as well as a scattering of the faithful from Thomas Road Baptist Church, some waving signs that said Welcome Home, Jerry; or We're with You All the Way.

He'd never before had to come home like that, humbled by defeat, having to look deep inside himself to ask where things had gone wrong. Maybe he had trusted too much in his own infallibility. Maybe in some subtle way he had fallen victim to pride and had felt himself destined to win every battle as long as he went into it reverentially, with a prayer on his lips, a Bible in his pocket, and a Jesus First pin in his lapel.

"Yes, it is true," he kept saying. "If I'd known the extent of the depravity down there I almost certainly would not have gotten involved." He would have more reason than ever now to brood upon the nature of sin and its often-unforeseen consequences. At Wednesday night prayer meeting, on his first week back in town, he would find edifying parallels between David's transgression with Bathsheba and Bakker's liaison with Jessica Hahn.

"It's never well to take sin lightly, is it? I keep thinking of Mr. Bakker wanting to get back on TV, get back into the ministry, take over PTL. It's just the reverse of what David did, isn't it? We remember how Nathan the prophet came to David and spoke to him of Uriah and Bathsheba in the parable of the ewe lamb stolen by the rich man who had immense flocks of his own. We remember that David's anger was greatly kindled against the man. 'As the Lord liveth,' he said, 'the man that hath done this shall surely die.' And Nathan said to him, 'Thou art the man.' And what did David do? Did he whine and offer excuses and complain that he had been betrayed by others into committing that great sin? No. David got down on his face before God in sackcloth and ashes. David got down on his knees before his Maker, and the mourning of that great man still echoes to us down through the centuries: 'Against thee have I sinned, O God! Against thee only! . . .'"

19

Home at last, home to stay. Maybe nobody really believed him at the time. Yet on that last day in Lynchburg I felt that I had seen something in Falwell I had not seen before. Despite all his years in the headlines, his reputation as the conscience of Reagan conservatism, and the foreign excursions that had won him the kind of attention ordinarily reserved for high-ranking diplomats, he still liked to think of himself as the self-less parson of a down-home congregation in a little Virginia town that had become famous only because he'd made it a byword for biblical fundamentalism.

It would not be many months before he would disband Moral Majority, Incorporated. And we heard scarcely a word from him when all the bad headlines started coming out about Jimmy Swaggart. Home to stay, to belong, to remain what in some ways he had always been: the man who had spent the early years of his ministry knocking at doors where signs of welcome were hard to find, being bitten by dogs, poked by shotguns, howled down by ignorant laughter.

"Go on and take your 'message' somewhere else, 'preacher'!"

He had never thought of giving up. He had hung on to "save" many of the people who had once sneered at his teachings, to serve them and thousands of others as pastor, intimate counselor, "brother in Christ." He could still think of himself in that role, and one could see it in him at Wednesday night prayer meeting or at Sunday worship service. He would remain in the pulpit until the last parishioner who wished to do so had come up to shake his hand, exchange a bit of town gossip, or inquire after the latest piece of dirt on Jim Bakker.

That was a part of Falwell most of America had never seen. The other Falwell was something else entirely. Driven by demons as implacable in their own way as any that ever drove man to fleshly pleasures, Falwell could never have rested until he had built the nation's largest church, its largest "Bible-believing" university, its biggest born-again political action committee. He had become at once the most hated and most beloved preacher in all the land; yet to his Thomas Road congregation he was the same genial and even folksy parson whose message harked back to an era many of us have mourned as forever lost.

But he was hurting now. PTL had cost him dearly. Six months of lost time and bad headlines and shrinking church donations—and something else that may not have occurred to him yet: the advantage that had come from knowing he had made all the right enemies. It just wasn't the same now. From the day of his first PTL press conference, way back in March, he had been all wit and charm; and he couldn't go back to being just plain old hated Jerry Falwell anymore.

"Sure," the reporters would say as they gathered in bars or on curbstones outside the Heritage Grand. "Falwell is OK. He always did right by me."

That was more than many of the fundamentalist church leaders who had inspired his early ministry could say about him. This, perhaps, was the strangest and most exasperating irony of all. But it was nothing new. Falwell had been losing ground with these men for years, ever since he'd first got mixed up in politics and begun to consort publicly with freethinkers.

Strangest of all, it wasn't the abortionists and smut peddlers and learned hirsutes of the New Left who had denounced him most fiercely; it was his own people—men who preached a gospel primitive even by the standards of the conservative sect that by this time had seized control of the Southern Baptist Convention. They were not a part of the convention; neither was Falwell. The larger question, though, was whether he was still, in the truest sense, a fundamentalist. The "scriptural inerrancy" of which he'd spoken over coffee one morning all those months ago at the Lynchburg Radisson had sounded vaguely heretical by comparison with the fundamentalist theology that had been drummed into me as a child.

"I do not mean by inerrancy that two good men cannot arrive at different interpretations of what the Bible is telling us," he had said. "If the Bible is not accurate on its surface, as we look at it, it is not because God is wrong. It is because we either don't know what is being said there, or because we don't have the knowledge available to comprehend it."

That was it, then: God wasn't wrong. It was just that we didn't know enough. Such talk was enough in itself to get him condemned as a contaminator of the word. And then to turn political agitator, against all that was "holy" in the "Anabaptist" tradition—well, that only confirmed a growing and really quite spiteful feeling among his former friends that the man was no true Christian at all. By getting into politics he had flouted his sect's deeply held belief in church-state separatism (though no Anabaptist I know of ever objected to the idea of children praying Christian prayers in public-supported schools) and had put himself forever beyond reconciliation with men who had been his spiritual guides and for whom he himself had once been something of a prophet.

"The most dangerous man in America," the Reverend Bob Jones had called him. Jones, the furiously reactionary president of the South Carolina fundamentalist university that bears his name—and also the name of his father, who founded the place—hadn't spoken to Falwell since the day the Lynchburg minister had been quoted in the papers as saying he would "feel comfortable" voting for a Catholic or Jew or even an atheist "if he or she agrees with us on the vital issues."

Vital issues? What kind of talk was that from a man for whom there supposedly was only one vital issue: the death, burial, resurrection, and redeeming power of Christ Jesus? The political Left, meanwhile, had been able to see little distinction between Falwell and the more typical agents of Baptist bigotry. When Bailey Smith, a former president of the Southern Baptist Convention, assured the faithful that "God Almighty does not hear the prayer of a Jew," Falwell, an unapologetic Zionist, learned that people were blaming him for this madcap utterance, and he thought he knew why. As he explained it, it was just one more way for political liberals and other critics "to drive a wedge between me and the Jewish community around the country.

"They forgot that the Jews and I share a common Judeo-Christian heritage. They forgot that my Master was a Jewish rabbi and that the writings of the Law, the Prophets and Wisdom Literature of the Old Testament, are as much a part of my faith as are the Gospels and the epistles of the New Testament."

Not everybody wanted to hear that kind of talk. During the 1980 presidential campaign Democrats dredged up the old statement and delivered it to a gleeful Jimmy Carter. Carter, a south Georgia Baptist fundamentalist who had partly redeemed himself with religious skeptics by confessing that he had sometimes felt "lust in his heart," and his vice presidential candidate, Walter Mondale, who would never have confessed to any such thing, were preparing to air a commercial attributing the contemptible statement to Falwell when they learned, regrettably, that they had the wrong man.

· · ·

To Bob Jones there had been more than enough reasons for him and his brethren in slander to repudiate Falwell, what with his refusal to shun or condemn men of other faiths. Now there was a worse reason: he had refused to throw himself into a plot to bring down the pope.

There had never been a better opportunity. For most of 1987 South Carolina had been racing to prepare for an autumn visit by John Paul II, the first Catholic pontiff ever to venture into the heart of the Protestant South. What could be his game? Extremists among the Bakkerites had long ago concluded that he was coming to set up his Abomination of Desolation in front of the Heritage Grand Hotel and summarily take over the world. But I was never quite convinced that that was what he had in mind. Somehow the papal visit had more the feeling of a reconnaissance mission. Heritage USA wasn't even on the agenda. Columbia, the state capital, was as close as he would get to the notorious theme park.

After a meeting with University of South Carolina officials in that city, he and his entourage would be toasted at the oldest Catholic church in town and then paraded to the USC football stadium along streets that had once echoed with the thunder of Wade Hampton's Confederate cavalrymen. When Bob Jones learned that the visit had been arranged with the connivance of liberal Baptist clergymen, his printing presses went into overdrive. Echoing the Bakkerites, he raged against the pope as Antichrist and took out newspaper ads condemning the Protestant ministers who had conspired in his visit as men "willing to betray Christ, deny the Bible and turn their back on those faithful Christian martyrs who [the Catholic church] had down through the ages imprisoned, tortured, mutilated and slain."

Tabernacle Baptist College, a Greenville, South Carolina, institution closely allied in spirit with its neighbor, Bob Jones University, had gone even further, mounting a billboard campaign that was to condemn and at the same time "save" the pope. I sounded out Falwell about the project and found him incredulous. "I would hope that I wouldn't be treated in such a fashion if I were to decide to go to Rome." Later I asked the people at Tabernacle about it and found that that was precisely what they might have expected from their most famous apostate.

"Falwell?" sneered Tabernacle dean Jerry Clark. "He's way too ecumenical for us."

The Tabernacle preachers were a hard-eyed lot. I had seen them on the streets of Charlotte and other cities, wearing their scowls of righteousness as they distributed fundamentalist literature and shouted their unrelenting message of redemption to passers-by. I found one of them standing outside my hotel one evening and made the mistake of informing him that his message was indeed a wonderful metaphor for divine truths that had been true in all ages and in all cultures. He came toward me bristling with rage, square jawed, fists clenched.

"Hell is real, mister! *Hell is real!* I've warned you now! I've warned you!" He kept shouting at me and coming out after me as I walked off into the dark. "I was a drunkard—lying in the gutter—nowhere to turn—and look what the blood of Jesus Christ has done for me! I've warned you, mister! Just remember: Your blood is not on my hands!"

I had a bit of difficulty finding out exactly how the Tabernacle billboard campaign was supposed to work. The way I finally got it was this: the billboards that were to line John Paul's parade route would be inscribed with biblical texts underscoring the fatal errors of Catholicism and urging him—while there was still time—to "accept Jesus."

I guess it was supposed to work with him the same as with anyone else. One moment he would be riding along looking out the window of his popemobile, smiling beatifically and waving his crosier at the crowds. Then all at once he would see the billboards, each bearing its message of inspiration and condemnation. Little by little he would begin to feel the same inward stir that Jerry Falwell had felt on that long-ago morning when he sat over a big batch of hoecakes in the kitchen of his Lynchburg home: a voice—not a voice exactly—a feeling—something, anyway—calling him to penitence and forgiveness.

What to do?

By the time he reached the stadium where he was to speak and bless his admirers, his smile would have vanished. The indictment would be heavy on him now, and at the last turn he would see yet another billboard with its climactic message, a text from First Timothy:

"For there is one God, and one mediator between God and man, the man Christ Jesus!"

He would realize then that he could no longer evade the truth. He would understand now that he had invested a lifetime in blasphemy. Suddenly the tears would sprout and he would leap from the popemobile with crazy abandon, flinging skullcap, crosier, and vestments aside and throwing himself on the mercy of the Tabernacle preachers, shouting, "Save me, Lord! For I have sinned mightily against Thy holy name! Against Thee have I sinned, O Lord! Against Thee only! . . ." And the preachers all hooting with joy, screaming at him as he knelt in the gutter:

"That's right, mister! We've warned you now! Your blood is not on our hands!"

The whole lot of them would be there—square jawed, hard eyed—calling on him to "repent and be saved lest he perish by the way" and then bursting into a rousing refrain that would doubtless set him to bawling again:

> What can wash away my sin?
> Nothing but the blood of Jesus . . .

At least that was the way it was supposed to work. "And then we're going after the homosexuals in Atlanta," student-preacher Ben Chapman, founder of the billboard movement, told me on the afternoon of my Tabernacle visit. He had greeted me alone in a big empty sanctuary, in front of the altar, wearing a black suit and tie, his manner fevered and anxious and a bit arrogant.

"Be not deceived!" he said as he strode back and forth in his preacher's suit, glaring at me sideways, his eyes shining. "The effeminate shall not inherit the kingdom of God!" A pause as he stared at me more intently. Had he taken me for one of the effeminate? Then: "We are going to inform the homosexuals of Atlanta, Georgia, that they are not going to Heaven. We plan to do that next spring some time."

As far as I know he did not do it in the spring or any other time. I guess his failure to save the pope had thrown a real snarl into all his plans. He had not so much as put up the first billboard. Everybody at Tabernacle knew why: the rich Catholic community had conspired to thwart the school's design by buying off both the billboard companies and all the people who owned land along the parade route.

Even without the billboards to promote their cause the Tabernacle preachers had all been out in force to taunt the pope. They lit into him in a powerful big way when he came out of the Catholic church and got into his popemobile and started down Assembly Street toward the stadium. I figured they would feel really bad that their campaign was a failure and would take it out on the rest of us. Since the pope did not get to read the Scripture that might have saved him from eternal torment and had gone home as lost to the Lord as on the day he arrived, I was afraid that the rest of us might be dragged to one side and forced to read it instead.

There were a lot of Tabernacle people out there that afternoon, ganged up on the wide concrete median across from the Catholic church—big, tough guys with glittery eyes and the hot, sulfuric breath of the very demons they despised. Probably a lot of former street fighters and eye gougers in the bunch. You had to be careful around guys like that. They had been howling out their gruesome message of "redemption" for a long time before the pope got there. So it wouldn't be easy getting away from them. Not an easy time for anybody who happened to be in their vicinity that day.

Yet the preachers did not seem entirely dissatisfied with their work, take it all in all, and they began to drift away from the scene in relatively good spirits. Maybe they were feeling good because the pope hadn't drawn much of a crowd down here in Protestant land, nothing at all like what had been predicted. Which meant, I suppose, that his visit would have to be counted almost as much of a failure as their own campaign to set him on the Glory Road.

Or maybe they weren't quite ready to be caught up in the Rapture and were just as glad that the pope had not proclaimed himself the Antichrist and announced that the days of the Great Tribulation were at hand. Always a few more good deeds to impose on the world before resigning yourself to eternal bliss. Or maybe it was just that they felt they had done all they could to warn him of the terrible evil in his life and were no longer burdened with the knowledge that if they had stood and said nothing, his blood would have lain heavily on their souls in the Great Day of Judgment.

Your blood is not on our hands mister you remember that now your blood is not on our hands

20

The pope was safely out of the country, no longer an immediate threat either to national security or to Baptist fundamentalism or even to Heritage USA, and he had not been gone long before PTL was again off the front pages. But we had not heard the last of the bankrupt ministry, and we sure hadn't heard the last of Jim Bakker and all the conspiracies that had brought him low. And even if we could have forgotten all that, we could not have forgotten Jessica Hahn, who had suddenly emerged from almost three months of saying nothing and enjoying her hush money into a blaze of public fury and recrimination, complaining bitterly about a plot to besmirch her good name and prevent her from becoming one of the first ladies of the American stage.

Not long before that she had come to Charlotte for the first time, summoned to testify at a grand jury probing Jim Bakker's old crimes. It was about the same time that we first heard about the million dollars *Playboy* was paying her to pose nude and recount the always-fascinating tale of the ravishment she had "suffered" at the hands of Bakker and fellow evangelist John Wesley Fletcher. This was the big cover story that was supposed to redeem her good name and prove to the world that she was indeed a God-fearing church secretary who had been violently wronged.

As we understood it, the story was even to restore her as some sort of model of Christian virtue. I was so much a victim of my fundamentalist background that I could not understand exactly how all the nude photos were supposed to help. Would *Christian Century* have been a more suitable outlet? Well, *Christian Century* probably didn't have a million dollars, and, besides, she doubtless would have been running real low on hush money by this time.

Anyway, I had a chance to ask her about all that during a press conference after her grand jury appearance.

My question was simple. I wondered if it would sound naive: How, indeed, were nude photos supposed to promote her good name and convince everybody of her resolve to spend her life in the service of mankind?

"When you read the story you will see. It will all be clear then."

I read the story. It still wasn't clear.

I guess I just never would understand it. A maddening thought to realize that after all this time you were still unable to free yourself from the stultifying effects of your early Baptist training. I had to confess, though, that the photos were really very good. If there had been breast implants, they had certainly taken well, even if the face-lift was not all that it might have been. Not exactly a display to redeem her good name, but certainly a nice complement to her story of that old dirty business with Jim Bakker. If anything, the prose was more explicit than the photos. All the smutty details were there, from the first moment she had seen Bakker down by the pool on that fateful afternoon until the moment he entered her room wearing only his beach robe.

The way she told it, she was still at that moment the virginal church secretary, perhaps hoping to enjoy some good, enlightening talk about God and the Bible and the Hereafter. Instead, that dirty little rat walks over almost without an introduction and unceremoniously thrusts his phallus into her mouth. Not exactly the best of manners, but maybe no more than you could expect of a man brought up in an orange cinder-block house (so it was in his memory, so it would ever be) in the working-class town of Muskegon, Michigan.

Well, so what. You couldn't exactly refuse the most famous television preacher in the land his measure of satisfaction. But she did complain that she had felt sick later. I was never sure whether that was before or after Bakker and Fletcher had finished with her.

The tale immediately drew howls of derision from men who said that they had known Jessica, in the biblical sense and otherwise, long before she had met Bakker. On the day we spoke with her she had not yet become the venomous harridan of the television talk shows. She seemed almost shy, almost believable, as she stood there speaking softly in the warm November sun. But that had all changed by the time *Playboy* hit the stands.

Suddenly she seemed to be everywhere—on radio, on television talk shows, in newspapers and magazines—railing against Jim Bakker as a slimy, good-for-nothing cheat for whom life imprisonment would be far too mild a punishment. Did Jessica Hahn have true star quality even after all the plastic surgery and silicone implants? She was harsh, shrill, profane, humorless, unforgiving. It began to look as if what she really needed was a personality implant.

No style, no class. So I guess we weren't surprised when we learned that her first big break in show business was as the impresario of a women's mud-wrestling contest. She defended the work in a television interview. It was just a start. There would be better work later and a lot more of it. But for some reason the better offers never came. We tried not to miss any of the mud-wrestling contests. Later she would try her hand at an extended late-night TV commercial exploiting the fantasies of the lovelorn. We tried to miss all of those. Nothing but more mud wrestling in a slightly fancier guise. So I guess we finally began to understand, and surely she had begun to understand, that she had been irrevocably typecast in roles unlikely to make her the toast of the New York stage. A Hollywood bit player at most—and only then with an awful lot of luck.

Long after Jim Bakker had gone to jail and Tammy Faye had started talking divorce, entrepreneurs would still be bidding to make something big and useful and appropriately garish out of the old Heritage USA theme park. Maybe someday they would succeed.

But by that time the once-famous mud queen who had started the fateful downfall of its founder would have stalked out of our lives forever.

.   .   .

For the Bakkers it was back to the street corners and sidewalks, back to all the starving little mission churches that had given them their start, back to Florida again. Before the end of the tumultuous year of 1987 we learned that he and his wife were back in business, sort of. They had taken over a newly vacated retail outlet, a cramped, shabby little place, in an Orlando shopping mall and were furiously pressing their case of Righteousness Undone.

Running yes it's true Jim and I running like little scared animals all the time running

As in the bad old days in South Carolina, they came and went in separate cars.

No one who had ever been to Orlando and its dazzling Walt Disney

World could have doubted its allure for the builder of Heritage USA. But from what we heard, he and his wife were preaching mostly to street people and curious vacationers. Anyway, one thing was for sure: the money was no longer coming in. Was the competition of Walt Disney World too great, or had people finally caught on to the pair?

They moved around a lot that year. After almost six months they were still unable to raise enough cash even to pay the rent on their grubby storefront mission. Sometimes they preached to derelicts in second-rate hotel lobbies, and at least once in a commercial showroom (emptied for their convenience by a sympathetic businessman), passing around their empty gift-wrapped offering box again. At every stop you might have thought the whole audience of "Nightline" was listening, ready to shell out more cash.

In the early summer of 1988 they finally signed a lease for an abandoned Tupperware warehouse in a mostly abandoned industrial park south of the city. A real dismal place. They also found a name for their enterprise: the New Covenant Church. It sure wasn't much. Here, as everywhere else, they found themselves preaching mostly to the cynical and the curious. And sometimes even to the very worst sort of people who had wandered in off the street. You sure wouldn't have seen anything like that in the old days at Heritage USA. But that was all right. "Let the poor people come," said Tammy Faye. "Love has no nose. Poor people sometimes don't smell too good, so love can have no nose."

They preached and cried and sang and tried all the old gimmicks that had worked for them in the early days. But almost nobody wanted to carry their show. A dozen cable channels, that was all. A good, promising start, perhaps, for somebody new to the business of TV hucksterism. Not much compared with the 171 channels that had carried the "PTL Club" during the last great days of its popularity.

Orlando zoning officials tried more than once to shut down the New Covenant Church, citing fire safety regulations. The fight went on all summer, Tammy Faye carrying on alone after her husband had gone back to Carolina to stand trial on twenty-four counts of fraud. The court finally found in their favor after the American Civil Liberties Union, lover of unpopular and sometimes perverse causes, sent in a team of lawyers and threatened to make a federal case out of it.

During all of this Bakker had never quite forgotten Carolina or given up his absurd dream of getting his hands on PTL again. "That is our dream eternally," he kept saying. He would often leave the affairs of New Covenant in the hands of his wife and daughter while he raced back to South Carolina on the pretext that he had backers clamoring to bankroll his bid for the theme park. After a Canadian businessman had put up $1 million in earnest money as a token first payment in a complicated $113 million deal that depended on payoffs from Heritage's undeveloped assets, Bakker boasted: "I can beat any offer these other guys make."

But where was the money? Did Melvin Belli have it all? Bakker went on to say that he was willing to pay at least $77 million in cash at once. Nothing came of it when the PTL trustee, M. C. Benton, learned that one of his backers had a prison record. Only the most committed Bakkerites could keep from laughing at him now.

If he had any part of the millions he had supposedly stolen from the old PTL, he had certainly managed to hide it well, perhaps against the day when his prison stay would be over, because by now even he must have known that that was where he was going. But he never talked of anything and apparently never thought of anything except the day when he would make his triumphal reentry into Heritage USA. Frail man on a donkey come to reclaim his eternal legacy.

Empty boasts, hollow posturings, as though he were not in a race with dozens of the world's most powerful financiers in his futile bid to get his hands on the Heritage park. Some had come from as far away as Australia. Plenty of them could have afforded to buy the ministry even at the exaggerated asking price of $113 million. The best offers were nowhere close to that—or even to the $70 million which had been its estimated worth at the time Falwell and his people had sought Chapter 11 financial protection.

The ultimate survivor of the bidding wars was a California evangelist named Morris Cerullo and a group of Malaysian investors. We heard nothing of the Malaysians at first, only of Cerullo and his plans to spend $15 million on the restoration of the Heritage park. The next thing we knew Cerullo was out of it and the Malaysians had taken over. Nobody would say what led to the falling out, but Cerullo had what he wanted anyway: the PTL satellite network, which, in the discredited lore of the faith partners, Falwell had never given up trying to "steal." Cerullo had paid $7 million for the network before bringing the Malaysians and other "friends of the ministry" in on the deal. Together, the partners put up another $42.5 million to acquire the rest of the Heritage complex. But how good a deal was it for the Malaysians? How would they fare without the gimmicks that had originally made the theme park a success? Even the selling of "family fun partnerships," which, as Richard Dortch had confessed, was the true source of PTL wealth, was not a factor in New Heritage's marketing plans.

No more partnerships, no more "PTL Club," which had been the big draw in former times and which was still reaching some ten million homes when, in the fall of 1989, Hurricane Hugo swept across the grounds and, like a cold blast right out of the Vatican, forced trustee Benton to close the place for good—or until a new owner could be found.

Bakker had just gone to trial at the time of the big hurricane. But everybody who thought the storm was meant to call attention to Bakker's sins had it all wrong. The warning, said Tammy Faye, was really for the people of Charlotte. CHARLOTTE, TAKE HEED! said the headlines out of Florida. "People are saying the storm had something to do with Jim and Tammy Bakker," Tammy Faye explained. "It had nothing to do with Jim and Tammy Bakker, but it does have everything to do with the way the people of Charlotte, North Carolina, have treated God's people."

. . .

Our laughter had become a little strained by the time Bakker went to trial. I guess nobody really wanted to laugh at him anymore. He no longer looked as if he quite meant to be believed—a pale, shrunken little man still full of the boasts that would help him hide all the old feelings of fear and inferiority and memories of the mythical deprivations of his childhood. The low point had come when old crony John Wesley Fletcher had taken to the pages of *Penthouse* to describe his own long love affair with Bakker and to brag that he had often procured other men for the former PTL host.

The preacher, as usual, denied everything, never accepting the blame for the slightest indiscretion, never offering any excuse or explanation, never admitting that he was guilty of anything except his onetime encounter with mud queen Jessica Hahn, never stopped pretending that he would one day return to glory as host of the "PTL Club."

One way or another he and his wife managed to dominate the headlines for years after their ministry had gone bust. Even as the federal government was issuing a twenty-eight-page indictment charging him with all those counts of fraud and conspiracy, he was still lurking about the grounds of Tega Cay and Heritage USA, tirelessly seeking to devise some scheme whereby he could get his hands on the bankrupt ministry.

To the great disappointment, and even disgust, of those who had hoped his trial would prove to be one long verbal foray into the byways of sexual debauchery, federal prosecutors had decided to focus exclusively on the preacher's financial wrongdoing. Not that there weren't moments of high drama. One day, while providing new and damning details about Bakker's excesses, Steve Nelson, who had once directed PTL's foreign missions program, suddenly fell out of his chair in a faint.

The next morning it looked to a lot of people as though the episode had given Bakker ideas. By the time court was ready to convene, Bakker had retreated again to his familiar fetal position. The way a psychiatrist described it to the judge, the preacher was "lying in the corner of his attorney's office with his head under a couch, hiding."

Judge Robert Potter, known as "Maximum Bob" to those who had followed his career, sent the defendant off to a federal correctional institution for further psychiatric evaluation. He came out in the arms of two federal marshals, shackled hand and foot, teeth clattering as he begged his keepers not to throw him to the "animals." He either did not recognize or pretended not to recognize the hundreds of Bakkerites who had gathered to pray for him and shout words of encouragement. "Please don't do this to me," he screamed as he curled up in the back seat of the car. "Please don't do this to me!" Psychiatrists believed it was all for real, that he actually believed he was being thrown to the animals, that he himself was turning into an animal.

There was talk that Bakker might be so far gone that the trial could never resume. Nobody ever knew how much of the episode Bakker had concocted to gain sympathy and perhaps to force an indefinite stay of his trial. Even his critics wondered if it was, in a sense, real—one of those rare and eerie occasions when reality broke through the wall of delusions he had built around himself and frightened him with visions of Hellfire. Or had he simply decided after those first days of damning testimony that he'd rather spend his time in the padded cell of an asylum than in a prison yard?

From the first days until the final terrible news that Maximum Bob had sentenced the preacher to forty-five years in prison, with no hope of release for at least a decade, the Bakkerites were always there en masse, clapping and singing or sometimes just standing there in prayerful silence, throwing up their hands and shouting at him as the marshals brought him to and from the courtroom.

"Amen, Jim! We're praying for you, Jim!"

Tammy Faye, who had somehow escaped the indignity of a federal indictment, was often at the courthouse to lead the singing and bamboozle the press with her tearful stories of Falwellian oppression. Many of the people who gathered at the courthouse each morning had lost everything in PTL and didn't even care. Some would prove to be the most impassioned of Bakker's character witnesses. Seventy-four-year-old Marjorie Grey, who had bought thirty-two lifetime partnerships, struck a common theme. She blamed everything on Falwell and said she would gladly give Bakker another $32,000 and more if he could just get his ministry back. "One of the best people I've ever known," she said.

Witnesses echoing the same theme came by the dozens and by the score, and it began to look as if they would never stop coming until one day Maximum Bob Potter banged down his gavel and said he had heard more than enough, warning defense attorneys to stick to the merits of their case, if any. The judge was angry and perhaps a little shaken. When the jury found Bakker guilty on all counts, he was a little reluctant to grant bail. He had heard enough to convince him that the Bakker people were cultists with a "Jim Jones mentality." Could you really trust these people? Would they help Bakker flee the country? Would they even follow him into some insect-ridden South American jungle and drink poison with him, as Jim Jones's followers had done?

His forty-five-year sentence, widely perceived as unjust—and later reduced after Bakker at last agreed to accept responsibility for his crimes—appeared at first to be the end of the story. But we again underestimated the ability of this pair, even in their estrangement, to dominate the headlines. When events did not warrant coverage by the big dailies, the supermarket tabloids took over. The pictures of Bakker in prison showed a man who seemed more than content with his new life. The tabloids explained why: his love for a fellow prisoner had finally brought him true happiness. They had just about worn out that theme when they found new cause for sensationalism in the affairs of "homewrecker" Tammy Faye.

Bakker's wife, "the Betty Boop of spiritual sancti-money," *People* magazine later called her, had petitioned for a divorce after falling for family friend Roe Messner, the loyal charismatic and now-bankrupt Kansas contractor whose idle crane atop the unfinished Heritage Towers had long been a symbol of the failed ministry. Messner's last words to Bakker before the preacher went off to jail: "Don't worry, Jim. I'll take real good care of your family."

Like everything else that had ever come out of the PTL scandal it was all a little difficult to take in, especially for Messner's wife, Ruth Ann, a striking fifty-six-year-old feminist who, unlike her husband, had a taste for cigarettes and good Scotch and who eventually walked out on him more in puzzlement than anything else, explaining that "any man who would want Tammy Faye is not the man for me." She promised a lot of lively copy—stories enough to keep the PTL controversy alive at least until the middle of the new decade. Richard Dortch, fresh out of prison and author of a book describing his long trek back to the comforts of the Old-Time Religion, gazed on Messner with "Christian contempt," much as he had once gazed on the *Charlotte Observer* in the days before it had begun to have second thoughts about its anti-PTL crusade. And Messner mostly just kept his mouth shut.

We stopped laughing at Bakker and the whoremongering Jimmy Swaggart long enough to laugh for a while at the lovestruck charismatic. Nobody could figure it. What could Messner, who still had his looks, possibly see in the fast-fading Tammy Faye, who had not come off well in her first encounter with middle age? Neither her manic faith nor all her cosmetics could save her now. The tabloids talked again of her lewd poses before clandestine cameras, of wanton public displays with her new beau. There was talk of all sorts of incriminating pornographic material uncovered by Ruth Ann's lawyers as they were rummaging through her old home for evidence against her husband. Kinky photos reminiscent of Tammy Faye's days with Gary Paxton. Tammy Faye wearing see-through nighties and skimpy lace panties and high-heel shoes and mesh stockings "with her big bottom stuck up in the air."

There were other stories of mobster lists said to have been found along with the sexy pictures. Big Mafia names like John Gotti, who would himself shortly be off to prison. Hints that the mob had found the old "PTL Club" a convenient outlet for its money-laundering operations. "The most sensational exposé of the 90's" is the way one paper described Ruth Ann's coming legal confrontation with Messner. There were other

stories of how Messner had been embarrassed, perhaps not so much by his lover's lewd poses as by her taste for gaudy K-Mart fashions. He had paid money, it was said, to send her off to fashion schools where she supposedly was to learn how to dress more decorously, at least in public.

There was just no way of figuring it at all. Had he decided on an affair as partial payment for the $14 million he had been unable to collect for his work at PTL? I saw him only once more. He had come back to the Heritage grounds on the day I happened to be there for my first interview with the Malaysians. An embarrassing moment for us both. For Messner because he realized he had been seen by a hated member of the press. For me because I had promised myself so many times that I would never again set foot on the place.

I did not recognize him at first, maybe because I had not expected to see any of the old Bakkerites in what had become alien territory for them all, and for none more than Messner, whose failure to collect the money still due him from the bankrupt ministry had ruined all his hopes for financial recovery. Without the papers to back up his claim, he was no better off than the hundreds of lifetime partners whose classification as "unsecured creditors" made it impossible for them to get back any of the money they had put into the ministry.

But why was he there? Had he thrown in with the Malaysians? Had he worked out a deal to put Tammy Faye back onstage? No, he had only come back to arrange with the new owners to get his crane down from atop the still-unfinished Heritage Towers, where it had sat ever since the day in 1987 that Falwell ordered builders to stop work on the facility.

Messner and a black-suited companion were just coming out of the Heritage office complex when I drove up to the place. By the time I got close enough to recognize him he'd already had enough time to make a fast getaway. I turned on the run and got back to the parking lot just as he and the other man hopped into their car and sped away.

"Messner! Roe! Wait a minute! Goddammit, don't you see, this is important!"

I flung away my notepad in disgust, watching it swirl upward in the fumes of his exhaust and then flop crazily down on the gravel, like a bird with broken wings. Like my own broken hopes for at least one more big story. Messner had apparently recognized me from the old days, even though we had never talked. He was mostly in hiding back then, and very few of us ever saw him at all. So nothing had changed. Just another flubbed opportunity to score big with a banner headline in next day's edition:

ROE PRAISES TAMMY AS HOT MAMA NYMPHO
WITH HEART OF DROSS AND PEWTER

But at least I wouldn't have to worry about my latest failure reaching the ears of Kovach and his chief newsroom enforcer, both of whom had left the *Journal-Constitution* in a huff after learning, somewhat belatedly, that Anne Cox Chambers of Atlanta and Barbara Cox Anthony of Honolulu, sole owners of the newspapers and two of the nation's wealthiest women, did not sympathize with their editors' empire-building tactics or share their vision for reforming the economies of the Third World. But I felt bad about it, all right. No telling quotes about his new love affair, no more inside dope—if any was left—on the dirty backstage antics at PTL. Hell, I never even found out how he got his crane back.

. . .

A lot had changed since my last visit back in 1989. That was only a couple of days before the big hurricane hit. But the hurricane was an anticlimax. Back then, the old theme park was only a sad mockery of what it had been in the days of its glorious decline. No trams running, no teenagers waving joyfully at you as you came in past the entrance gates, no crowds packing the Hall of Faith every day to watch the Bakkers, Richard Dortch, and all the other grinning gospel-mongers shout out their religion of joy and prosperity and long life for all. No pitchmen to warm up the audiences before the show, no psychedelic fudge to bring visions of a paradise full of water nymphs ready to compromise the chastity you had guarded so diligently throughout life.

It was quite a shock, really, to see how far the old place had fallen. Clumps of Johnson grass and jimsonweed had shot up through the concrete pavement, and all the lovely pastel colors of the buildings along Main Street USA had faded badly, and even the canopy in front of Heritage Grand had developed an ominous series of cracks. But at least Messner's rusty old crane was still there, way up in the air atop the Heritage Towers, unfailing reminder of what might have been. Here and there an elderly couple wandered about, looking forlorn, wondering what they had to show for all those lifetime partnerships they had bought. The pope and the Antichrist had placed their signets of doom on everything, but the forces of Gog and Magog would have found the pickings of the once-grand water park mighty thin indeed. Rust and decay and memories of beds falling down in the middle of the night and bums full of liquor on the steps of the Heritage Grand. And what was that in the wind as dusk came on? A faint burst of mocking laughter from on high or only my imagination?

With Bakker sitting in the dock and bids for the park going nowhere, I wondered if the trustees would ever find anyone to buy the place. Or would it inevitably lose itself in the weeds and dust, until in another generation it would have been forgotten entirely, like some windblown gold-rush town in the Old West, to be rediscovered, if at all, in some distant age by teams of zealous archaeologists anxiously scouting for the ruins of our decadent twentieth-century civilization?

It is fitting, I suppose, that the Malaysians, who had lived among the ruins of ancient civilizations for so long, who had walked, perhaps, among the decaying remains of ancient Islamic temples and fallen castles where sultans had once ruled, should have been the inheritors of Bakker's old water park. Good Christian men from a faraway Moslem land, we were told, with billions to spend turning thousands of acres of undeveloped Heritage land into golf resorts and retirement retreats.

On the day of my scheduled interview with the president of the new corporation, broken off at the last moment, I walked again down the long hall from the parking lot past the conference rooms and the big auditorium where Jerry Falwell had held his famous X-rated press conferences. Workers were everywhere, redoing the brickwork, the paint, the carpet, frantically preparing for the grand opening—now less than a week away—of what was now being called the New Heritage Carolina Corporation.

Although I had not been closely following the affairs of New Heritage, I had gathered that there would be no attempt by the new owners to recapture the spirit of the original PTL, no attempt to introduce Christian themes of any kind. I had even supposed that after my long, tiring trip back to South Carolina I could relax with a cocktail or a fine Hav-a-Tampa. Not so, explained a certain Ronald Iwasko, the new director of ministries.

The new owners are "all fine Christian men," Iwasko said, "and they are determined to make this a truly Christian resort," something we all knew it had never been except perhaps briefly in the time of Jerry Falwell.

So that was it, then: no booze, no cigarettes, no mate swapping, not even among the people who ran the place. I could see that Iwasko wasn't kidding. I kept the flask of gin I had brought along carefully tucked away in my jacket pocket.

It was a big gamble for the Malaysians. Could they really make a go of it without any of the old gimmicks that made the old PTL work? The "PTL Club," as I say, had always been the big draw. Now even that was gone. Only the mall, the hotel, the water slide, and good, clean Christian fun. No more lifetime partnerships to bring in the faithful. I had noticed in my long walk from the parking lot that there was very little to remind one of the days when Bakker was at the height of his power. Everything was gone, all the gold and the gilt and glitter . . .

Well, not quite everything. On a wide expanse of wall overlooking the water park was a familiar tablet inscribed with a passage from Matthew, the words emblazoned in huge red letters, to remind the visitor that the new ministry was indeed paying obeisance to the old, reminding the visitor that very little had changed after all, that New Heritage was to be essentially what it had always been: a charismatic ministry celebrating the joy of Christian life, spreading gladness over the land like a rampant crop of kudzu or clover:

"Again I say unto you, that if two of you shall agree on earth as touching anything that they shall ask, it shall be done for them of my Father which is in Heaven."

Ask in my name and ye shall receive . . . I am come that ye might have life and have it more abundantly.

Big cars, fancy houses, gold filigree, diamonds big as the Ritz, all the wanton glories of antique Samarkand. Troubling echoes from a past we had thought was long behind us. Crowds would swarm the park on opening day, but how many of the new people would keep coming no one could guess. How many would make it a part of their lives, as thousands of PTL partners had once done? The partners themselves, at least, would be no part of it. The Malaysians had seen to that.

"We would like to be able to do something special for them because we feel for them," Iwasko told me. "But the problem is if you do that you in effect are admitting that you have some legal responsibility for them. And we don't. The bankruptcy proceedings took care of all that."

All new faces. No Jerry Falwell or Richard Dortch or Sam Johnson to come back and be a part of the new ministry. "No," Iwasko said, "we have no plans to invite any of those people back."

It was a big gamble, all right, now that the owners had dispensed with all the old gimmicks, all the old loyalties. They were in no hurry to explain how they would make it work. I kept thinking of all the times I had tried futilely to break into the "Old Time Gospel Hour" up in Lynchburg. The same thing all over again. But you had to figure that if the Malaysians couldn't make a go of it, there was at least one large body of claimants still waiting to take over the place: the remnant of an old Catawba Indian tribe living in squalor on a state-owned "reservation" just south of the theme park.

This had all been Catawba land once, up until about the middle of the nineteenth century, and tribal leaders had been in court for years fighting to get it back. The more than two thousand acres of land bought up by Jim Bakker in the late 1970s and early 1980s was only an infinitesimal part of the fifteen-square-mile tract the tribe was claiming. The Catawbas, who had pressed their case both in the federal courts and in Congress, contended that the white man cheated them out of their land with the kind of promises we had seen broken a thousand times in third-rate western movies. The heart of their appeal was the 1840 Treaty of Nation Ford, under which white settlers acquired all the Catawba territory in exchange for assurances that the Indians were to receive an equally sizable tract in the Cherokee mountain country of North Carolina. The deal never panned out. And now the Catawbas wanted back everything they had lost.

They had built up a good case. They even had a Crown patent to the land dating all the way back to prerevolutionary times. And they wanted a lot more than the land occupied by the Bakkers' old theme park. They also wanted the towns of Rock Hill and Fort Mill, the booming lakefront community of Tega Cay, and bustling Carowinds, the giant amusement park that lay just west of I-77, which ran right down through the heart of the old Catawba property. And I guess they wanted the highway too.

"But we know, realistically, that the courts aren't gonna say, 'OK, you white people just go on and get off this land and get out of these cities and move on away from here: this land all belongs to the Catawbas,'" tribal chief Clifton Blue had told me once. "Of course that's not gonna happen. But they will, in effect, have to say that the Catawbas were cheated and their land is there and that you're going to have to work some kind of deal with them."

Money? Sure, and a lot of it. But not just money. "If it's gonna be fair, it's got to include land as well." That was what made the old Bakker property look particularly vulnerable. By 1992, as a final settlement of the question was being taken up in Congress, attorneys representing the tribe had isolated at least four hundred acres that could not be defended by current owners under South Carolina's complex statute-of-limitation laws. The rest of the acreage? Some was surely more vulnerable than the rest—good land that included thousands of undeveloped acres. Weed-grown fields and woodlands and river bottoms. The talk was that tribal leaders were close to an arrangement that would satisfy all parties to the dispute. Maybe so. The threat of eviction for potential new owners of the theme park was still real enough to deter at least one hopeful buyer, a Canadian financier named Stephen Mernick, from closing on a $65 million deal that had seemed like a sure thing for months. His complaint: no one would write him a dollar's worth of title insurance to the place, a consideration that apparently had not troubled the Malaysians and their backers. The reason was simple. The last trustees of the ministry had discreetly suggested to many of the insurance companies who had loaned money to Bakker and who were now in bankruptcy court trying to get some of it back that maybe they would like to write title insurance for the new owners as a condition for validating their claim.

A slick deal all accomplished with the utmost discretion through what Falwell had called an "old-boy network" of South Carolina lawyers.

. . .

It was just dusk of a midsummer evening when I finally left the old park for the last time. The sad last dead time of day when all I had known of civilization, if that is the word, seemed to lie far from the ruined towers of Heritage USA—far out along the interstate toward the Southeast's newest great boomtown of Charlotte, North Carolina. At such an hour in the old days you might have seen the lifetime partners romping about in mocking derision of Falwell, shouting out their joyous songs of death and everlastingness (and yet there was a little something sad about it for all that) and hailing the great Day of Judgment and casting out demons from "unbelievers"—men and women actually foolish enough to believe they could join in these mysterious rituals of the dying day without betraying themselves instantly to the people who walked always in the great light of the Holy Ghost. None of Falwell's "plants" had ever got away with it as far as I knew. To Paul Wood their true identity would be as obvious as if they had already been wearing the fatal brand of the Antichrist on their foreheads.

Now there was nothing, only the dusk, no sound, except the dying cry of a mourning dove somewhere off beyond Tega Cay, only the wilderness spreading away to every side, so that as I turned out of the gate onto a broken, rutted side road I could almost sense that I was in a world little changed since the coming of the first white settlers, since the bitter day in 1840 when they had cheated the Catawbas out of their ancient heritage. For a moment it was almost as though I were no longer in the twentieth century at all and that there had never been any such thing as Heritage USA and that there had never been any such thing as the Bakkers and their feel-good-all-over religion and that even now the Catawbas were lurking in the pine woods just opposite the Heritage gate, all done up in feathers and war paint, glaring insolently at me as I turned west toward the interstate, back toward life and reality again—never again to return (so I kept assuring myself) to that sad, dead part of the world.

It would be enough to know that the tribe had finally won back its inheritance after all. I couldn't help thinking of those old Catawbas and

SMILE
PRETTY
AND SAY
JESUS

old Chief Blue and the sorry "reservation" that had been their home now for more than a hundred years. Nothing but a lot of tarpaper shacks lining what the white man called Reservation Road, a narrow stretch of blacktop that ran south of Rock Hill through great stands of hardwood and scrub pine and weedy clearings.

So if anyone were to gain the right to plow up PTL, certainly it should not be the druids or George Bush or the Antichrist and his walking computer or any of the other insidious forces that had cast their demonic spell over the place. The world's largest and most garish medicine show. So why not just let the Catawbas have it? Deprived of its gauds and baubles and gilt, maybe it would never be worth much as a theme park again. But who could doubt that it had the makings of one of America's great Indian reservations? A little ostentatious, perhaps, compared with what the Catawbas had been used to in their grim shacks along Reservation Road. But who could imagine a more fitting end to the story— or, for that matter, a surer way to get all those tourists back?

The land had once been good for Blue and his people. Why not again? "We'll clear it all out," he liked to say. "We'll make it a good and fertile land again. The fields yielding corn and tomatoes and all kinds of vegetables, the forests yielding a great bounty of game. We'll bring in dredging machines and make bigger, richer river bottoms."

Maybe it would never happen exactly like that. But for the first time it looked as though, out of all that was lost, they might at last be getting a little something back. Dark was coming fast as I drove farther along the narrow, ill-paved highway, thinking about Bakker alone in the cell up in the Rochester prison that would be his home for at least another four years, maybe with his lover or maybe just sitting alone on his bunk and reading again those lovely, agonizing lines from the Book of Job. I thought of old Dortch, out of prison at last, free again, and all the others: Sam Johnson, Messner, the genial and indefatigable Paul Wood, David Taggart, once Bakker's closest confidant, and his brother James, the interior designer, both men also out of prison after serving terms for tax evasion (though, as far as I know, James never had to spend so much as a day in jail for what seemed to me an even more heinous offense: the extravagant and tasteless decor that had been characteristic of almost all his work at Heritage USA); of Jessica Hahn, John Wesley Fletcher, and, finally, of Falwell, who had risked everything in a venture that he knew from the beginning might well fail and bring a long, long spell of spiritual darkness over the land.

And I guess most of all what I thought of as I turned at last onto the interstate was Tammy Faye Bakker and her teary supporters standing in front of the courthouse in Charlotte on the morning that the federal marshals spirited away a handcuffed Bakker to begin serving the forty-five-year sentence—*Say it ain't so, Jim*—that even Falwell felt was overly harsh. Tammy Faye singing softly at first and then more loudly as she led her little coterie of hard-core Bakkerites in a last sad, ironical chorus that for me marked the true ending of this whole unseemly affair. With some embarrassment I realized that I was humming the same mournful little tune as I drove back onto I-77 toward Charlotte, back into life again:

> On Christ the solid rock we stand;
> All other ground is sinking sand.

21

We spend our years as a tale that is told. . . .
Return, ye children of men.

Psalms 90:3 and 9

For months after Falwell walked out on PTL I kept coming across the old memorabilia: the form letters imploring me to send money lest the "Old Time Gospel Hour" fall on its face, the cassette tapes bearing "a special message from Jerry Falwell," the newspaper clippings, already beginning to turn yellow, the two Jesus First pins that had come in the mail with a thank-you note for the donation I had never got around to sending.

I did not display the pins prominently. They went into my chest of drawers and were straightaway forgotten, except for the times I happened to stick myself while rummaging around for a pair of socks or underwear. Then—sometimes—I would take one of them out and look at it and wonder at the implications. Jesus First. Wear it proudly in your lapel so that the world will recognize you as one of those who has chosen to stand up for the living Christ. Or maybe I would play one of the tapes and hear again the familiar Falwellian voice—warm, resonant, reassuring—coming to me out of a vast, nameless solitude, intoning a peace that passeth all understanding; and then I would always wish that I had sent him a little something.

I had given nothing to the May Emergency or to the June Crisis or to the July Crusade or to the August Last Chance. So it was no good: I was still lost, impenitent, sticking myself from time to time with the Jesus First pin and being reminded all over again that the hour was short and the day of reckoning near—that it was long past the time when I should have been out on the street corners of the world, blessing the multitudes and shouting out the old sweet story of the blood atonement and the risen Christ.

For he who confesses me before men him will I confess before my father which is in heaven . . .

I would think about all that and a great deal more as I stood in front of my dresser drawer: the blood rescue, the endless propitiation, the stone rolled away from the mouth of the cave, resurrection, and a new dawn with brass horns sounding—the oft-told tale of a thousand myths, elevated at last into the story of the True Cross and reflected now in a mere trinket, a blood-laden pin that had come unbidden in the mail. The gaudy vainshow of our ultimate redemption.

Sometimes I would almost feel that I had been through it all before, as though I had been standing there throughout all of what we call eternity, sticking myself repeatedly with Falwell's little lapel pin. Blood on my socks, blood on my fingers. And the memory of street preachers shouting at me in the dark: *Your blood is not on our hands mister!* I would become vaguely aware of a dull, insistent gleam of light far off in the back of my mind, somewhere just below the mists of being, and feel again the old, dark longing, the rage and fear, the conviction that something "is wrong with us as we naturally stand." Then I would realize, as so often before, that I had been caught up in a wayward and disreputable life of my own choosing, and would have to go through it all again, times without number and beyond all reckoning, down through vast, dim, uncharted millennia, or at least until I'd got around to sending Falwell the check—and for no mere token amount, at that.

. . .

I had recently been to a lot of parties where people got drunk on expensive French wine and spent half their time talking about the "shameful" way Gary Hart had been hounded out of the presidential race and the other half about the fate of man and New Age consciousness and the role of karma in our lives—of existence itself as nothing more than a kind of monstrous conspiracy thrust upon us from on high, pointing

Then I would learn that in spite of everything—PTL, the bad publicity, my own niggardliness—the "Old Time Gospel Hour" had enjoyed its best year ever. Falwell would be ready with a quick, warm, satisfying explanation: when viewer donations dropped after news of the scandal, his wealthy patrons had rushed in to shore up the bastions of his falling empire.

So it would be all right after all. Come to think of it, my paltry donation would have been a mere travesty, unworthy of a true believer. Then I would think about all the corruption and hypocrisy (and we *still* didn't know the whole truth about Jimmy Swaggart) and go out and give it to the derelicts and panhandlers instead.

Say, mate, can you spare a copper?

Just out of Mississippi mister got my lungs all full of cotton can't you help a poor man mister can't you help? . . .

Give and it shall be given unto you. Sow and ye shall reap. Dimes in the gutter. Quarters in the attic. Sow the wind and reap limousines full of Popsicles, mink stoles, and cotton candy.

My lungs is full of cotton mister can't you help a poor man get rid of the Mississippi mister?

.   .   .

What Falwell had lost with the people who had inspired his early ministry he had gained with the more liberal Protestant sects. Elmer Towns, dean of Liberty Theological Seminary and an old Falwell confidant, had been especially well placed to observe the transformation. During the more than six months that Falwell had been in charge of PTL, Towns had traveled widely and spoken frequently to interdenominational groups, often to people who knew nothing of the old Falwell or the new Falwell or that there was a difference or that it even mattered.

"We found a groundswell for him—a tolerance—we had never seen before," Towns told me on my last visit to Liberty University. "It was phenomenal. I could see that he had become a statesman in this, a statesman for the whole body of Christ and not just for the radical Right of fundamentalism."

All true. Yet even tolerance has its limits. I had been back in Lynchburg often enough—visiting old friends, getting the other side of it—to know that in spite of Falwell's newly won respectability he still had a hard time getting into all those big important houses out on Rivermont Avenue.

our way forward or backward toward the celebration of some mighty sacrament for which we as yet had no name—of why, in short, there were some things a whole lot more important than whether I ever got around to sending Falwell a check.

Blood on my hands, blood on the soul, head full of gin, the thought of the tawdry pin glimmering in my lapel. (A good laugh for all the Hart supporters if they should ever see it there.) Always arriving too late at the station, always departing on the last train out. Always the long, hard fight through sunless jungles, whacking my way forward through the brambles and thickets of my own unsavory karmic destiny, a strange mud creature staring out at a world far gone in clamor and confusion, not knowing whether to declare myself to passers-by, beg for a quarter, or fling myself back into the comfort of the warm mud. I would vainly try to shake the profound melancholy that would always come over me, promising to avoid New Age ideologues the way I had once tried to avoid Holiness preachers and vowing with Yeats never again to take

> My bodily form from any natural thing
> But such a form as Grecian goldsmiths make
> Of hammered gold and gold enameling
> To keep a drowsy Emperor awake;
> Or set upon a golden bough to sing
> To lords and ladies of Byzantium
> Of what is past, or passing, or to come.

Perhaps I had been to too many parties and seen too many of the same mocking faces and heard too much of the same empty talk. I would leave the parties and walk out into the cold December dark, hating myself for entering into the spirit of the occasion and wondering where I could find a local chapter of Fundamentalists Anonymous. And I would think again about all the times I had stood at my dresser drawer, bleeding on my socks and underwear, feeling the old dull ache of longing and mystery and fear. I would think about all the times I had haunted the streets of Falwell's town, waiting for an interview, pounding at the doors of the "Old Time Gospel Hour," wanting to crawl back into the mud again. I would listen to the tapes and read the crumpled form letters, constantly sensing the desperation that lay behind the words: *Goddammit we're going broke can't you see that can't you see . . .*